Student Companion to

Mark
TWAIN

Student Companion to

Mark Twain

David E. E. Sloane

Student Companions to Classic Writers

Greenwood Press
Westport, Connecticut • London

Library of Congress Cataloging-in-Publication Data

Sloane, David E. E., 1943–
    Student companion to Mark Twain / David E. E. Sloane.
        p.   cm.—(Student companions to classic writers, ISSN 1522-7979)
    Includes bibliographical references and index.
    ISBN 0–313–31219–2 (alk. paper)
    1. Twain, Mark, 1835–1910—Criticism and interpretation.   2. Twain, Mark,
    1835–1910—Examinations—Study guides.   I. Title.   II. Series.
    PS1338.S56   2001
    818′.409—dc21   00–049059

British Library Cataloguing in Publication Data is available.

Library of Congress Catalog Card Number: 00–049059
ISBN: 0–313–31219–2
ISSN: 1522-7979

First published in 2001

Greenwood Press, 88 Post Road West, Westport, CT 06881
An imprint of Greenwood Publishing Group, Inc.
www.greenwood.com

Printed in the United States of America

The paper used in this book complies with the
Permanent Paper Standard issued by the National
Information Standards Organization (Z39.48–1984).

10 9 8 7 6 5 4 3 2 1

For Bonnie, Rachel, David, Sarah, and Elizabeth

Contents

Series Foreword

This series has been designed to meet the needs of students and general readers for accessible literary criticism on the American and world writers most frequently studied and read in the secondary school, community college, and four-year college classrooms. Unlike other works of literary criticism that are written for the specialist and graduate student, or that feature a variety of reprinted scholarly essays on sometimes obscure aspects of the writer's work, the Student Companions to Classic Writers series is carefully crafted to examine each writer's major works fully and in a systematic way, at the level of the non-specialist and general reader. The objective is to enable the reader to gain a deeper understanding of the work and to apply critical thinking skills to the act of reading. The proven format for the volumes in this series was developed by an advisory board of teachers and librarians for a successful series published by Greenwood Press, Critical Companions to Popular Contemporary Writers. Responding to their request for each-to-use and yet challenging literary criticism for students and adult library patrons, Greenwood Press developed a systematic format that is not intimidating but helps the reader to develop the ability to analyze literature.

How does this work? Each volume in the Student Companions to Classic Writers series is written by a subject specialist, an academic who understands students' needs for basic and yet challenging examination of the writer's canon. Each volume begins with a biographical chapter, drawn from published sources, biographies, and autobiographies, that relates the writer's life to his or her work. The next chapter examines the writer's literary heritage, tracing the literary influences of other writers on that writer and explaining and discussing the literary genres into which the writer's work falls. Each of the following chapters examines a major work by the writer, those works most frequently read and studied by high school and college students. Depending on the writer's canon, generally between four and eight major works are examined, each in an individual chapter. The discussion of each work is organized into separate sections on plot development, character development, and major themes. Literary devices and style, narrative point of view, and historical setting are also discussed in turn if pertinent to the work. Each chapter concludes with an alternate critical perspective from which to read the work, such as a psychological or feminist criticism. The critical theory is defined briefly in easy, comprehensible language for the student. Looking at the literature from the point of view of a particular critical approach will help the reader to understand and apply critical theory to the act of reading and analyzing literature.

Of particular value in each volume is the bibliography, which includes a complete bibliography of the writer's works, a selected bibliography of biographical and critical works suitable for students, and lists of reviews of each work examined in the companion, both from the time the literature was originally published and from contemporary sources, all of which will be helpful to readers, teachers, and librarians who would like to consult additional sources.

As a source of literary criticism for the student or for the general reader, this series will help the reader to gain understanding of the writer's work and skill in critical reading.

1

The Life of Mark Twain

When Samuel Langhorne Clemens died in 1910, newspapers carried the news around the world in boldface headlines. The people of the world had lost one of their greatest friends, the newspapers mourned, a friend who had used his authorial voice to battle imperialism, repression, inhumanity, and greed wherever he found it. "Mark Twain," the name under which Clemens wrote and lectured, was a household word at the time of his death; he was an icon of humanity at large, demanding justice and a reasonable degree of freedom from want for all people, especially for the downtrodden people of color who were crushed under the heel of Imperialism and racial prejudice at home. Powerful though his voice had been, his personal life had been a roller-coaster. it was brightened by astounding recognition for a writer who began as a mere "Phunny Fellow" in the 1860s but ended up holding degrees from Yale University and Oxford University, and it was darkened by the humiliation of bankruptcy and the deaths of his wife and three of his four children before his own passing. His reputation today has grown rather than diminished, powered by the debate over *Adventures of Huckleberry Finn*, a book that has been recognized since its publication in 1885 as our nation's foremost candidate for the title "The Great American Novel," but severely criticized today for its use of the nation's most repugnant racial epithet.

Mark Twain—Samuel Langhorne Clemens—was born in the tiny crossroads of Florida, Missouri, a few miles back from the Mississippi River, on March 10, 1835. So small was the rough-hewn cabin where he was born that it is now preserved by the U.S. Park Service inside a modest covered dome near its original site. Shortly after Sam's birth the Clemens family—including his father, John, his mother, Jane Lampton Clemens (who bore seven children but outlived four of them), and older brother, Orion, and sister, Pamela—moved to Hannibal, Missouri. A depot town and steamboat stop on the Mississippi River, Hannibal supplied the young Samuel Clemens with the scenery and characters that brought much of his later fiction to life. His father was a justice of the peace; a cold and austere man, his pretensions as a descendant of the "First Families of Virginia" were never matched by his income, and economic hardship forced him to sell the last family slave in 1841 and mortgage land in Tennessee that he had counted on to make the family rich. He died when Sam was eleven years old, leaving the family poorly provided for. The type of life enjoyed by boys in Hannibal, however, and the richness of summers spent on the farm of his Uncle John Quarles, a few hundred miles downriver in Arkansas, provided Clemens with the experience of dialects, folkways, and backwoods humor that informed his writings throughout his life. It was at the Quarles Farm, for example, that young Sam met "Uncle Dan'l," who appears in *The Gilded Age* and provides the model for the portrait of Jim in *Adventures of Huckleberry Finn*. The local and regional characteristics of Mark Twain's works owe much to this personal background.

At age thirteen Sam Clemens was apprenticed to a printer named John Ament. The apprenticeship system allowed for little formal schooling, and Clemens's was limited to a few years of grade school in Hannibal. However, typesetters were exposed to vast quantities of literature and gained a broad experience of nationalist political rhetoric through their trade. Clemens set type for both Ament and his brother Orion, and he worked as a journeyman printer in St. Louis, Cincinnati, Philadelphia, and New York in the early 1850s. Along with the sense of humor and religious philosophy he inherited from his mother, his experience as a printer introduced him to a rhetorical tradition and provided him with an ironic attitude that formed another important part of the persona that would become Mark Twain.

The period before the Civil War was one of intense nationalism. John L. Sullivan coined the term "manifest destiny" in 1845 to describe the westward push of the United States of America, subduing the continent from sea to sea. The idea of the American frontier held powerful sway over the popular imagination. Tall-tale heroes boasted in story after story that they could lasso the Earth with nets made from the lines of latitude and longitude. The "universal Yankee nation" (only later was the term *Yankee* limited to the North by the "Southern" insistence on states rights and the perpetuation of slavery) was a "go-ahead" nation, to use the frontiersman Davy Crockett's proud term, chock full of enterprise, self-reliance, and commercialism. Americans were impatient with monarchy and the repression of individual rights and behaviors, whether on the basis of economic or social class. Slaves in the South were an embarrassing exception to the promise of egalitarian democracy, an anomaly seen with foreboding by various critics such as (1) the French statesman Alexis de Tocqueville as early as 1838 in his book *Democracy in America,* and (2) newspaper writers like William Lloyd Garrison, who had been mobbed in Boston in 1835 because of his then unpopular anti-slavery views, and Henry Ward Beecher, whose "Beecher's Bibles" (i.e., guns in boxes labeled as prayerbooks) would become part of the legendry of "Bleeding Kansas" in the 1850s. Harriet Beecher Stowe's *Uncle Tom's Cabin* (1851–1852) hardened feelings against slavery in the North; twenty years after her book was published she and Twain became next-door neighbors at the literary colony known as Nook Farm in Hartford, Connecticut.

Clemens's brother Orion was the first of the family to take up the newspaper trade, and Clemens worked with him, setting his first pieces in print in the early 1850s. Over forty published letters appeared in local papers in 1852. He continued sending Orion letters for publication at various times throughout his travels in the 1850s, and by 1853 he was sending pieces to publications in the East. In fact, the story considered his first real publication—"The Dandy Frightening the Squatter," a one-paragraph sketch of a crude river confrontation between a tough frontiersman and a "dandy" well-dressed gentleman from the East—appeared in B. P. Shillaber's (Boston) *Carpet-Bag* in March 1853. The publication of this story and one or two others is evidence of Clemens's ambition, but his path to a career as a writer was not direct.

In Keokuk, Iowa, working for his brother Orion, he amused young ladies with his tomfoolery and was more often than not seen carrying a book. He read and smoked extensively, often lying in bed late at night with book and pipe. Typesetting was dull work, and he thought of going to South America to make his fortune. Instead, he met Mississippi River pilot Horace Bixby and managed to convince Bixby to take him on as a "cub" pilot for $100 cash and $400 due from his piloting wages once he was licensed. In March 1866 he wrote to Orion that he could no longer correspond with Orion's paper because learning the river did not allow time for anything else. Even in the letters from this period (now reprinted in the University of California Press edition of Twain's letters), however, his narratives are pictorial and descriptive and his writing reflects an awareness of great authors and a direct but sophisticated literary style. The death of his brother Henry on June 21, 1858, from injuries in a steamboat explosion, darkened this period. In 1859, Twain later claimed, burlesques of Isaiah Sellers he published led to his taking up Sellers' pen name in 1863: a term for safe water, "Mark Twain."

Setting other people's words in type was not the kind of challenge a mind like Clemens's would relish as a life's work, although he was involved in publishing ventures throughout his life. Like other young people in Mississippi River towns, Clemens was fascinated by the glamorous life aboard the steamboats carrying goods and passengers up and down the river. As a cub pilot, he had to master the dynamics of steamboating and memorize the characteristics of a river that was a central conduit for life in the American Midwest and South. Its banks always changing, its conditions dangerous, competitive, and all but unregulated (his pilot's license was granted by the district of St. Louis, not by a state or federal agency), the Mississippi River was Mark Twain's incubator. Even his pen name reflected the writing career of a windy oldtimer, Captain Isaiah Sellers of New Orleans, who had used the leadsman's call for two fathoms ("Mark Twain!")— safe water for a steamboat to navigate. Clemens took over the pen name in Nevada a few years later, partly out of regret for having thoughtlessly lampooned the harmless old man, partly as sheer opportunism. Clemens received his pilot's license on April 9, 1859, but this period of his life ended a scant two years later when the Civil War interrupted river commerce.

When regular steamboat traffic on the river was shut down by the Civil War, the event not only ruined the wealthy merchants of the South and ended one of the most colorful eras in American history, it also ended Clemens's career as a riverboat pilot. After spending a few weeks flirting with the cause of the Confederacy (in which he may have killed an innocent man under the mistaken belief that he was a Yankee spy), and fearful of being forced to pilot Yankee gunboats, Clemens reached the same decision that many young Americans reached during the Vietnam War a hundred years later: the war was not for him and the issues involved were not ones that he cared to fight and die for. When his brother Orion, a supporter of Abraham Lincoln, was appointed secretary of the newly organized Nevada Territory, making him second in rank to the governor of the territory, Clemens was invited to go along as Orion's clerk—which office he filled briefly in the fall of 1861, although he managed to get himself listed as assistant secretary of the Territory in the 1862 territorial directory. The trip and its aftermath later became the basis for his second major travel narrative, *Roughing It*. The brothers arrived in Carson City, Nevada, on August 14, 1861, and immediately began the experience of flush times in the silver mining country. By December, Sam Clemens was himself mining in Humboldt County.

The western years from 1861 through 1866 were crucial for Twain's development into the mature reporter who burst into national prominence with "Jim Smiley and His Jumping Frog," later titled "The Celebrated Jumping Frog of Calaveras County," in 1865, and *The Innocents Abroad* in 1867 (as newspaper letters) and again in 1869 (as his first major book). "The Notorious Jumping Frog" and other collected western sketches had been published earlier as a slim volume of short pieces consistent with the writing of other humorists of the 1860s. Clemens had sent some letters signed "Josh" to the Virginia City

Territorial Enterprise in early 1862 and responded to its offer of $25 a week to turn reporter in August 1862. It was the most momentous decision of his life. Fellow reporter "Dan De Quille" (the pen name of William F. Wright) was a skillful comic writer and reporter, and editor Joseph T. Goodman encouraged his reporters to write expansively and adventurously, supporting the comic writer now finding his voice as Mark Twain. Indeed, Twain's "Petrified Man" hoax outraged editors, and his piece "The Bloody Massacre at Dutch Nick's," in the fall of 1863, ended up by attacking manipulations of mining stock; Goodman backed his reporter against editors angry at being tricked into printing Twain's criticism. Reporting on the Nevada legislature for the Virginia City *Territorial Enterprise*, Twain learned how to mock the jargon of power brokers, political fakers, and greed-driven capitalists. By the summer of 1863 he had attained celebrity status in San Francisco for his mix of reporting and comic commentary—usually with a strong ethical and moral tone. Some Nevada legislators were so angry at his reports that he claimed to have taken on the shorter name to make their denunciations less lengthy; but on December 11, 1863, he was given the comic honor of election to the "Third House," the delegation of reporters of legislative matters, and his humorous lecture was considered the best of its kind ever heard there, providing the basis for his coming career as a humorous lecturer and speaker. By 1864, at the age of twenty-nine, he had established a substantial reputation as a newspaper reporter.

Twain also met Artemus Ward, a literary comedian and comic lecturer who developed a profitable literary persona as an "old showman" modeled on P. T. Barnum. Ward's comic letters to the New York comic weekly *Vanity Fair* offered burlesque interviews with public notables, absurd trips to visit varied religious communities known as "Shakers" and "Free Lovers," and a jaundiced eye toward religious pretension and falsely inflated historical claims. The real person underlying the persona, Charles Farrar Browne of Maine, was a sophisticated deadpan lecturer on the platform, offering the young Mark Twain new insight into the flexibility of comic voice. Ward and Twain drank and cavorted together for a week or two at the end of 1863 in Nevada before Ward's lecture tour as the "Wild Humorist of the Plains" called him onward to Salt Lake City and the Mormons. Twain, already known as the "Moralist of the Main," would soon become known in the East as the "Wild Humorist of the Pacific Slope." Many of Ward's strengths as a writer, self-parodist, and sophisticated deadpan lecturer feigning naivete subsequently became part of Twain's repertoire of techniques.

Resisting Ward's entreaties to come east and stop wasting himself among the sagebrush, Twain went to San Francisco, writing for newspapers and learning to polish his skills under the tutelage of the writer Bret Harte, then a popular editor of *The Californian*. In 1863 Twain had arranged to become the Nevada correspondent for the San Francisco *Morning Call* and wrote "How to Cure a Cold" for the literary San Francisco weekly *Golden Era*. In 1864 and 1865 he reported for the *Call,* the *Golden Era,* and *The Californian*. In 1865, still writing for various papers, he visited Angel's Camp in Calaveras County because his criticisms of San Francisco police were causing him difficulties there. Even his general popularity was not a shield against a police force that resented his attacks on corruption within its ranks and its poor treatment of Chinese immigrants. Corresponding to the Sacramento *Union,* he visited Hawaii and scored a scoop on a disaster at sea in 1866 that was published in *Harper's Monthly* (but with his pseudonym misprinted as "M. Swain"). Most important, he convinced the editors of the *Alta California* to send him traveling to the East and Europe and the Holy Land and send back newspaper correspondence in the slangy, pragmatic viewpoint of the "new" westerners; he departed from San Francisco on December 15, 1866, his career more fully launched than even he realized. The letters, which began to appear in print in 1866, were tremendously successful, and the book that followed, *The Innocents Abroad* (based on a trip to Europe and the Holy Land aboard the steamer *Quaker City*), was even more so, remaining Twain's best-seller to the end of the century.

By 1869, now a prominent writer, Twain was courting Olivia Langdon, known as Livy, the daughter of an Elmira, New York, lumber and coal magnate and entrepreneur whose family adopted Twain into their lives. After Livy Langdon and Samuel Clemens were married in 1870, Twain bought a part interest in the Buffalo (New York) *Express,* a new life for the western humorist. The couple's happiness was soon darkened by the death of Livy's father, who had given them a handsome brick house as a wedding gift and admired Twain considerably. Then in 1871 Hartford, Connecticut, which boasted the literary colony Nook Farm, beckoned. There the Clemenses designed and built a more extravagant house, which was to be their home from 1874 to 1891 (it was sold in 1903). Their social life was punctuated by Twain's lecture tours, trips to Europe, and summers spent in Elmira, New York, at Quarry Farm, home of Susan Crane, Twain's sister-in-law. There Twain accomplished much of his best writing in the octagonal study that Susan had built on a bluff overlooking the Chenango River Valley for his special accommodation. A variety of books followed: *Sketches, New and Old* (1875), *The Adventures of Tom Sawyer* (1876), *The Prince and the Pauper* (1882), and *Life on the Mississippi* (1883).

Hartford was a northeastern intellectual city with a publishing bent. Livy's friends, the Hooker family, resided there. The Clemens's house would be less than 100 yards from Harriet Beecher Stowe's, and the Beechers were a prominent part of the life of both Hartford and Elmira, where the Langdons had some involvement with the Underground Railroad, carrying slaves to freedom in Canada, water cures, and other ideas that were advanced for their time.

Twain's lifelong friend, Joseph Twichell, pastor of the Asylum Hill Congregational Church, had come to Hartford on the recommendation of Horace Bushnell, a leader of the "meliorist" philosophy, that expressed tolerance of diversity and optimism about improvement of the human condition. Twichell and Twain both belonged to the Monday Evening Club, founded by J. Hammond Trumbull, an intellectual stimulus. The Clemens family rented a pew in Twichell's church, although they were not members, and he officiated at their marriages and deaths, beginning with the marriage of Sam and Livy in 1870. Twichell and Twain took a number of trips together, and Twichell figures most notably in *A Tramp Abroad* (1880). Another Nook Farm resident was Charles Dudley Warner, a popular humorist and editor of the Hartford *Courant* who co-authored with Twain *The Gilded Age* (1873), Twain's first success in the novel form. William Dean Howells, editor of the *Atlantic Monthly*, could visit easily, and Twain and Howells, known as the "dean" of American literary realism and a major figure in the development of American literature in the period 1870–1910 became close personal and literary friends. Howells and Livy counseled Twain on matters of taste and style in his books, leading to later charges by critics that he had been emasculated and made falsely genteel in an ordeal of censorship.

Hartford was also a center for religious publishing in the United States and the home of the American Publishing Company, which became Twain's publisher. The company sold books "by subscription," sending sample books door-to-door with salesmen who solicited advance payment. Less dignified than publication by a recognized major publishing company, the medium nevertheless was lucrative for Twain. His lecture tours in the 1870s also helped to bolster this kind of sales. He eventually founded his own ill-fated firm, the Charles L. Webster Company, run by a nephew. Never a money-maker, it contributed to Twain's bankruptcy after his extensive but unsuccessful investment in the Paige typesetter machine caused Twain's fortune to be lost in the early 1890s. Later, after Henry H. Rogers, a Standard Oil vice president, reorganized Twain's finances, Twain published with the Harper & Brothers Company. His literary properties were subsequently reorganized and turned over to the Harper Company, which put his works into sets of "uniform editions," beginning in 1903, befitting "classics" ("Classic: a book which people praise but don't read," Twain once commented). The ethical model created by the payoff of his debts "cent per cent" and the appearance of the uniform editions cemented his reputation as an icon of American life and letters. Although the original books had garish woodcuts throughout, the Harper editions had only frontispieces without further illustrations. In this way the style by which Mark Twain, the vulgar comedian, had risen to fame was modified, formalized, and made gravely classical, far different from the texts his original readers relished.

Further literary successes followed *Innocents Abroad*. These included *Roughing It* (1872) with outrageous tales of the "mother load" and "flush times" in Nevada and California. To make the length needed to sell the work door-to-door as a subscription book, Twain concluded the volume with a pre-vision of his later anti-imperialist writings in deft comic literary reportage on his visit to Hawaii in 1866. The novel co-authored with Charles Dudley Warner, author of the gently humorous *My Summer in a Garden* (1871) and *Backlog Studies* (1873), gave a label to its era, *The Gilded Age*; the political satire was published in 1874. Short stories as well kept Twain's name before an eager public. In 1874 "A True Story," one of his best short pieces (although he felt it was a departure from his regular comic line), brought him into the pages of the prestigious *Atlantic Monthly*, now edited by friend and literary confidant William Dean Howells; "Old Times on the Mississippi" would appear there as a serial soon thereafter, thoroughly identifying Twain with the old Southwest and the Mississippi River as well as with the Western Slope and California and Nevada. A major gaffe by Twain in 1877 was an ill-fated burlesque of the American literary eminences Emerson, Holmes, and Longfellow for the "Whittier Dinner" convened by the *Atlantic Monthly* to honor the poet John Greenleaf Whittier on his birthday (and incidentally the magazine as well); Howells consoled the distraught humorist after his jokes on pretension fell flat, but a few newspapers criticized the upstart's irreverence.

Twain's social irreverence toward institutions and popular reputations might have been an outward manifestation of his deep-seated concerns about spirituality. The narrow and literalistic Presbyterianism he saw around him was ill fitted to the broader and more universal love he craved. Twichell reminisced that Twain got down on his knees beside him at his bedside one night and prayed for faith, but such a literal request was not likely to succeed. Indeed, Twain's quarrel with God was based on his distaste for a world in which death seemed a blessed relief from worse pain inflicted by chance or human depravity, and where man seemed a self-centered machine. Even Livy's faith was shaken by Twain's iconoclastic attacks on religion, but Twichell's sympathetic musing that Twain was a desperate man, a Calvinist who didn't believe in God, characterizes the faith Twain never completely stopped wishing he could restore in the face of his own skepticism.

For every plaudit of praise, there was a brickbat of disapproval or a caution. P. T. Barnum sent clippings and tried to interest Twain in a joint venture but was so identified with the art of money-getting and "humbug," Twain did not join with him. Thomas Nast, the cartoonist, soon famous for undermining New York's Tweed ring, the corrupt Democratic administration from "Tammany Hall," power brokers looting New York City's municipal treasury, offered to do on-stage charcoal illustrations while Twain talked. P. V. Nasby and Twain flirted with the idea of a joint lecture; pioneer realist J. W. DeForest suggested a joint collection of satiric short stories, but he was a minor writer—his letter to Twain remains, but the response, if any, is unknown. Thomas Bailey Aldrich's wife refused to invite Twain to dinner in the 1860s because she thought on the basis of his odd mannerisms that he was drunk; by the 1890s, his drawling lecture style was internationally famous. B. P. Shillaber, who had published his early piece in 1853, cautioned him in the mid-1870s to make hay while the sun shines. The comic magazine *Life* in 1885 lambasted *Huck Finn* as coarse and inelegant, but Joel Chandler Harris, famed as "Uncle Remus" and later Brander Matthews, the critic, considered the novel the best candidate yet for the title "The Great American Novel." Twain lectured with fellow author George W. Cable in 1884 and 1885, billed as "Twins of Genius." Although Twain learned much from Cable's views on southern racism, he was frustrated by his piety. Popular humorist Max Adeler (Charles Heber Clark) accused Twain of plagiarizing *The Fortunate Island* in *A Connecticut Yankee* in 1889. "Mere" humor was little prized in America in the later half of the nineteenth century, and many humorists seemed more ashamed than proud of their livelihood. Twain wrote many pot-boilers to support his expensive life-style, but the majority of his work contained moral and ethical insights that thoughtful critics praised. To reach the level of moral purpose accomplished by Twain at the time of his death was an unusual and extraordinary achievement. His fiftieth birthday, celebrated in the pages of *The Critic* in 1885, and his seventieth birthday banquet were the major literary events of the age with astonishing guest lists of writers and publishers.

Twain's family grew like his reputation, but not without personal tragedy. His first child, a son named Langdon (after Livy's father), was born in 1870 but died of illness in 1872—Twain blamed himself for exposing the child to cold weather. Three girls followed: Susy (1872–1896), Clara (1874–1962), and Jean (1880–1909). Twain was probably a difficult father: unpredictable, effusive, and irrascible by turns, and frequently absent, while attending to professional matters. His bankruptcy in 1894 was a humiliation that disrupted family life. In 1898 his creditors were paid off; he had escaped from bankruptcy, but his beloved Susy had died while he was absent, and for several years after her death the family celebrated no holidays.

Twain once remarked that Livy not only edited his books, she edited him as well; but Twain was always a social challenge, fond of cigars and addicted to profanity, given to large social gaffes and deep remorse. He was likely to get up from the dinner table and regale guests with an old-fashioned country "break down," a shuffling country dance, or folksy stories and bang out "O Dem Golden Slippers" on the piano. At one dinner he spat hot soup on his plate, glared at the woman across from him, and burst out, "Some damn fools would have swallowed that." Yet he sat up nights nursing his dying father-in-law and his infant son, and he paid the scholarships of several Negro students, one to Yale Law School, remarking it was part of the debt owed by every white man to every black man for the fact of Negro slavery. So powerful was his endorsement of the touring Fiske Jubilee Singers in London in the early 1870s, and so grateful were the black collegians raising money for their *Alma Mater* Fiske College for it, that he had to fight their manager in the lobby to pay his own admission to the show. For the last thirty years of his life Twain was a powerful and sought-after literary lion who lived with incredible intensity, reaching deep into his own childhood for folk meanings that informed eveything he wrote. When news of Livy's death was brought to him, he threw back his head and burst out with "Swing Low, Sweet Chariot."

Throughout the late 1870s and 1880s Twain's books and stories appeared in profusion: *The Adventures of Tom Sawyer* in 1876, *A Tramp Abroad* in 1880, *The Prince and the Pauper* in 1881 (a family favorite that was made into a front-porch play for which the girls made tickets), and more stories. *Adventures of Huckleberry Finn* was published in England in 1884 to secure British copyright and shortly thereafter in America (in 1885). Like Twain's other books, it was sold by subscription. The story was told in the first person by a slangy river boy who spoke and acted the part of a lower-class child of 1845, offending readers such as those at the Concord, Massachusetts, public library, who threw the book out even while others such as the author Joel Chandler Harris, author of the popular "Uncle Remus" stories, praised it as "The Great American Novel." In 1888, Yale University awarded Clemens a Master of Arts, his first honorary university degree.

The last eleven years of the century brought darker times. Twain had always fancied himself something of a businessman, and he held patents for a self-pasting scrapbook and a suspender-garter for stockings. He was among the first American writers to use a typewriter, if not the first, as he boasted to Howells in 1874. It was expensive to maintain the Twain family household, and such sources of revenue augmented royalties. Twain's ill-timed investment in the Paige typesetting machine, the prototype of which still sits in the cellar of his Hartford home, grew out of this interest but brought Twain to bankruptcy in 1894. By then, however, the family had already begun a painful reconstruction of its lifestyle, living in Europe as expatriates to reduce expenses. Some critics argue that Twain's pessimism from his deteriorating finances might have been reflected in *A Connecticut Yankee in King Arthur's Court* (1889), *The American Claimant* (1892), and *Pudd'nhead Wilson and Those Extraordinary Twins* (1894). Livy's health was equally a cause for concern. It deteriorated throughout this period, some claim in response to Twain's goading about religion before her death in Italy in 1904. Emotionally, Livy and Sam never fully recovered from the unexpected death of daughter Susy from spinal meningitis, with Joe Twichell at her bedside, in 1896, while Livy speeded across the Atlantic to nurse her daughter.

An extended stay in Vienna, Austria, in 1897–1898 seems to have influenced Twain's brooding views at the end of the century. Anti-Semitism and political bickering mixed with advanced social thought stimulated him to begin "The Mysterious Stranger" as well as to write about American imperialism. His bankruptcy and determination to make good on his debts had caused him to undertake an around-the-world lecture tour in 1896 that completed his standing as a citizen of the world. The result was *Following the Equator* in 1897, published a year after *Personal Recollections of Joan of Arc*, a book at least partially modeled on Susy. Twain's personal fortunes began to recover, but more pessimistic works followed—among them many manuscripts that Twain considered unpublishable because of their despairing message. "The Man That Corrupted Hadleyburg" was published in 1900, but the "Great Dark" manuscripts and "The Mysterious Stranger" were only resurrected by later editors. "Extracts from Captain Stormfield's Visit to Heaven" appeared in 1907–1908 and was not too skeptical for popular sales, as Twain had thought since conceiving it as a burlesque of *The Gates Ajar* (1869) by Mrs. Elizabeth Stuart Phelps Ward, many of whose ideas he apparently adapted. American and European imperialism in the Philippines, Cuba, Africa, and China came increasingly to outrage Twain, and he thundered against what he saw as these international abuses in "To the Person Sitting in Darkness" (1901), "Battle Hymn of the Republic (Brought Down to Date)" (1901), "The Czar's Soliloquy" (1905), "The War Prayer" (1905), and "King Leopold's Soliloquy" (1905), among others. More broadly stated were pleas for decency and humanity in "Does the Race of Man Love a Lord," *What Is Man?* (1906), and other cries from the heart. Twain attempted to compensate for the loss of his own family by adopting various "Angelfish," young girls whom he befriended and enrolled in his pool of surrogate grandchildren, the "Aquarium Club." At the same time he was truly a literary lion, sought after for newspaper squibs, brief quotations, and after-dinner speeches everywhere. Book revenues enabled him to construct an Italian villa, "Stormfield" (named after the story), in Redding, Connecticut, in 1908.

Daughter Clara was married to Ossip Gabrilowitsch at Stormfield on October 6, 1909, but the mixture of joy and grief continued. Twain's daughter Jean died there on December 24, 1909, the victim of an epileptic seizure. Twain's biographer and executor, Albert Bigelow Paine took Twain to Bermuda to recover from his loss, but his health rapidly deteriorated. As Halley's Comet streaked through the sky, as it had done when Twain was born in 1835, Twain passed away at Stormfield on April 21, 1910, and was buried alongside

Langdon, Susy, Livy, and Jean in the cemetery at Elmira, New York. He was acknowledged at his death to have been one of the great benefactors of, and spokesmen for, humankind.

One could say that Twain had grown bitter in his later years, but one could also say that he represented the maturation of America itself, from the booming monopolies and political corruption of the 1870s, which he satirized, to the deeper—and more intransigent—problems of world power and responsibility in an age of imperialism. Democracy was Twain's point of absolute idealism, and his own life represented its possibilities in a capitalist economy; but the authority of absolute monarchies, established churches, and even village aristocracy suggested an unredeemed world, one that Twain saw as perversely constructed around pain rather than joy. It is not surprising that his last works expressed some of his deepest and most desperate thoughts about God and humankind, but those thoughts had always underlain his moral vision.

Twain's Career and Contributions to American Literature

The post–Civil War period in American literature has long been described as a battleground where the war for literary realism was fought and won against literary romanticism and popular sentimentalism. "Realists" seemed to favor photographic portraits of everyday events, whereas writers of "romance," featured exotic far-away places and heroic actions. Sentimental romance and didactic religious writers couched their stories in moralistic admonitions, which the realists preferred not to do, letting characters and events bring the readers to their own ethical and moral realizations. Mark Twain, a professional writer well aware of popular taste, knowingly "donned the cap and bells," playing the jester, as many aesthetic literary critics complained, rather than writing the "serious" literature that they felt would have been a "proper" calling. Like other literary comedians, he burlesqued sentimental writers and lambasted the devices of romance writers such as James Fenimore Cooper. In fact, Twain's career was actually several careers rolled into one—writer, popular lecturer, newspaperman, publisher, and, perhaps, investor—and the styles in which he wrote, including the sentimental and melodramatic, were equally varied. Later he gained a broader role as literary statesman and took up the cause of international humanitarianism, writing as a world spokesman. Much has been made of many unfinished and very pessimistic manuscripts produced at the end of Twain's career, but from the outside, and as presented in the Harper Company's "uniform editions" of his works, his career presents a facade of unparalleled success: an American dream come true.

MARK TWAIN'S CAREER

"Mark Twain" is a literary creation, developed over a period of eight to ten years by a small-town Missouri boy who had been a typesetter and riverboat pilot up to the time of the outbreak of the Civil War in 1861. Although some called author Samuel Langhorne Clemens "Mark," many friends called him "Sam" and his wife called him "youth." Like newspaper humorists John Phoenix and Artemus Ward before him and Orpheus C. Kerr, Petroleum Vesuvius Nasby, and later Max Adeler and "Josiah Allen's Wife," he wrote under a pen name because humorous authorship was not a particularly well-respected profession in America at that time. Joseph C. Neal, a Philadelphian writing under his own name in the 1830s and 1840s, was recognized as the "American Dickens," but few other serious writers (with the exception of songwriters), wished to be identified with a popular audience. The Southwestern humorist Augustus Baldwin Longstreet had simply published his popular *Georgia Scenes* in 1835 as written by "A Native Georgian." To the newspaper humorists like the majority of those just named, humor came naturally, yet not always without soul-searching. Before committing himself to the "low" calling of humor, Twain underwent a struggle with his conscience and even spoke in one letter to his family from San Francisco (October 20, 1865) of "pistols or poison" if he was not out of debt in three months. By January 20, 1866, however, he boasted to his mother and sister of his literary success: at thirty years of age, his career was launched.

Clemens's life was vibrant, and thus provided ample material on which to base his writing, but literary models were also numerous. He later cited Cervantes' *Don Quixote* and Oliver Goldsmith's *Citizen of the World* as his favorite models of good writing; he certainly also encountered the work of John Milton. Of course he knew Shakespeare and among English humorists was familiar with Laurence Stern, Tom Hood, and London's *Punch*; Charles Dickens, William Thackeray, and Tobias George Smollett; and among lesser known humorists Albert Smith, who originated the comic travel lecture in the 1840s. Twain read the works of Jonathan Swift but forgot how powerful Swift's writing was until rereading *Gulliver's Travels* while courting Olivia Langdon. He shows evidence of reading American humorists from the Southwest, including A. B. Longstreet, J. G. Baldwin, J. J. Hooper, and G. W. Harris. From the Northeast, he knew Seba Smith's "Jack Downing" vernacular political satires and the work of B. P. Shillaber, and T. C. Haliburton, along with sketches by Joseph C. Neal and G. W. Curtis's *The Potiphar Papers*. Most notable in the 1850s would have been comic sketches by John Phoenix, "The Veritable Squibob" (pseudonym of George H. Derby) and Artemus Ward (Charles Farrar Browne)—the two writers were the most important literary comedians before Mark Twain. Petroleum V. Nasby and Josh Billings would have been among his readings in the 1860s. As a class, the American literary humorists were experimental in their use of language and fond of exaggeration, often reported or wrote in slang, and freely intermingled political and economic satire in their social satires, literary burlesques, and caricatures. Literary polish, as such, was less a goal than depicting unique and evanescent local scenes. Satire and grotesque exaggeration blended to attack oafishness, snobbishness, and various forms of meanness. Indeed, the urgent idealism of the American democracy was often seen through satires of its deficiencies.

Newspapers were a major publishing outlet before the Civil War, followed by an immense number of usually short-lived periodicals—monthly magazines mostly, but also weeklies. B. P. Shillaber's Boston *Carpet-Bag* (1850–1853) was one such weekly oriented toward railroad travelers, featuring humorous pieces of varying lengths from various regions, including Down East, urban, Southwest, and frontier. Another was *The Knickerbocker*, a more literary undertaking based in New York City with lengthier articles and a sophisticated style resonating with echoes of England and Europe. Finally, William Trotter Porter's *The Spirit of the Times* combined racing news for horse lovers and hunters with comic stories, many identified with the Old Southwest and supposed to be authentic combinations of folk story and frontier experience uniquely American. It is important to note the diversity of regions and styles: southwestern humor, for roughness of dialect and character as well as grittiness of episodes; western humor for tall tales and exaggeration; northeastern humor for irony and the use of wit, language, and style; and the literary comedians and Artemus Ward for posed naivete and the dead-pan narrator. As the newspapers and periodicals of the period 1870–1910 developed, a new wave of domestic and political humor replaced older, similar forms and displaced most of the more formal-seeming Augustan satire and stilted invective of the Federal era. Many humorists wrote newspaper columns, and even Twain himself edited a humor department for the *Galaxy* in the early 1870s for a brief time. "Old Times on the Mississippi" ran in the *Atlantic Monthly* as a serial in five monthly installments. Each piece had to be self-contained, but it also had to suggest a continuity with other chapters and a developing theme that would be worth following. Humor at this time was a breathtakingly diverse genre, harder to generalize than most critics seem to acknowledge, and it was rapidly becoming a recognized national genre.

"Mark Twain" was born—or, more accurately, inherited—when Samuel Clemens, a young newspaper reporter in Carson City, Nevada, decided to borrow the pen name of Isaiah Sellers, a Mississippi steamboat pilot and occasional contributor to the New Orleans newspaper the *Picayune*. The articles signed "Mark Twain" for the Virginia City *Territorial Enterprise* in 1863 were breezy, slangy reports of the doings of the Nevada Territorial Legislature, often written in mock-heroic, pseudo-biblical, or mock-political language. No rules applied to such writing. The medium was well fitted to develop comic invective, irony, and pseudo-realistic descriptions. It also dissolved into parody and literary hoaxing. Indeed, some of Twain's most notorious early pieces were hoaxes. For example, in "Petrified Man" (1862) limestone petrifies a man with one thumb pressed against his nose and the fingers extended while the other thumb holds one eye open in an exaggerated wink. Even this nose-thumbing wasn't enough to tip off some editors that they had a hoax on their hands. "A Bloody Massacre near Carson" (1863) detailed a grisly murder to bait readers into criticizing San Francisco newspapers for their complicity in allowing fraudulent mining schemes to go unexposed. Subsequently much criticism was directed at Twain by readers who probably would have skipped over an exposé of mining frauds and newspaper complicity, and by editors who would not have printed his attacks if they had been written directly as ethical statements.

If Twain's only capacity had been in the writing of hoaxes, it is not very likely we would know his name now. Throughout his private letters his sense of morality is strong, even though frequently shown in reverse as he teases his mother. That same moral sense led him to write exposés of stock frauds in Nevada. In fact, his reputation as the "Moralist of the Main" seems to be what caused Artemus Ward to seek him out in 1863; he was a writer with strong ethical positions. In San Francisco, Twain found the brutal treatment of Chinese immigrants so outrageous that he satirized it sharply, but his writing was rejected by cautious editors fearful of offending racist white readers. Twain's attitude is best represented by "Disgraceful Persecution of a Boy," a story written and published in *The Galaxy* in 1870 and reprinted in his collection *Sketches, New and Old* in 1875. His San Francisco editors were not ready for such a dose of moral protest against racism; his pieces were repressed and he had to seek work elsewhere. The jumping frog story represented a big break for Twain. The frog story was a "local color" piece sent east to be included with Artemus Ward's *Travels among the Mormons*; but, missing that publication, it was printed in Henry Clapp's *Saturday Press* on November 18, 1865, as "Jim Smiley and His Jumping Frog." It became an instant national sensation; its key line rang in every ear; "I don't see no points about that frog that's any better'n any other frog." Twain's ensuing national celebrity caused the San Francisco *Alta California* to hire him as a traveling correspondent, first to the East and then to Europe and the Holy Land as part of a tour on the steamship *Quaker City*.

Twain's letters to the *Alta* were to become his first major book. *The Innocents Abroad* (1869) chronicled a trip to Europe and the Holy Land, the sort of new experience that commercial success was enabling many affluent middle-class Americans to seek. This was a mirroring in American culture of the European

"Grand Tour," which had initiated young Englishmen to continental culture earlier, but with a sanctimonious bent that suited the religious heritage of burgeoning American capitalists. Twain, however, took the trip as a westerner, a pragmatic skeptic ready to skewer the cheap merchandising of culture and religion by cynical Europeans and degraded Arabs. Allusions in the original letters to P. T. Barnum as an exploiter of mass culture and gullibility were frequent. Twain satirized the falseness and hypocrisy of the pretentiously religious pilgrims at the same time. It was a hilarious combination, and American readers loved the book for its dry irony about "pieces of the true," which were numerous enough to make several crosses. Subtitled "The New Pilgrim's Progress," the comic travelogue was an innovation as profound as Twain's later novels, for it provided a comic work with a serious moral message in popular language. Twain's subsequent comic lectures expanded the book's profitability. The American Publishing Company, which had specialized in religious books, went on to become one of the nation's foremost publishers, of humorous works; it also offered the comic writings of "Josiah Allen's Wife" (in reality the unmarried suffragist Marietta Holley) which paralleled Twain's from a feminist perspective without reaching their stature.

Having already begun a career as a popular lecturer, even before his "Sandwich Island" lectures in 1866, Twain was astride a popular wave of literary enthusiasm, bolstered by lecture opportunities in educational "lyceum" programs and expanding outlets for his comic copy. The writer most like him, Artemus Ward, died in March 1867 from pneumonia at the age of thirty-three, making Twain appear all the more unique. Ward had matured by the time of his death into a sophisticated travel humorist able to integrate a sense of history into his burlesques and was recognized by the most important humor magazine of the age, *Punch* of London, for his unique American voice. Thus in a sense his passing was fortuitous for Twain, who might have rested uncomfortably in his shadow for several more years; even so, comparisons continued for a decade or more. In the meantime Twain capitalized on the westernness of his "voice" by lecturing on topics related to Nevada and, in 1872, publishing *Roughing It*, the story of his trip from Missouri to Nevada, incorporating tales of mining and outlaws like "Slade," and concluding with the exotic Sandwich Island chapters from his trip to Hawaii. Short stories written for various periodicals also kept his name before the public. He was a triple threat as a literary figure, and his acceptance by the Hartford literati was, in a sense, a national as much as an individual accomplishment.

Twain's career throughout the 1870s sustained success after success on the literary front. *The Gilded Age* built on his strengths: the reportorial voice; the western exaggeration, irony, and sarcasm; the ability to draw colorful characters and provide slangy comic references; and the strong underlying sense of democratic responsibility, history, and humanity. In January 1875, "Old Times on the Mississippi" began appearing in the *Atlantic Monthly*, marking Twain's claim to the South as well as the West as his regions of expertise and bringing him into the inner circle of recognized literary writers in America. Western sketches and more recent work were joined to make *Sketches, New and Old* in 1875. His collaboration with Charles Dudley Warner on *The Gilded Age* gave him the confidence to venture further into the novel form, which he did with his first major "boy book," *The Adventures of Tom Sawyer*, in 1876. The terrifying character Indian Joe and the adventures of Tom Sawyer with the cat and the painkiller and his rescuing of Becky from a caning in school were engaging to Twain's readers, but the sequence involving Tom's conniving to get other boys to white-wash Aunt Polly's fence while paying him for doing the unwanted painting chore has made the book a world-renowned classic since its publication. Pirated editions of Twain's works in London and Toronto were irritants, and many reviewers dismissed him as a literary clown, but a growing number of authors and critics recognized the hero Tom's accuracy to life and Twain's importance as a writer.

By the 1880s Twain was well established. After publishing *A Tramp Abroad* in 1880, he moved to the Boston publisher James R. Osgood (who was better at billiards than book selling, perhaps adding something of a cultural cachet to his publishing venue, although still selling books by subscription). *A Tramp Abroad* purported to relate a European walking tour with Twain's friend Joe Twichell, but it was a "tramp" book featuring "gossip" about Europe, a collection of burlesques, western stories, and reportage; its best pieces are stories from the American West, in fact. Some critics felt that *The Prince and the Pauper* (1881) was a limp departure from his best vein into medievalism and a sort of soft sentimentalism marred rather than enhanced by a tendency to western slang. Yet Twain's wife and children loved the book, and many others, including Howells and Norwegian-American realist writer H. H. Boyesen, found its purity to indicate a valuable deepening of Twain's capabilities as a writer. (More than any other of his works, it inspired a powerful film experience in 1937 with Errol Flynn as Miles Hendon, one that many viewers have never forgotten.) In 1882 another volume of short stories, *The Stolen White Elephant*, also appeared. Sales were reasonable but not outstanding. As Twain's work came to the attention of serious literary critics such as John Nichol, a dour Scot who published one of the first full-scale literary histories of America in 1882, brickbats flew, Nichol labeled him "degenerate."

If Twain needed an answer to this criticism, it came in the form of three of the most characteristic books in American literature: *Life on the Mississippi* (1883), the last book he published with Osgood; *Adventures of Huckleberry Finn* (1885), published by his own firm, Charles L. Webster and Company;

and *A Connecticut Yankee in King Arthur's Court* (1889). *Mark Twain's Library of Humor* (1888), compiled with and written mostly by Howells, provides an index to the kind of humor Twain favored and knew. The Mississippi River book used material from the *Atlantic Monthly* and added chapters to update the history of the river to modern and more mundane and prosaic times as a commercial conduit.

Unlike the serial novels of Charles Dickens, Twain's works were visionary reportage involved with travelogues, a medium best described as semi-fiction and well suited to American newspaper readers. Even Twain's novels adopted some of these characteristics. *Adventures of Huckleberry Finn* featured one of Tom Sawyer's sidekicks in a purposeful effort to make a sequel and companion; the "voice" of the book escaped into an exotic new form, a first-person narrative that was slangy, naive, vulgar, and horrifyingly dead-pan in describing a range of topics previously unacceptable in Victorian American parlors and drawing rooms: drunkenness, child abuse, thievery, murder of animals and men, and crude violence. Critics were divided on the book. Some praised its voice and vision, others decried its portrayal of vicious aspects of life and its vulgar model of boy life in the character Huckleberry Finn. The book's importance in the development of an American voice and conscience continues to be examined by scholars and literary historians over a hundred years after its publication.

A Connecticut Yankee in 1889 infuriated many British critics as an attack on honored Arthurian chivalric traditions and decreased Twain's book sales in Great Britain. The transmigration of a Yankee mechanic back 1,300 years into a stronghold of aristocratic privilege and mystical trickery, however, gave the author an opportunity to elaborate in varied plot events on his egalitarian beliefs, his love of entrepreneurialism, and his intense empathy for the victims of slavery and economic oppression. Hank Morgan, the tale's title character and narrator, like Huckleberry Finn, undergoes a number of travel adventures, but over medieval roads and through medieval dungeons rather than on a river raft. His travels expose a variety of social failings; some of the failings, as with Huck, are even embodied in himself.

The 1890s appeared to be a time of diminishing power for Twain, at least initially. Both his and Livy's mothers died in 1890; and the Paige typesetter, Twain's largest commitment to a bid for wealth as a capitalist entrepreneur, became a consuming problem that finally led to his bankruptcy in 1894. Further, Twain suffered from rheumatism and other illnesses, including gout. Much of his writing at various points during this period was not intended for publication. Nevertheless, his production of short stories and books continued. *The American Claimant* was published in 1892; *The Tragedy of Pudd'nhead Wilson and the Comedy of Those Extraordinary Twins* followed in 1894; and *Personal Recollections of Joan of Arc* followed in 1896, after appearing in *Harper's Maga-*

zine in 1895 anonymously so it would be taken "seriously." In 1895 and 1896 Twain undertook personal adventures that fully established his standing as a world-class moral spokesman. H. H. Rogers, a Standard Oil vice president, took over his affairs in 1894, and in 1895 Harpers began acquiring the rights to Twain's works that would lead to major "standard" editions. Twain also determined, at the urging of Rogers and Livy, to pay off his creditors penny for penny after his bankruptcy. In 1896 he began an around-the-world lecture tour, which led, in 1897, to *Following the Equator.*

The turn of the century brought increasing recognition and extensive social demands for Mark Twain the personality, and Twain met many of them. He also felt increasing outrage at American foreign policy, which led to brutality in the Philippines and China. "To the Person Sitting in Darkness," "Battle Hymn of the Republic (Brought Down to Date)," "King Leopold's Soliloquy," and a variety of other works protested the evils of colonialism and the repression of the "confiding" people of color of other lands; this was a distinguished conclusion to a career of protest against the inhumane treatment of Chinese immigrants and African Americans in the 1860s. "Was It Heaven? Or Hell?," "A Dog's Tale," "The Diary of Adam and Eve," "Extracts from Captain Stormfield's Visit to Heaven," and "What Is Man?" all appeared during this decade, but "The United States of Lyncherdom," "The Mysterious Stranger," and a variety of manuscripts touching on pessimistic themes did not see print. Twain's "Autobiography," rambling dictation, also appeared. Following his death, Albert Bigelow Paine began publishing his speeches, letters (censored), and biography, and thus the modern Twain industry began.

Despite the appearance of a rather snide critique in 1906 entitled "Is Mark Twain Dead?" implying that he had published nothing "new" in some time, Twain's works continued to emerge in the first couple of decades following 1900. Partly, Twain's concern that he was "writing with a pen warmed up in Hell" caused him to place certain injunctions on the publishing of his works. His daughter Clara's judgment also restrained some publications. Still, some of his harsher writings were released in books by Paine, by Bernard DeVoto, and after mid-century through the ongoing Iowa-California Edition of Mark Twain's works, which brought out the "Great Dark Manuscripts." This last "complete" edition of Twain's works—including massive compilations of his letters, notebooks, many manuscripts, and newspaper writings lost since their original publication and never reprinted before—should run to roughly seventy-seven volumes and finish *perhaps* in the year 2024. A controversial decision by the editors of this series caused them to completely redo an already completed volume of *Roughing It*, largely because it was published without illustrations and with some information and editorial decisions that were in need of correction. The point is that Twain's books are now understood in their totality to be cultural documents as well as "a good read." In the meantime, Oxford University Press brought to market a "complete" works of twenty-nine volumes in 1996 that features texts of the first editions, all with original illustrations. Previously unseen Twain works continue to emerge, and scholarly books on Twain appear at the rate of four or five a year in the United States. There is even more publication abroad, some encouraged by Mark Twain Circles in various countries.

MARK TWAIN AND AMERICAN HUMOR

Although it was common among critics from 1920 through 1970 to more or less ignore Twain as a literary humorist, except in relation to the Southwest, humor—specifically "American" humor—was the envelope that carried his message. From as early as Thomas Morton of Merrymount's false report in *New English Canaan* (1637) that American Indian babies were born white but stained brown by being dipped in walnut juice at birth, Americans have been particularly adept at the exaggerated lie to strangers. The western humor of the mining camps was loaded with such material, including the tale of the mine shaft that was so long it stuck out of the other side of the mountain 200 feet in the air. Preposterous jokes abounded in newspapers and could be blended with the weapon of political satire, which also represented a major American political force from its use during the American colonial insurrection onward. Twain fused these traditions during the course of his career. Even though and while his political writings of the 1860s and 1870s might have appeared to be mere newspaper ephemera, they were a continuous strand that broadened throughout his novels and into his anti-imperialist writings in the 1900s. In this, Twain stands alone.

In his eulogy on Twain in *My Mark Twain* (1910), William Dean Howells also saw Mark Twain as a lone figure: "Emerson, Longfellow, Lowell, Holmes—I knew them all and all the rest of our sages, poets, seers, critics, humorists; they were like one another and like other literary men; but Clemens was sole, incomparable, the Lincoln of our literature" (p. 84). As a humorist Twain had fused "jokes" with an intense sympathy for suffering humanity, and he had raised a minor art to the level of vision. Egalitarianism, empathy, and entrepreneurialism are his three major themes, and within them he championed the downtrodden of every race and color. The fact that he included caricatures of minorities as well as majorities in his works makes them confusing to superficial readers, but this practice is illuminated by Twain's comment that you didn't have to tell him if a man was black or white, once you said that he was a human being you had said the worst possible thing about him. In 1896 Brander Matthews noted this complexity in an essay entitled "The Penalty of Humor"; the penalty was being misunderstood by readers who did not understand satire and the capacity of burlesque and caricature to further the ends of political protest. The enriched use of history as the stuff of comedy, carried by Twain's predecessors as literary comedians such as Artemus Ward, became in Twain a full-blown fictive world: in England, where two dramatic anti-slavery novels take place as "medieval" life; and in the American South in the 1845 period, where *Adventures of Huckleberry Finn* and *Pudd'nhead Wilson* are set. American slave narratives, the life and writings of P. T. Barnum, personal experience, southwestern humor and literary comedy, and even the blending of dialect with cacography (the use of misspelling for comic effect rather than as dialect) provided an array of literary tools that Twain, uniquely, fashioned into a canon of major and sustained proportions.

The literary comedians contributed to the national thread in Twain's humor. Thomas Chandler Haliburton, a Nova Scotian writing tales featuring a Yankee clockmaker named Sam Slick, gave a model of humane comedy that was sympathetic to its subjects' welfare even while decrying their economic innocence and showing a sharp trader taking comic advantage of them. Artemus Ward gathered history and politics into his comedy, but as literary material rather than satiric attacks on "issues," thereby jumping from the mundane to the universal and offering the possibility of converting such material to a truly literary format. John Phoenix added the strain of literary foolery and whimsy that could still touch a human issue. Lowell in *The Biglow Papers* might have presaged this development. One could even say that a sense of the "literary" as a possible outcome of comic writing was developing (1) in England with the writings of Dickens and Thackeray, as well as with the prominence of *Punch*; (2) in America; and (3) through increasingly available historical writings such as Cervantes' *Don Quixote*, regarded in Spain as something of a literary indiscretion because of low statue of humor in Spanish culture, but to Twain one of the most exquisite books ever written. In Cervantes he found the picaresque form—a rogue's adventures embodied in a traveler's experience. The format was close to that of travel reportage but gave Twain the medium in which to express jokes and comic anecdotes as plot material, practices typical of the picaresque genre but departing from the more photographic realism of other writers. Don Quixote's skeptical sidekick, Sancho Panza, also provided a powerful literary precedent for undercutting attitudes expressed by the romance writers. Because Twain saw romanticism as distorting American life and sympathies, especially in the South, he could blend this voice with his own reportorial voice or put it in the mouths of various characters. He did both.

Southwestern humor was traditionally regarded as the central influence on Twain by scholars during the first part of the 1900s. Arguments for the importance of southwestern humor in Twain's work are strong. As pioneer humorists of the frontier and its local beliefs, writers such as A. B. Longstreet, Joseph G.

Baldwin, Thomas Bangs Thorpe, Johnson J. Hooper, and George Washington Harris, brought forth a body of work that was folksy, vernacular, rough-hewn, and rough in character, incident, and detail. The limits of vulgarity were often exceeded; the language was racy and colloquial, and the incidents were exaggerated, slapstick, and brutal by turns. Twain borrowed these humorists' free-wheeling anecdotalism, inserting brief sketches and stories inside travelogues and novels. Especially in the Sut Lovingood tales by Harris, women could be either the butts or practitioners of ugly practical jokes as well as men; this was perhaps the only point on which Twain diverged, for his women are consistently the repositories of motherly virtues.

The verbal yarn was a dominant mode, and Twain himself depended heavily on the verbal element in his composing and writing—dictating most of his autobiography, for example, and reading his day's work to the family on many evenings at Quarry Farm. As with Ward and the literary comedians, obvious borrowings from other writers occur, such as a camp meeting that was viewed by Huck Finn and seems a close copy of a similar meeting visited by J. J. Hooper's rogue Captain Simon Suggs. Most important is that the borrowings translate consistently from the lesser to the more important works. In whatever way one approaches Twain in terms of the history of American humor, it can be said that he successfully elevated a minor literary genre into an international literary phenomenon.

LOCAL COLOR IN TWAIN'S WORK

When Twain sent "A True Story" to William Dean Howells for publication in the *Atlantic Monthly*, he noted that it was "rather out of my line." It had "no humor in it," he thought, being close to a literal transcript, and he admitted feelings of uncertainty about it. He had been writing as a humorist rather than as a local color author. Under the impulse of Howells's enthusiasm, Twain admitted to working hard on getting the Negro dialect correct. The combination of local color and comedy leads to a richness of humanity that is extraordinary in any short story. The "local color" school might be said to have replaced earlier pastoral stories and poems, following the Civil War, with a more realistic interest in the regions. Harriet Beecher Stowe, a neighbor and friend of Twain at Nook Farm, had been a pioneer in this sort of writing, beginning in 1862 with *The Pearl of Orr's Island; Oldtown Folks* (1869) and *Sam Lawson's Fireside Stories* (1872) added stories with a figure whose skeptical voice may have influenced the ironist in Twain's later material. Bret Harte's short stories legitimized the local color mode, according to scholar Claude Simpson, in *The Local Colonists* (New York, 1960), making details of language and action that were not "genteel" acceptable in periodicals directed at middle-class American homes.

Before Harte, the southwestern oral tale and the humor of *The Spirit of the Times* had been for men only. Although Jack Downing of Portland, Maine, and Lowell's *Biglow Papers* had been influential as dialect protest humor, they were not recognized as literature. After Harte, the works of several writers represented various regional characters; these included Richard Malcolm Johnston's southern tales, Edward Eggleston's "Hoosier" schoolmaster, and works by Maurice Thompson, Constance Fenimore Woolson, and Sarah Orne Jewett. These were followed in the 1870s and 1880s by George W. Cable, Joel Chandler Harris, and Mary N. Murfree; still later came Charles Chesnutt, Thomas Nelson Page, and many more.

Twain explored and developed a rich vein of local color in both his western and southern writings. Literary "maps" of the nation in the 1890s always showed his name along both the Rocky Mountains and the Mississippi River. He used the slang of the miners and the dialect of the poor whites and Negroes to depict their wily individuality. His ability to capture scenic detail in fresh language was most ably demonstrated in his novels, but his short stories also conveyed a vivacity of language and incident that made them unique, embodying important national values in plain language (as in the "lightning pilot" episode of *Life on the Mississippi*; Mary Ann Cord's story as Aunt Rachel in "A True Story"; or the jumping frog story) brought Twain his first important notice. Twain's sense of detail and incident and his use of language inculcated values in his works that rose above the writing of others in the same vein. Even as he benefited from the vogue of a national literary movement, he also became its outstanding practitioner.

TWAIN AND REALISM

The Civil War, catastrophic event that it was, ushered in the era of literary realism. "Idealism" sent many men off to die, and writers such as Rebecca Harding Davis noted that the high purposes clothed in rhetoric did little to apologize for the men murdered and women outraged on the borders between slave and free states where the warfare was most bitter. "Romance" was replaced by a demand for a more pictorial record of real life, a movement paralleling the development of the camera and the art of photography (which was yet to be regarded as an art at all but was increasingly prominent as a medium for capturing images of individuals and of American life). Only a hundred years later would careful visual historians demonstrate that Matthew Brady's shockingly realistic photographs of the battlefields were sometimes created by artfully repositioning available corpses. To critics of the period, realism meant the literal capturing of the real, a confusion about the difference between "artistic representation" and "real experience" that has complicated analysis of the genre ever since.

The realist writer attempted to depict real life as events that happen to normal people in normal settings, as in the novels centered around Huck Finn, Tom Sawyer, and Pudd'nhead Wilson, which is not to say that some events may not be exaggerated. But at least plots and characters were not supposed to be sentimentalized romanticism. Twain's knights in shining armor sweated and yearned for a smoke (the basic joke that originated *A Connecticut Yankee*), and his heroic noble savages were degraded to being no better than Baltimore and Ohio Railroad directors (the lowest form of moral life on earth to Twain). Twain once expressed surprise that it made people mad that he spoke of the biblical Joseph of Arimathea's backyard as if it were his own backyard, but he held to the principle that human beings had much the same characteristics in every time and place, granted some national variations. The author, as a voice in realistic fiction, was expected to remain distant, letting the story tell itself. Such terminology disguises the fact that literary realism is just as contrived as any other art form, and Twain was not respectful of such conventions. Typically, though, realistic authors tried to use commonplace language, avoid overly fantastic or sentimental plots, and refrain from lecturing on morality. The refusal of realists to make moral judgments about their characters, even when those characters behaved in sordid and immoral ways, led to trouble, for many readers did not understand that to portray something might be a way of discrediting rather than advocating it. In fact, many nineteenth-century critics feared that to depict evil actions or bad conduct and language was to endorse it, violating the responsibility of the novelist to inform and uplift.

Twain's semi-fictional travel burlesques, *The Innocents Abroad* and *Roughing It*, were part of the realism movement and the genre of travel narratives—featuring Americans abroad and geographical descriptions through reportage. They were eyewitness accounts, although the views had a strongly western perspective. *A Tramp Abroad* and *Following the Equator* were continuations in this genre, although less inspired, thrown together out of whatever materials came to hand. The first two were connected by a unifying vision of the naif, or "innocent," being introduced to a world in which the sublime and ideal in history, religion, nature, and humanity were obscured by self-interested promotions by sellers and buyers, and even by missionaries and pious pilgrims. Twain described alkali dust, rocks, sagebrush, sand, flies, and saddle sores. He complained about degraded human beings and sentimental falsifications of scenes. These burlesques made the coyote and the "jackass" rabbit into notable examples of comic realism. Twain's highly individualized focus was on the physical perceptions of the moment rather than on romantically reconstructed emotion. He was a reporter far from the romanticists following Wordsworth in their sentimental writings. Partly exposés, Twain's travel burleques had a western newspaperman's style; after all, they were based on his own notebooks and letters home, many for publication in newspapers originally. They have the voice of a "real" speaker rather than a literary writer. In fact, critics who value Twain's authentic frontier voice, beginning with his personal friends from Nevada, cringed when his passages took off into the sublime and the seemingly literary. Nevertheless, his capacity for unifying the real and ideal capabilities in a narrative that involves readers is what sustained his popularity across social lines and accounts for the power of his greatest works.

The Gilded Age (1873), Twain's first novel, co-authored with Charles Dudley Warner, demonstrates his varied capabilities blended with his co-writer's. The novel begins with the local color of backwoods Tennessee, where the Hawkins family and Colonel Sellers seek their fortunes. The scene shifts to Washington, D.C., where lobbyists and corrupt senators are freely satirized as Laura Hawkins lobbies for a bill that will make her family rich. Although able to manipulate senators, she is herself seduced and then murders her lover; she is subsequently tried, convicted, released, and finally humiliated to death on a lecture platform. The panorama of the nation's capital and its life offers opportunities for criticizing the search for easy wealth and the hypocrisy of characters like Laura's mentor, Senator Dilworthy. As a novel of contemporary life, the book is an engaging satire; in fact, Laura and other characters were modeled on real-life people. Twain published the story's sequel, again featuring Colonel Sellers, in 1893 as *The American Claimant*. Seldom discussed except as a potboiler written to generate revenue to pay bills, this later work blends science fantasy with science fiction, as Colonel Sellers attempts a variety of loony futurist inventions (including using sewer gas as a lighting resource and reinvigorating the dead to put real corpses in the Congress); the novel ends, after various demonstrations of democracy and aristocracy as competing philosophies of life, with Sellers traveling in space to harness sunspots. Through such works Twain illustrated the various uses to which comic realism could be adapted. Satiric passages attack the jury system, social upstarts, and the irreverence for history symbolized by the unfinished Washington Monument. The crooked "Knobs Industrial College" bill that Laura lobbies for plays on the misuse of the cause of the freed slaves, and in one memorable moment a Negro corpse is even made to reprimand a would-be doctor, Ruth Bolton, for coming to dissect him after the years of abuses of blacks by whites in America.

Twain's major novels were also varied in their realism, modified by his exaggerated humor. Twain presented himself as a stickler for realistic writing in "Fenimore Cooper's Literary Offenses" (1885), lambasting Cooper on points of language and the improbability of the events portrayed. Yet Twain's own Connecticut Yankee travels through time, employs chance eclipses as tools, and creates an industrial empire out of little more than imagination. Indeed, Twain could make the gritty and industrial into the stuff of fantasy, the ultimate artistic device of the genre. Col. Sellers in *The American Claimant* ends up flying through space to harness sunspots, although the plot up to that moment has been reasonably well domesticated in the boarding houses of Washington, D.C. The ability to encapsulate the appearance of being involved in local life and times held the key to the realist's success, and society became the symbol. Twain's use of language and his ability to create characters were very powerful in this regard. Of the triumvirate of major realists, Twain, James, and Howells, Twain was the most given to social satire, lower class language, and scene and seemingly the least preoccupied with his characters' inner thoughts. Of the three, he gives the most exaggerated representations of American culture in the thoughts of his characters. Yet his works are more intellectual than is sometimes thought. Thus, his portraiture of Huckleberry Finn is an impressive contribution to the genre. Crane, Norris, London, and Dreiser wrote novels of a more naturalistic bent later, sometimes called "sterner realism." Twain's more naturalistic manuscripts, chiefly scientific or vaguely religious fantasies, gloomier than his published works, did not seem to him to fit his role as humorist spokesman for the world; they remained largely unpublished at his death.

HISTORICAL AND CULTURAL LITERARY INFLUENCES FROM ENGLAND AND AMERICA

Twain's reading in English and American cultural history was as extensive as it was undisciplined. *A Connecticut Yankee in King Arthur's Court* is an example of a "historical" book, a consistently popular genre in America. The cultural historian W.E.H. Lecky, whose ideas Twain used frequently, is even footnoted in the text. Lecky's sense of the church as a force for evil influenced Twain, and several incidents (including scenes in the Valley of Holiness and the hanging of the young mother) are derived from him, according to Harold Baetzhold in *Mark Twain and John Bull* (Bloomington, IN, 1970) and Joe B. Fulton in *Mark Twain in the Margins* (Tuscaloosa, AL, 2000). Twain was strongly influenced by Lecky's attitude toward medieval abuses. Likewise, Twain was well aware of Sir Thomas Malory's *Le Morte d'Arthur*, which he had purchased and read in the mid-1880s at the suggestion of George Washington Cable. Every educated person knew of Alfred, Lord Tennyson's *Idylls of the King*, a high Victorian representation of Arthur's knights of the round table in heroic guise, as well, and many critics of Twain's book accused him of besmirching the lofty ideals of Malory and Tennyson. The burlesque of Malory was an annoyance for reverential British readers. Setting toothpaste against pig-royalty was particularly galling to reverencers of the past; the sale of Twain's books in England di-

minished as a result. Twain was walking a fine and somewhat perilous line between the upholders of culture and a popular audience in treating such conventionally idealized subjects in burlesque and satire. Even the idea that you couldn't
tell a king from a commoner if you stripped them naked, however, was derived
from Thomas Carlyle's *Sartor Resartus* (1838), one of the earliest and strongest
attacks on Victorian complacency and self-satisfaction. Twain was aligned with
major Victorian critics and satirists. Howard Baetzhold's *Mark Twain and
John Bull: The British Connection* (1970) provides detailed analysis of these and
other borrowings from the British tradition in various of Twain's works.

Twain's reading of American sources also figures in some of his texts. Slavery
narratives contributed to the texture of *A Connecticut Yankee* in its most horrible aspects. Charles Ball's *Fifty Years in Chains; or, The Life of an American Slave*
(1860) provided scenes of forceful separation of families and whipping of
young women in *A Connecticut Yankee*, according to Twain's own notebooks.
Frederick Douglass's autobiography, *The Narrative of the Life of Frederick
Douglass: An American Slave* (1845), furnished the phrase "Give a nigger an
inch and he'll take an ell" for Huck Finn's recollections as a representation of racial prejudice. Twain had read extensively in slave narratives, and those stories
were adapted to show the pathos of treating individuals and families inhu-
manely. He would return to it in *Pudd'nhead Wilson*. The persona of P. T.
Barnum is another historical/literary influence. Twain was familiar with
Barnum's *Life*, originally published in 1855, and *Struggles*, a later update—both were widely read biographies of Barnum, who was a politically active individual and a social philosopher advocating the idea that a little
"humbug" could be combined with profitable instruction. Twain could very
possibly have read Max Adeler's *The Fortunate Island* (1882), forgotten it, and
rediscovered the memory as a plot idea later for *A Connecticut Yankee*, as Adeler
thought he had. But Twain himself had combined industrialism and medievalism in columns as early as 1870, and after 1879 Thomas Edison, "The Wizard
of Menlo Park," was seen as a kind of Merlin, so the imagery for Twain's book
was in the air throughout the decade of the 1880s.

TWAIN'S INFLUENCES ON OTHERS

Twain's central place in the world of American letters was well established by
1885, but even before then he seems to have possessed a magnetism that drew
the attention of others. During his lifetime Twain received a range of letters
from various authors; many of the letters are in the Mark Twain Papers at the
University of California at Berkeley, and some at the Mark Twain House collection in Hartford. Twain's success brought him into contact with a wide array
of important authors. First he encountered literary comedians such as Artemus

Ward, Petroleum V. Nasby, B. P. Shillaber, and Josh Billings. In the late 1860s he had contact with authors, some of whom had a similar midwestern background, such as William Dean Howells, and Thomas Bailey Aldrich. Later Twain interacted with not merely the showman P. T. Barnum but also the literati, including Oliver Wendell Holmes and Ralph Waldo Emerson. Furthermore, he invested himself actively in good causes. For example, he was impressed by Frederick Douglass and interceded in his behalf for a government appointment. He used his own prominence in England in 1872 to boost the Fiske Jubilee Singers, on tour singing Negro spirituals. Twain even delivered a speech on Plymouth Rock castigating Pilgrim harshness in punishing the weak, a theme he often wrote about in terms of savage laws impacting the poor. From the late 1890s onward he spoke and wrote actively on issues of imperialism, relating the treatment of people of color worldwide to the treatment of Negroes in the American South. He was not admired by everyone, however. J. T. Trowbridge, another author of numerous "boy books" who demostrated good style but was heavily overshadowed by Twain's success, never warmed to him. Many of the more academic critics saw his influence as a bad one.

Joel Chandler Harris, author of the Uncle Remus stories, admired him. Oliver Wendell Holmes, the beloved "autocrat" of the breakfast table, contributed a poem for his fiftieth birthday recognition by the *Critic*. Authors Bret Harte, John Hay, and others whose names are historically memorable were glad to work with him. His respect for President Ullyses S. Grant caused him to read proof for the dying hero's memoirs, published by Twain's own company and ensuring the financial well-being of Grant's widow. Henry James found him uncomfortably buffoonish, but writers like Howells recognized his passion and his lawlessness as great strengths, and Harris and Brander Matthews acknowledged *Adventures of Huckleberry Finn* for the breakthrough in American language that it was.

Humorist George Ade, in an essay on the power of Twain in making the standard subscription book into something appealing to a generation of young readers, cited Twain's breezy freshness as a positive value. H. L. Mencken, as well, was positive about Twain, calling *Huck Finn* "one of the great masterpieces of the world." James T. Farrell wrote an appreciation and Sherwood Anderson's work shows Twain's influence, although Edgar Lee Masters criticized Twain as selling out to capitalism. Ernest Hemingway gave Twain his greatest boost in the recognition of *Adventures of Huckleberry Finn* when he stated in *The Green Hills of Africa* (1935) that "all modern American literature comes from one book by Mark Twain called *Adventures of Huckleberry Finn*" (p. 22). The value of language as Twain opened up local, vernacular dialect was most important to these later writers. In Twain's works, most centrally in the voice of Huckleberry Finn, the descriptive power of "plain" English seemed to be fully exploited for the first time, blazing a trail that Hemingway, Anderson, and others could follow in developing their own voices.

Toni Morrison and Ralph Ellison, hardly alone among such other important African American writers as Langston Hughes and Richard Wright, consider Twain to have been a valuable influence on them. Ralph Ellison's collection of essays, *Shadow and Act* (1964), bears particularly good evidence of Twain's value to Ellison and also of Ellison's awareness of and insight into the difficulty of a white writer interpreting the character Jim in *Adventures of Huckleberry Finn* in terms that show him as fully adult in the readers' own terms. Ellison said he found in *Huck Finn* a valuable tool in language, in irony, and in problems of representation of African-Americans that had to be overcome and had even led Hemingway and the critic Leslie Fiedler to misjudge the issues within the novel. Toni Morrison, in her "Introduction" to the Oxford *Huck Finn* volume, praises the book's freeing of language and, more important, its silences, for the effect they had on her own "alarm" at reading the book. She finds it a true classic, undertaking the most troubling and sophisticated issues of race, childhood, and culture. Certainly, as long as relations between Anglo Americans and African Americans remain clouded in America, the portraiture Twain created will provide a touchstone of awareness of self and possibility that is likely to retain its fascination for sophisticated readers of all races.

Less significant revisions of the novel, which indicate the force of Twain's popular appeal, include *I Been There Before* (1985) by David Carkeet and *The True Adventures of Huckleberry Finn* (1970, 1987) by John Seelye. Carkeet resurrects Twain in 1985 to create a detective trail of "delirium Clemens," holding the reader in suspense to the last page. Seelye's novel deepens and intensifies the uglier aspects of Mississippi lower-class life—its villainy, racism, and sensuality. Peter J. Heck has turned Twain works into mysteries, including *Death on the Mississippi* (1995) and *A Connecticut Yankee in Criminal Court* (1996). Another mystery novel, *The Adventures of Huckleberry Fiend* (1987) by Julie Smith, revolves around the mysterious disappearance of the first half of the manuscript of *Adventures of Huckleberry Finn*. The real disappearance of the first half of the manuscript was resolved finally in 1991 when the daughters of the head of the Buffalo (New York) Public Library, James Fraser Gluck, who had originally solicited it from Twain, recovered it from a trunk in which it had sat for 100 years. Its recovery was not without drama, both in prompting legal negotiations and in causing scholar Vic Doyno, who had just completed *Writing Huck Finn* (1991) on Twain's method of composing *Huck Finn*, to undertake a second volume. The second book will complete an analysis of the manuscript evidence indicating Twain's artistry and intent; Doyno has found historical precedents for Twain's depictions and has supplemented the evidence of Twain's "creative process" in developing a masterpiece through careful revision.

The discovery of the *Huck Finn* manuscript was front-page news, and further testimony to Twain's importance as an American spokesman lies in the appearance of relatively recent news relating to him as front-page stories in newspapers such as the *New York Times*. On the occasion of the discovery of a letter in 1985 identifying the black college student Twain had funded at Yale Law School, Warner McGuinn, international and national papers covered the story. Shelley Fisher Fishkin's book *Was Huck Black?* (1993) likewise attracted major coverage in magazines such as *Newsweek*, where discussion of the book included interpretations of Twain's intent and academic liberalism. Fishkin's title was intended to question interracial influences with a tongue-in-cheek reference to the notorious "one drop of blood" rule (to determine racial origin and enforce segregation) that dishonored southern history; Fishkin claimed to have found the drop in "Sociable Jimmy" published by Twain in 1874. Her work infuriated some and amused others but also provided a thoughtful platform for an inquiry into race in American cultural history. Fishkin's *Lighting Out for the Territories* (1997), partially an academic book and partially informed reportage, goes further in exploring the cultural attitudes of those who promote the Twain heritage, such as the annual Mark Twain Festival in Hannibal, Missouri. She provides insight into our culture through a study of how the symbols and characters Twain created are integrated into the life of the places where he lived.

Finally, the list of writers of prologues for the twenty-nine volumes of scholar Shelley Fisher Fishkin's *The Oxford Mark Twain* (1996) is an impressive index to Twain's importance to contemporary writers: (in chronological order of works introduced) Roy Blount Jr., Mordecai Richler, George Plimpton, Ward Just, Lee Smith, E. L. Doctorow, Russell Banks, Judith Martin, Willie Morris, Toni Morrison, Kurt Vonnegut Jr., Anne Bernays, Bobbie Ann Mason, Malcolm Bradbury, Nat Hentoff, Sherley Anne Williams, Justin Kaplan, Walter Mosley, David Bradley, Gore Vidal, Cynthia Ozick, Ursula K. LeGuin, Charles Johnson, Frederick Busch, Garry Wills, Arthur Miller, Erica Jong, Frederick Pohl, Hal Holbrook. It would be hard to imagine a more distinguished collection of Pulitzer Prize winners, important novelists and political humorists, and creative writers and members of the theater. Some of the essays even had other printings in major literary venues. Yet detractors remain. Author Jane Smiley attacked Twain's major work, assessing Harriet Beecher Stowe's *Uncle Tom's Cabin* as more worthy of classic status. In the early 1990s, when the idea of renaming a Hartford, Connecticut, community college after Mark Twain was under discussion, one Puerto Rican student representative declared that Mark Twain did not speak for him; he also revealed that he had read no Twain. Hartford and the State of Connecticut feel otherwise, pinning significant hopes for a downtown Hartford renaissance around the development of the Mark Twain House as a tourism magnet.

3

Twain's Early Short Stories and Sketches

Mark Twain first came to prominence through his short stories. "Jim Smiley and His Jumping Frog," published in 1865, quickly took on a life of its own and became a national phenomenon. Other early stories show the development of Twain's dramatic voice, which included the devices of the comic narrator and the coloring and characterization that came to distinguish his fictional characters in longer works. With "A True Story," in 1874, he added another dimension with the sincerity of expression found in a transcript of a former slave's narrative of real-life events. Finally, some domestic pieces and western tales round out the chronology of Twain's early stories and show they have an important moral dimension. "Sketches" must be addressed as well as stories because Twain semi-fictionalized—that is, transmuted into humor—much material that does not technically fit the definition of a short story.

"THE DANDY FRIGHTENING THE SQUATTER" (1852)

This brief sketch appeared in *The Carpet-Bag* of Boston. The sketch is in the mode of the southwestern humorists and would not be recognized today if it had not been Twain's first publication in a major periodical. It purports merely to relate an event—freezing a moment in time "about thirteen years ago," which would have been when young Clemens was four years old. Therefore, it is a "set piece," conforming to other stories of this type which its young author had read, not an observation. The setting is the primitive landing of Hannibal,

Missouri, before it had even become a town; the occasion is the landing of a steamboat, a symbol of the larger world. Two character types are identified: the "brawny woodsman" and the "spruce young dandy, with a killing mustache," the two dominant stereotypes in American humor at that time. The young dandy is full of pride and attempts to make an "impression upon the hearts of the young ladies." He invites them to watch him challenge the "squatter" with a false threat. When he delivers the threat to make the squatter into a barn door and "drill the key-hole myself," the squatter bashes him between the eyes and throws him into the river. The squatter yells at the "crest-fallen hero" sneaking back on board the steamboat, telling the dandy not to forget him the next time he comes around drilling key-holes. Dialect words suggest to some critics that the folksy squatter is somehow more practical and worldly than the young dandy. He is certainly more directed in his behavior. The simple country attitude embodied in the squatter confronts the complex social behavior of a naive and self-centered youth, the dandy. The youth is re-paid for his failure to recognize his own stature (or lack thereof) in the world and is educated accordingly.

The piece is steadfast comedy: no one is seriously injured, and the realism that might have made for a grimmer story is subdued into a festive moment and the expression of a code of behavior appropriate to the frontier. The Pike County dialect (representative of vernacular speakers and simple people), ver-sus formal English signifies two different worlds coming into conflict. Because the only comment is by "the ladies," who vote the dandy's weapons, a knife and pistols, "to the victor," rather than by the author, the sketch can be classified as comic realism. Throughout Twain's writing, similar themes of naivete coming to comic correction are often found.

"JIM SMILEY AND HIS JUMPING FROG" (1865)

"The Celebrated Jumping Frog of Calaveras County," one title this story goes by, was first published in the New York *Saturday Press* on November 18, 1865. It immediately became immensely popular, and Howells remembered that the line, "I don't see no points about that frog that's any better'n any other frog," was heard everywhere. The democratic theme of proving oneself on one's own merits despite the trickiness of opportunistic opponents, resonating American capitalist ethics, appealed to readers across the nation. The story is framed in a supposed letter to Mr. A. Ward—Artemus Ward, in whose *Travels Among the Mormons* (1865) it would have appeared had Twain gotten it to New York soon enough.

The framing narrator of the story tells the readers that he feels imposed upon, the victim of a practical joke orchestrated by Artemus Ward. This frame establishes that the entire story is part of a world where foolery is the fabric of personal interaction. Yet the speaker pretends not to be part of that understanding. Mark Twain was supposedly something like this when he was in Nevada, capable of playing jokes on others but receiving sourly any practical jokes played on himself. The initiation of the story might be a joke intended to disarm critical readers by falsely suggesting that the story is as "useless" as it is "infernal." Humorists can mislead readers as part of the humor; perhaps readers wouldn't have thought about "usefulness" if the writer hadn't mentioned the idea. The emphasis is on being trapped—as the narrator has been, and as the character Jim Smiley will be by his own enthusiasm in an event that becomes, as it is distanced from the reader, a sort of myth.

Setting

The story inside the frame is set in the mining camp of "Boomerang," somewhat like Angel's Camp, California, a real mining camp where Twain once tried his hand at mining while in retreat from newspaper reporting. The setting is "by the barroom stove of the little old dilapidated tavern." Therefore it is identifiably "local color," possibly a little vulgar and common, not "elevated" or sublime. But from that setting, the story drops back one more level to "the winter of '49—or maybe it was the spring of '50 when the 'big flume' wasn't finished building." Of course, '49 is the year of the Gold Rush, and that aura is added to the story. By now the reader has dropped back another dimension into another layer of local detail—folk-dated by remembered events rather than characters. But, really, the setting is the character Simon Wheeler's dozing mind, with its hazy recollections of time but its detailed memory of scene and event. The teller is dead-pan, blockading the listener. The sense of memory, "I remember," "drifting along through such a queer yarn," provides the real frame for the story.

Plot

It is a fantasy in reality, and beginning as a stiff, rather wooden narrative, it becomes the tale of a mind that records bizarre events without interpretation. When Mark Twain tries to make his getaway, after Simon Wheeler is called from the room, and escapes being "buttonholed" (grabbed by the front of his jacket), he mutters "good-naturedly," "O, curse Smiley and his afflicted cow!" Life is local and mundane, and its mysteries exist within an unmysterious context of swamp and barnyard; the themes are democratic and entrepreneurial: no one gets anything they don't earn on their own merits.

The plot of the inner story is simple. Jim Smiley loves to bet, and he trains animals for various contests including horse races, dog fights, and, finally, a jumping frog contest. A stranger comes to town and shows skepticism about the prowess of Smiley's jumping frog. While Smiley foolishly leaves the frog in the stranger's care and hunts for a second frog, the stranger fills the frog full of buckshot and subsequently wins the frog jumping contest, escaping with the money from their wager before Smiley realizes that he has been cheated.

Characters

Two sets of characters shape the story. The first set provides the frame, the second the presumed action. The first character is the narrator, Mark Twain. He is somewhat starchy, a busy man. The second is the "sociable" Simon Wheeler, who tells the tale without any special animation in a colloquial voice that denotes his limited place in life, in a mining camp, in a barroom. These characters' framing presence makes the story an intellectual event: a "story" men tell to each other.

The most obvious set of characters, however, includes Jim Smiley, "the feller" who comes to camp, and the array of animals, two of which are partly anthropomorphized into American political figures: Andrew Jackson (the first president to represent the raw and vulgar side of democracy), the fighting bullpup, and Dan'l Webster (the great New England statesman reviled for his compromise on slavery), the jumping frog itself. The involvement of these animal characters with Jim Smiley places them in a world where everything depends on a bet. Indeed, Wheeler tells the reader that Smiley was the "curiosest" man he'd ever seen because he would bet on any side of any contest, just so long as he could bet. The comic climax of that immediate observation is Smiley's countering Parson Walker's thankful remark—that his wife, with the blessing of Providence, would overcome her illness— with "Well, I'll resk two-and-a-half that she don't, anyway." In this comment the slight overtone of the sacrilegious blends with the personal audacity of the oblivious Smiley. His blindness to others is foreshadowed here, and it will be punished in the outcome arranged by the stranger.

Smiley's mare is an emblem of fraud. Although looking asthmatic and distempered, at the "fag-end" of a race she would come up "scattering her legs around limber," to finish "about a neck ahead, as near as you could cipher it down." The sense of exaggerated animal madness is made comic through the effortless dead-pan narration of Simon Wheeler with its casual slang and its own sense of narrative truth.

Smiley's bullpup, Andrew Jackson, effusively described in the language of a steamboat, is a dog with a special ability: it can grab the hind leg of an opponent in a dogfight and just hang on until the other dog gives up. The bullpup is imposed upon when Smiley arranges a fight with a dog that "didn't have no hind legs, because they'd been sawed off in a circular saw." Always offering the extra bit of useless detail, the story maintains an air of gossipy truth as a sort of intellectual problem. Like the reference to the flume of 1849 or 1850, the verisimilitude is so evident as a device of the story-teller that the story takes on a life of its own. Yet the deeper theme of Smiley's betrayal is that the dog's heart is "broke" and it is Smiley's "fault." Added on is the concept that Andrew Jackson was a dog of "genius" who would have gone further with his special talent if not for that last fight, after which he "limped off a piece, and laid down and died" in a fashion that makes him almost supernatural. In real life, Twain the author was keenly aware that General Andrew Jackson's success at the bloody Battle of New Orleans in 1815 actually was a futile waste, as the war had already ended when the battle was fought. Thus, Smiley's defeat in the final episode of the story is fully foreshadowed.

The animals up to now have represented Smiley's character and foreshadow his fate. Smiley catches and "educates" a frog and carries him around in a box, having trained him to "outjump any frog in Calaveras county." Finally, a stranger remarks that he "don't see no points about that frog that's any better'n any other frog" and says, "I ain't got no frog—but if I had a frog I'd bet you." Smiley thrusts Dan'l Webster into the stranger's hands in an act fully as naive as matching the bullpup Andrew Jackson with the legless dog. The stranger, now turned frog custodian, after he "set there a good while thinking and thinking to his-self," fills Dan'l up with buckshot; in the contest that follows, the amazed Smiley is unable to get his frog to jump or make any gesture beyond a Frenchman's shrug. The stranger exits with Smiley's forty dollars and the famous tagline, soon followed by the furious Smiley. Of course a sequel exists, involving a one-eyed yellow cow with a tail like a "bannanner," but the storyteller escapes Simon Wheeler. The experience is encapsulated, as isolated historically as any story by Edgar Allan Poe or Nathaniel Hawthorne, but seemingly a tale of modern life in California.

Thematic Issues

The power of the story and its importance lie in its democracy. The reason the story's tagline became so popular—"I don't see no points about that frog that's any better'n any other frog"—was that the task of having to prove oneself is the central component of a democracy, and especially of a capitalist democracy. This theme is the underpinning concept of American society fableized—

and made fantastic, furthermore, in a context so localized by voice and manner of telling that it seems unquestionably real, even when it is obviously a fictional exaggeration. The only way of proving oneself in Smiley's world is to win a contest, in most cases reversing the apparent probabilities. All his animals are unpromising, but they prosper, as in Dan'l's case, by means of "education." Aristocratic pride of place has no part in this world. Even skill and education succumb to chicanery and shrewdness. Everything in the universal American Yankee subculture endorsed this outcome, and Smiley's vulnerability is the fulcrum on which the comic story turns. The message is plain: don't make yourself vulnerable through innocence of the world (in its negative sense), because if you do, none of your other trained and honed abilities can cause you to rise above the buckshot.

Twain later declared the story a "villainous backwoods sketch" in a letter to his mother. However, the jumping frog also became one of his representative images. He returned to the story in 1875 as a French translation and again in 1894, giving its "private history." It remains an American classic, generating frog-jumping contests from California to Hartford, Connecticut, in our own time. Furthermore, it represents in lowly life the philosophy by which most of our nation's institutions operate ("You can fool some of the people all of the time . . .").

"CANNIBALISM IN THE CARS" (1868)

"Cannibalism in the Cars" is another so-called frame story in which a narrator appears at the beginning and end of the story and pretends to relate a story within the story.

Setting

The setting is in a railroad car around 1867, where a pleasant political discussion is taking place between the narrator and the story's "source," a man who seems to know his way around government and think by association, because a passing remark triggers his reminiscence. After the story is told, a conductor approaches the narrator and explains that he has been talking to a (harmless) madman.

The inner story is also set in a railroad car bound from St. Louis to Chicago, but back in time to 1853. The company are twenty-four gentlemen who are convivial and knowledgeable about politics, specifically with no women and children aboard. This railroad car becomes stranded and isolated in a snowdrift in the middle of the prairie. Wood is plentiful for the engine, but no food is available.

Plot

The plot arises from a storm on account of which all aboard are threatened with starvation. As a result of five days of being isolated the starving occupants of the car finally propose cannibalism, in lanaguage echoing a congressional report: "Nature had been taxed to the utmost—she must yield." The parliamentary phrase then leads into an account in the format of the *Congressional Globe*, which carries the formal reports of legislative doings in the Congress. During the remainder of the enclosed story, various parliamentary resolutions and stratagems are employed with flowing rhetoric to support them, but with the purpose of cannibalizing the car's inhabitants to feed the remaining occupants. *Roberts Rules of Order* prevails. Finally the story-teller must leave, and the reader is left aghast and relieved.

Characters

Characters in the frame include the narrator and the story-teller, who is prompted only by an overheard conversation of two passers-by who mention "Harris." The other characters are encapsulated within the story, including "Harris," the first passenger to be cannibalized. All the rest of the characters within the story represent a spectrum of American political personages, each designated by their state of origin just as they would be in the minutes of a report of speeches and legislation in the U.S. Congress. Additionally, each is designated by type according to how he would be as a meal: stringy, tough, tender, and so on. The conductor of the train on which the narrator rides concludes the story by explaining the story's origin, and the framing narrator concludes by announcing his relief.

Thematic Issues

The theme of the story lies in the uses to which the political forms are corrupted. Although the story is that of a madman, the suavity of the starving gentlemen in their use of *Roberts Rules of Order* to eat each other raises questions about whether they could do similarly savage things in the real Congress of the United States. The point of Twain's satire is that such men could, and do, create such nightmares under the pretense of parliamentary gentility. The story satirizes the nation's political system and the human tendency to disguise selfish inhumanity by making it seem inevitable and logical within a given context. Parliamentary form prevails in the railroad car; even when some passengers protest, they do so in parliamentary forms, validating the absoluteness of the dominance of form over sense. The outrageousness of the story as a funny tale lies in the enclosure of human behavior in forms that kill; the internal "logic" of what happens, clothed in the conventional rhetoric of government in the 1860s, is inescapable. Jonathan Swift in his even more outrageous "A Modest Proposal" (suggesting solving the Irish famine by eating babies), made a harsher attack on a specific abuse than Twain's more universalized tale, but the two stories have the satiric element in common.

"SOCIABLE JIMMY" (1874)

Students who worry that there is nothing new to be discovered about major authors will be interested to learn that this story was little known and virtually undiscussed until the early 1990s, when scholar Shelley Fisher Fishkin brought it to national and international attention by using it to link the voice of Huckleberry Finn to the voice of African Americans in Twain's rendering of Huck Finn's Pike County dialect. To most Twain scholars the piece came as "new" information, and it has continued to be heavily discussed. The sketch has no plotted story, but rather it represents a young African American who acts as bell-hop to the traveling reporter/lecturer Mark Twain. In the course of his talk, Jimmy speaks with a naive innocence that enables the events of the stories to unfold without criticism, taking on their own comic absurdity. The style of the speaker and his simplicity both seem to foreshadow Huck Finn's voice as narrator of the later novel. Because Jimmy is "black," the suggestion was made by Fishkin that under the notorious "one drop" rule by which some southern states assigned "race," Huck must be part of the African American heritage in American literature. "Sociable Jimmy" and "A True Story," no matter what they represent otherwise, are insightful records of speech and deeply humanized foreshadowings of the awfulness of slavery as subdued in the character Jim's gentleness in *Adventures of Huckleberry Finn*. Just as Jimmy's talk innocently reveals the vulgar, commonplace behavior of his relatives as if in a photograph with his voice being the frame, so will Huck reveal a more sinister society.

"A TRUE STORY" (1874)

Perhaps the best documented of all Twain's short stories, "A True Story" is important in terms of the discussion surrounding his satires of American racism. When he sent it to William Dean Howells of the elite *Atlantic Monthly*, his accompanying note was apologetic. The story seemed to him something out of his line and virtually without humor, an assertion that most readers will disagree with.

Setting

As with some of Twain's other stories, "A True Story" is a framed narrative in which the teller of the story offers up another person's tale. A brilliant analysis of this story by Twain scholar Horst Kruse, however, finds much more significance in this frame than in some others. The frame of the story is set on the front porch of a farmhouse "on the summit of a hill." The actual house, in fact, still exists in Elmira, New York. In the frame, the character Aunt Rachel is being teased and laughs heartily, but when the character Misto C—supposes that she has never suffered, she responds with her story.

Aunt Rachel's story is set in the South before, during, and at the immediate end of the Civil War, a time when the lives of Southern slaves were especially chaotic. Aunt Rachel describes being separated from her husband and children at a slave sale, serving Union soldiers, and finally being reunited with one of her sons, Henry, the youngest. A brief return to the frame completes the action.

Plot

The details of the plot make it poignant. Aunt Rachel's little son Henry promises to find her again, showing the innocent faith of a child in positive outcomes. Her own acceptance of her role as a cook, first for her Southern master and subsequently for Union officers, is identified by her as "what I's *for*." She identifies with her own role in life, but she also maintains hope that she might find Henry again. Foreshadowing the final revelation of identity, she mentions to the officers Henry's identifying marks. The rowdy events of an evening dance in her kitchen provide a sort of carnival atmosphere in which the final events are worked out as she vents her dynamic character fully. She is not repressed or withdrawn. Dialect indicators, heavily used and carefully reworked by the author, enhance her role as a "folk" character, distancing her from the formality of educated gentry and from their resources. Consequently, when Henry identifies her and reveals himself to her, the discovery has the effect of a special gift more than a planned outcome. Such a feeling may justify the positive interpretation she makes of a life summarized in reversed terms: "*I* hain't had no trouble. An' no *joy*."

Characters

Characters are extraordinarily important in this story. Aunt Rachel, the central speaker and actor, is based on the real person Mary Ann Cord, the Negro house servant of Susan Crane, Twain's sister-in-law, in Elmira, New York: a former slave. The reader understands her to know the differences of class and race because she sits on the lower step of the porch, "respectfully." But she also seems assertive beyond her station, because she touches the narrator's hand and forehead at the end of the story—and by that time, a sensitive reader will believe she has earned that right of familiarity, for she has bared her life.

The most important element of Aunt Rachel's character is her strength in adversity. She maintains her identity as the daughter of "one o' de ole Blue Hen's Chickens, *I* is!" Because she maintains this identity so strongly as a point of personal pride, the story is resolved in joy rather than sorrow. Yet it is her sorrows that show her strength. Some are too great to be accepted, and she fights and is beaten into submission when her husband and children are seized and sold away from her. Her simplicity is another important virtue, for it allows her also to accept her life as a cook, identify with it, and endure. It also causes her to bring her story to Union officers, at which point her innocence is revealed both to her and to the reader, for she does not realize that her little boy, sold away from her thirteen years earlier, has grown up. Action and events conclude the story. Characteristically, despite the intense personal tragedy that permeates her life, she finds the joy of getting back one of her "own ag'in." She may well be one of the greatest portraits of the African American spirit, and the larger positive "American" spirit, in the nation's literature.

Misto C—, who seems so unimportant, is crucial to the story, for it is (presumably) the white Misto C— whose casual racism initiates the story. Like Aunt Rachel, he is innocent about an important fact of life—the reality of her life. This literary figure (beware the biographical fallacy here of seeing Twain as insensitive) assumes that Aunt Rachel has had no trouble in her life because she is so jolly. This assumption is a white racial generalization about the smiling Negro, akin to the myth of the contented slave in the South and the belief in social advancement in the North. Both perceptions do not square with the perceptions of African Americans on the same subjects (as opinions on the O. J. Simpson case revealed widely in the 1990s). Misto C— is naive about the nature of human suffering and must be educated to the intensity of suffering and the meaning of the joy that may be derived from it.

Thematic Issues

Aunt Rachel, within her own story, experiences a long series of events originating in times of slavery. The true human cost of slavery is the obvious theme of the story. The second thematic message is that the outward appearance of a person gives little clue to his or her history or suffering. A further thematic message is that the assumptions white people hold regarding black people—that they are less "feeling" than whites, either because they don't show conventional white mannerisms of suffering or because they are naturally joyful—are simply incorrect. The power of the negative words and exclamation points in the immeasurably positive statement with which the story ends reemphasize this theme. This is Twain's most concise statement of racism by whites toward blacks. He shows the historical events, but he also shows how whites mistake the language and culture of blacks, failing to read their experience and its meaning because of cultural naivete on their own part. He had previously dealt with these issues in terms of both Chinese immigrants and black Americans, but to newspaper audiences or in other magazines. This statement, made to the premier reading audience in America, is thus of great importance.

OTHER TALES AND STORIES

Because Mark Twain wrote hundreds of short stories, tales, and sketches, selecting all that are worth discussion is impossible. Among tall tales that merit further study are "The Petrified Man" (1862), "A Bloody Massacre near Carson" (1863), "Jim Wolfe and the Tom-Cats" (1867), "The Facts in the Great Land-Slide Case" (1870), and others that exaggerate the newspaper correspondent's role into a vehicle for comedy carrying a message. Overtly moral tales that criticize the superficial morality of children's literature are plentiful: "Advice for Good Little Boys" (1865) and its counterpart for girls, "The Story of Mamie Grant, the Child Missionary" (1868), and "The Story of the Good Little Boy Who Did Not Prosper" (1870); all burlesque the standard format of the moral story for young people dominant in 1870. Other stories attacking the abuse of the innocent and the weak include, most notably, "Goldsmith's Friend Abroad Again" (1870) and "What Have the Police Been Doing?" (1866). "Buck Fanshawe's Funeral," from *Roughing It* (1872), along with "Tom Quartz" from the same source and "What Stumped the Bluejays" from *A Tramp Abroad* (1880), are often cited as among the best of Twain's backwoods tales showing the quirky humanity of the participants as they try to get along in the world despite their innocent misconceptions of how things work. These pieces were included in longer works, however, and did not originally appear as stand-alone stories. A series of stories based on the domestic life of the "McWilliamses" in the early 1880s reflects Twain's sense of his own household. "The Babies" (1879) and "The Private History of a Campaign That Failed" (1885) are both responses to the self-congratulatory idolatry building around the Civil War, in which Twain had little part; and his "Whittier Birthday Speech" (1879) shows Twain playing ironically with reputation and fraudulent misrepresentation, something that may have reflected his own emotional insecurity about his fame as a writer and that created a moment of powerful cultural embarrassment for him because of its cool reception as a speech. "The Curious Republic of Gondour" (1875) is Twain's vision of a meritocracy based on education and value to the community; Howells wished he would follow up with a story about the "place," but Twain never did. Long though this list is, it barely begins to name stories, tales, and speeches that attached human significance, moral themes, or civil or political protest to comic episodes, making Twain one of America's most overtly moral short story writers. "A True Story" might well be the candidate for the best American short story ever written, and a comparison with Hawthorne's "Young Goodman Brown," among other candidates, is justified.

4

The Personal Travel Narratives: *The Innocents Abroad* (1869), *Roughing It* (1872), *Life on the Mississippi* (1883), and Others

The Innocents Abroad (1869) and *Roughing It* (1872) defined Mark Twain for the reading audience of the nineteenth century, an image completed by *Life on the Mississippi*'s (1883) first version, "Old Times on the Mississippi" (1875). These works introduced the breezy skepticism of the American West to readers in the East, but Twain's readers in the West and Midwest also loved the typically American attitude that was practical, specific, humane, and sometimes downright vulgar. The "voice," partially inspired by literary comedian and comic lecturer Artemus Ward, represented a narrator who was a naif—an innocent not fully armored against worldly duplicity, cynicism, and greed but capable of sarcasm and dead-pan irony as well. Speaking through this voice, Twain described many slapstick comic adventures and recounted the rough-and-tumble experiences of both the American frontiers and the cultural frontier of "old world" Europe and the Holy Land.

The American story-teller is less committed to art than to practicality. His personal comfort is one of his major motivations, partly accounting for his own victimization by historical frauds, sentimental travel writers, and commercial sharpers ready to fleece the unwary with various schemes. His anecdotal adventures capture the clash of attitudes, encapsulating them in a series of personal adventures that are engaging and dramatic. Informal and structureless as Twain's travel narratives seem, they are sustained narratives with a tinge of bildungsroman, in which a young man develops mature viewpoints (in *Roughing It* and *Life on the Mississippi*), but mostly connected by strong moral themes and the author's mature realism measured against his youthful fantasies of travel and adventure.

The narratives also are moral projections of two different civilizations: (1) the old world of Europe and the Holy Land; and (2) the western world of flush times in American mining and commercial enterprises, and the years when "King Cotton" made the Mississippi River a booming conduit of American economic and social life. The narratives are expanded and capped by a visit to the recently Christianized island of Hawaii in *Roughing It. Life on the Mississippi* was Mark Twain's characterization of his own relationship to the river. His viewpoint belongs to a broad range of Americans, but the setting was vanishing into history, being transformed by modern commercial improvements. *A Tramp Abroad* (1880) and *Following the Equator* (1897) round out the list of travel memoirs by Twain, but neither holds the compelling interest of the earlier books.

Looking for a plot, as such, is not the best way to read these books. More enjoyable reading is to be had episode by episode, each with its own high point: a reader should look for moments such as glove-buying in Paris, Twain (expounding on Leonardo da Vinci and the other Old Masters, or pausing at the Tomb of Adam in *The Innocents Abroad*; Bemis and the Buffalo or the Old Ram story in *Roughing It*; and the cub pilot's training and experiences with Horace Bixby in *Life on the Mississippi*.

During the late 1800s the increased economic well-being of Americans led to a hunger for literature, and Twain's travel books occupied a special niche. As George Ade, a popular humorist of the period 1890–1910, recalled, their gorgeous bindings, illustrations, and humor made them a delight in the conventional parlor, with its otherwise overpowering seriousness. As travel works, the volumes pretended to be purposeful and educational, thereby escaping categorization as mere entertainment. The moral purpose underlying the humor was recognized by many reviewers as well, and Twain's place as a writer representing an American viewpoint on the world was assured from the moment *The Innocents Abroad* was published. Furthermore, the books had to be large and well illustrated to sell well, causing Twain to develop more copy, and leading to charges by later, more literary critics, that he sometimes used filler material. Only the reader can judge whether the books provide a coherent experience with a clear sense of values sustained by the story-telling.

THE INNOCENTS ABROAD (1869)

Setting and Characters

The Innocents Abroad, or, the New Pilgrim's Progress was first a series of newspaper letters to the *Alta California*, a San Francisco newspaper that paid Twain's way to go east and write back to San Francisco about his travels.

The lands visited are the subject of special expectations. Twain semi-fictionalizes his travels through the Azores, Paris, Florence, Venice, Rome, Damascus, the Holy Land, and Egypt by showing in each how impositions on the tourist conflict with his romanticized expectations.

The "American Vandal" is the dominant character in *The Innocents Abroad*. "Mark Twain" is an American literary character or persona made up by Samuel Langhorne Clemens to represent what a western "vandal" (a destroyer of cultural icons and artifacts) would think about storied places. He lacks reverence and likes his comfort. He wants an elegant French barber but gets roughly scraped; he discovers that an exotic lunch in Damascus is nothing more than dirty eggs; a luxurious Turkish bath leads to more scraping and being pounded. His urge to reverence the Old Masters, especially da Vinci, turns to frustration when he sees poorly maintained rubbish instead of great art, and the Vandal and the "boys," including an unnamed doctor and other young skeptics, turn to teasing guides—all of whom they name "Ferguson" for simplicity—by asking about mummies and others, "Is he dead?"

At the time Twain wrote these reports the cultivated and genteel may have thought him a lowbrow, but in fact he spoke for the average American. He represented the breezy informality of his region (the American West) and his own shrewd ethical and democratic vision. His travesty of the Turkish bath in Damascus, in *The Innocents Abroad*, had been preceded by a travesty of the same phenomenon in New York City. For newspaper readers of Twain's day in California, continuity existed between the American East and Europe—at least in terms of exaggerated claims of cultural superiority. Early in the book and again in the Holy Land, the unregenerate "boys" are set against the "pilgrims" to show the difference between casual decency—the western standard—and pious rigidity, at once self- and doctrine-centered.

The characterizations of various peoples and governments are important. In the Azores, Portuguese islands off the coast of Africa in the Atlantic, the first landfall on the European leg of the journey, Twain finds the people "eminently Portuguese—that is to say, it is slow, poor, shiftless, sleepy, and lazy." Throughout the remainder of the travels, such characterizations differentiate the cultural climate in Europe and the Holy Land from the American "go-getter" spirit. It might be more accurate to describe these characterizations as attacks on traits rather than on individuals, building the book's theme. Individuals such as the pretty Paris glove-seller or the Turkish bath masseuse usually get the better of the narrator as he loses his innocence about travel adventures.

In Europe his target is the tour guides, but in the Holy Land it is the sentimental tour books, the natives, and his own fellow pilgrims—a wide range of targets for moral and ethical burlesque and sarcastic comment. Twain reverses viewpoints when seeing remnants of the work of da Vinci and Dante, but the sword of an old crusader causes him to write seriously of conventional values of heroism and integrity, which he finds lacking in the places he tours. Nevertheless the Vandal represents a sort of idealism, even if many "sublime" passages are offset by skeptical commentary, a comic conclusion, or a moment of slapstick or burlesque.

Is the slangy, irreverent narrator the real Twain? Yes, but the "real Twain" is a persona, too, for Samuel L. Clemens. The viewpoint is both a projection of an American from the West and Twain himself. The two are intertwined. In *The Innocents Abroad* Twain was playing the role of Philistine, a practical traveler lacking aesthetic sensibility. Mocking the serious pretensions of the "pilgrims" ruffled some feathers, especially when he compared them to storks looking down their beaks at the other less sanctimonious travelers. However, Twain's egalitarianism, entrepreneurialism, and empathy—his major values—are evident in the Vandal's underlying character.

Plot and Thematic Issues

Whether or not *The Innocents Abroad* has a plot is debatable. As a travelogue, it doesn't require one. The series of events is connected by Twain's reports of the variations between mundane reality and glorified expectation. The naif finds his voice in critiquing from a vulgarian's viewpoint the inflated expectations of the sentimentalists. Twain's aggressive comic attacks on Europe and the Middle East drive the events in the most notable sections: joining and starting the trip; arriving in the Azores; and visiting Paris, Rome, Yalta, Damascus, the Holy Land (especially entering the Holy Land), Jerusalem and the Tomb of Adam, and Egypt. Rome, Greece, and Damascus set the stage for the Holy Land, where Twain exploits the dichotomy between his actual perceptions and what he was told to expect by sentimental travel books (especially those by William Prime, here burlesqued mercilessly as William C. Grimes) and the holier-than-thou travelers.

As early as the Azores, Twain vents his spread-eagle American attitude on the dirt, superstition, and backwardness in technology of Europe. This is *posed* writing—a persona represents an "American" viewpoint for comic purposes. It is partly reliable as an expression of the nation's culture, but it is also caricature. Twain satirizes both the setting and characters and "himself." The Roman Catholic Church is blamed for superstitious lack of progress, dirt, and ignorance; and Twain makes the people who demonstrate these traits the butts of his satire for the rest of the work. A reader should wonder if Twain in Paris is a little like Jim Smiley in the "Jumping Frog" story: shrewd on one hand, naive on the other. Readers have to draw their own implications when Twain is taken in by the flattery of a flirtatious French glove seller, for example. Is she corrupt, or is he too innocent? Both are true, otherwise the anecdote would be more of a set piece of conventional comedy and less funny.

Italy presents Twain a wide scope of thematic issues. His passages on da Vinci and the Old Masters show the vulgarian's failure to appreciate historical artifacts. Borrowing the question "Is he dead?" from an Artemus Ward sketch set in London in 1866, the "boys" torment their guides when viewing an endless series of relics. The "boys," acting like inspired idiots, ask the guides about the deaths of Columbus, a mummy, and da Vinci. In Rome, Twain extricates them from a monastery mausoleum decorated with frescoes of human bones before they can ask the question about the monkish skeletons. The chapters on Rome feature these moments as highlights among Twain's funniest burlesques. Also, Twain in Venice presents a paragraph that comments on racism in America. Using the phrases of the Civil War, Twain captioned this paragraph "Contraband Guide" in Chapter Twenty-three. He notes simply that a very cultivated American expatriate guide has no plans to return to America; Twain responds in three words, "He is right."

The Capuchin Convent in Rome is the locus of one of the best-realized literary comic moments in the book, although the lunch in Damascus rivals it. Vanity is the target, and the carefully set up "Is he dead?" joke, openly borrowed from *Artemus Ward in London* (1867) to emphasize how the reporter's attitudes were in the skeptical tradition of American literary comedy, provides a comic cap to get Twain out of what threatened to become an overly "sublime" reflection on the bones of the monks. The scene combines language, sentiment, and slapstick, exploiting much of the potential of literary comedy. Pious vanity is portrayed as grotesque, a gruesome underlayer of the profit motive which had Barnumized churches and innumerable pieces of the "true cross" and martyrs that populated church after church as money-making frauds.

A series of events develop the thematic idea that naive western travelers make themselves look foolish in the way they respond to exotic settings and new experiences. At Yalta, visiting the Prince of Russia, much is made of a speech authored by Twain that is patently silly. Then the Prince retires to count his spoons to see if the pilgrims stole any. This event actually did take place, and the printed broadside of Twain's speech is preserved in the Twain Collection of the Mark Twain House. The written scene, however, is developed as literary comedy with skeptical perspectives derived from the *Quaker City's* crew as well as from the author, and even implied in the gracious Prince's counting of his spoons. The attitudes of the narrator are woven into the action, and events are aligned to make a comic sequence that shows the pretension of the participants. In the Turkish lunch sequence, western poker terms juxtapose practical attitudes about cleanliness to false expectations about foreign grandeur.

The Holy Land provides an opportunity to magnify all the themes of naivete and relate them to religion and spirituality among both Americans and foreigners. Twain is most outspoken, however, about an act he perceives as "inhumane," a violation of the Savior's creed: the pilgrims insist on driving exhausted horses to their limit to avoid any "Sabbath breaking stain" upon themselves by traveling on the weekend. This leads Twain to argue that these men had elevated the letter of the law over its spirit, a life-long target of his humor. Chapter Forty-three is an important intersection of plot and theme in the passage on "Pilgrim Fidelity to the Law" with its rhetorical "Men might die, horses might die . . ." Twain's argument is that he respects these men but thinks their ideas of the Savior's message are distorted. Missing a boatride on the Sea of Galilee indicates that the pilgrims are so cheap they try to bargain for the cost of a ride on holy waters. Twain shows the irony of this as a criticism of the moral smallness of the people. They compare poorly to Godfrey of Bouillon in Chapter Fifty-three. As an old crusader, Godfrey represents the archetype of the professional. Indeed, professional men—pragmatic, realistic, but made humane by their apprenticeships—embody Twain's philosophy. They have been hardened like Godfrey's sword in the fire of experience, but they have also been taught a trade, and this privileged apprenticeship has made them wise, not cruel. Readers will recognize them in the characters of Miles Hendon, Hank Morgan, Huck Finn, Pudd'nhead Wilson, and others.

The Holy Land offered Twain a vast array of conflicts between elevated expectations and degraded reality, poverty, disease, and ignorance. For example, the Church of the Holy Sepulchre in Jerusalem features fighting monks. This anomaly may suggest that the narrator is actually a reverencer of the things he caricatures. A comic moment that undercuts false expectations involves Twain weeping at the Tomb of Adam, where he discovers "his" long-lost ancestor Adam. Pragmatic American readers knew this was all pretentious nonsense. The piece is sheer farce; all America laughed. Compensating, perhaps, Twain added "sublime" passages on the pyramids and the Sphinx in Egypt when revising the letters. A lot of criticism of the "sublime" passages—a form of fine writing frequently practiced in the nineteenth century to elevate the emotions of reader or viewer—has been vented as making the book seem stilted and false. The Egyptian sections show Twain trying to be both elevated and comic at the same time. This book was sold door-to-door by subscription, not in bookstores, and sat next to the Bible and John Bunyan's *Pilgrim's Progress*.

ROUGHING IT (1872)

In *Roughing It* and *Life on the Mississippi*, Twain describes the gaudiness, individuality, uniqueness in place and time, and romance of unusual settings.

His viewpoint, that of the worldly describer of his own naive adventures, adds the realistic element that makes these experiences "normal." He even wrote in *Life on the Mississippi* that there are "Two Ways of Seeing the River," and the professional pilot's way he has learned has taken all the romance out of the river for him. William Dean Howells, the dean of American editors and the general in the fight to recognize realism as *belles lettres* (high art literature), argued in *Criticism and Fiction*, later, that one would rather read in detail of a real grasshopper than see a gorgeous, tinseled fake—a romanticized one. In describing the cross-country stagecoach ride, the outlaw Slade, wretched Indians, the comic tall tales of the Sierra Nevadas, and even more comic interplay between missionary Christianity and Hawaiian paganism, Twain brings the exotic into focus as real adventures—uncomfortable and intimidating—and almost always in a self-deprecating way. Words and phrases, incidents, humor, and extended sequences and characterization are based on the interplay between the two schools of writing. Twain's narrator is even naive about his own culture. Much of the fun of both books comes from the interweaving of the viewpoint of the narrator with the unusual historic scenes, tall tales, and lore of these two exotic areas.

Setting and Characters

Roughing It is based on letters and newspaper clippings that Twain compiled during his stay in Nevada from 1861 to 1865. He left Missouri to assist his brother Orion, newly named secretary of the Nevada Territory, thereby missing the Civil War. He arrived in Carson and Virginia City, Nevada, in time to experience the flush times of the great silver rush. He tried placer mining but found his real calling in newspaper reporting with the Virginia City, Nevada, *Territorial Enterprise*, developing his confidence and aggressiveness under its editor, Joseph T. Goodman, and fellow correspondent Dan De Quille (a pen name for William F. Wright). At this time the country was changing rapidly and the mines were a boom industry with talented liars and colorful and unique characters; grossly exaggerated stories abounded. Twain's "Jumping Frog" story, sent east to the popular comedian Artemus Ward, was representative of the sort of hoaxes and tall tales that circulated throughout the mining country and that populate *Roughing It*. From 1865 to 1867, Twain reported for various San Francisco papers, visiting Hawaii in 1866. There he also found a society in a state of change; primitive and civilized elements mixed incongruously with traces of the boom times of the West.

Twain's reporting of the doings of the Nevada legislature allowed him to hone his skills as a flamboyant satirist, and that satirist became the chief protagonist of *Roughing It*. In fact, Twain's attacks on corruption in the mining industry led to his title as the "Wild Humorist of the Pacific Slope" and the "The

Moralist of the Main." He acidly commented on the new Nevada motto, "Volens et Patens," suggesting how willing the territory was to help out in the distant Civil War—that the residents would do better adopting a jackass rabbit as their state animal and the legend "volens enough, but not so damn potens." Add to this mix of images and ideas the ethical and moral voice of Mark Twain, and the setting of the rough mining country holds a lot of potential for meaningful comic experiences.

Twain paints his own personality with a comic aura of naivete that exposes him to the wily opportunists of the frontier economy and leaves him in awe of its more portentous figures, such as Brigham Young and the character Slade. Young, as leader of the Mormons, was subject to burlesque because he had multiple wives, but Twain ends by describing himself as an infant in comparison. Slade, a sort of outlaw figure who manages a stage line, exemplifies the wild life of the drivers and conductors of a dangerous new enterprise. Tenderfoot traveling companions like Bemis, the wretched Indians, and the natives of Hawaii make a full panorama. Bemis is a tenderfoot foil, or contrast, to the reporter; but the Indians and the native Hawaiians represent subject peoples—the former thoroughly degraded, the latter colorfully and ridiculously modified by missionary intervention into their customs of dress and behavior.

Plot and Thematic Issues

Chapters One through Seven introduce readers to a new and exotic world: "The West," land of riches and plenty. The luxury of lying on the baggage reading the dictionary is balanced by the first of an array of odd characters, a local woman, and the "jackass rabbit," filtered through the bemused perspective of Mark Twain, the celebrity writer. The coyote in Chapter Five represents an exaggerated tall tale of this landscape; he is an emblem of the forces lying behind the comedy of the stagecoach ride. The tall tale "Bemis's Buffalo Hunt" in Chapter Seven is emblematic of a world that has broken out of the standard rules and manners of town life. A buffalo is supposed to have climbed a tree in chase of a man, a lie equaled only by Twain's claim that he had seen a coconut-eating cat in Siam "years afterward" (another event that never happened because Twain hadn't been to Siam when the book was written). The joy of these episodes is that they are highly intellectualized humor—stories and attitudes—masquerading as anecdotes of local color.

Lawlessness and violence simplify rules of survival. Chapter Nine introduces the character Slade, a man who is a killer but is otherwise like the professionals/heroes of Twain's major works. Slade murders outlaws, but to the innocent traveler he is "romance, and I sitting face to face with it!" Romance turns to comic terror as tenderfoot encounters murderer and Slade courteously refills the narrator's coffee cup with the last serving. Silly moments exaggerate sillier romantic sensations for the readers' enjoyment, but Slade's death by hanging is detailed a few chapters later. One incident sums up the practicality of the region: in Chapter Twelve a conductor falls into a fourteen-foot ditch with his lantern and yells out, "Don't come here"; the stagecoach driver responds, "Think I'm a dam fool." Politeness is not a factor.

The Mormons had already been subjected to burlesque by literary comedians Artemus Ward and Max Adeler by the time *Roughing It* was published. Chapters Thirteen through Eighteen focus on the Mormons, playing on the group's plural wife system that scandalized easterners. As comic as Twain's meeting with Brigham Young is his shoe-shine by an "Injun" who remarks that the cheap tourist should keep his small tip in his pocketbook rather than in his soul to avoid getting it cramped so. Twain seemed to hate the frontier Indians, the Goshoots. (Actually they were Gosiutes, a Shoshone tribe whose members ate a variety of foods that whites found repulsive and who were collapsing as a people under pressure from other displaced Indians. Twain's dislike is an anomaly in his generally humanitarian attitudes toward the oppressed.) Crossing the alkali desert and encountering the Indians brings unpleasant reality to bear on comfortable fantasy in the chapters that follow, and James Fenimore Cooper, creator of the noble Indian savages in the Leatherstocking tales, is debunked. By Chapter Nineteen, Twain recasts the experience as social criticism, noting that the Baltimore and Washington Railroad directors are worse than the Indians. Lake Tahoe provides a beautiful counterpoise, which Twain sets on fire when his poorly banked campfire gets out of control.

Chapter Twenty-four introduces one of the book's finest stories, detailing Twain's ride on a "Genuine Mexican Plug." Elements of naivete, slapstick, dangers to the innocent in a democratic world, and "coming to knowledge" all figure in the story's comic construction. The story starts, as have others, with the tenderfoot's romanticizing of the sights of bronco breaking. In an auction frenzy Twain buys the "genuine" Mexican plug, not knowing that such horses are untameable. He then describes his impossibly wild ride. Reality and fantasy are so completely integrated in the narrative style that no reader could guess where one leaves off and the other begins. The steed Oahu will later provide a counterpoint comic horse story in the Hawaii chapters.

Various stories of mining follow, including one about Twain and Bemis nearly freezing to death in a snowstorm a few feet from their cabin—another great comic moment as they make promises to reform if they are saved. Twain also tells the story of how he lost a claim to a fortune, and he finally brings up his career as a newspaperman in booming Virginia City. Chapter Forty-seven offers a culmination of this experience in "Buck Fanshaw's Funeral." Scotty Biggs, using miner's slang, tries to arrange for a friend's funeral with a parson who speaks in a very formal manner. Once they finally understand each other, Scotty joins the parson and leads a Sunday school class. In a new world, a new language may be needed.

Roughing It shows up law and especially the jury system as ill fitted to the wild times, and justice takes a special turn in Chapter Fifty. The character Captain Ned Wakeman is outraged that a bully named Noakes has killed his colored mate (referred to only in reported dialect as "nigger"). Wakeman captures the man and hangs him, grumpily allowing a kangaroo court to convict him first only for form's sake (one of several attacks on the jury system in *Roughing It*). Twain brings forth the story as a curiosity, but not an uncommon one, and he is studiedly mute on whether he condemns or approves of the action. Rather, it is typical of the time and place.

Winding through various topics related to the silver rush, Twain comes finally to two of the funniest of his set pieces, or self-contained stories: "The Story of the Old Ram" in Chapter Fifty-three, and the story of the cat "Tom Quartz" in Chapter Sixty-one. Each story is a unique comic production, trailing through a series of non sequiturs (unrelated ideas that are improbable or impossible on their face) that are so textured by the teller that each slapstick fantasy takes on a feeling of reality. They are isolated representations of life in the Washoe silvermining country with its mixture of fabulous wealth, absurd doings, exaggerations, and social mundanity of everyday fights and business deals.

Twain's Hawaiian experience occupies Chapters Sixty-two through Seventy-nine. They expand the action from the exotic local to the exotic international, broadening the range of cultures but restating some of the themes of (1) innocence and chicanery, (2) the special quality of the landscape, and (3) religion, justice, and spirituality that were marked components of Twain's treatment of the Washoe. Chapter Sixty-four, "An Interesting Ruin," provides Twain the opportunity to offer ironic praise to missionaries who have improved the lot of the Islanders by teaching them about hell. Masquerading as history and "sublime" description of old customs, Twain's humor suggests a moral dimension that calls into question the colonial impulse to remake native cultures. The Hawaiian chapters provide an emotional, comic, and personal climax to the book. Yet even here, Twain tells western stories, for example, the "Incorporated Company of Mean Men" story—Chapter Seventy-seven—a comic song about Irish laborers. These chapters may have been added to expand the book for door-to-door sales, but the wider international/religious/personal commentary highlights aspects of Twain's ethics that readers admire elsewhere in his canon as well.

LIFE ON THE MISSISSIPPI (1882)

"Old Times on the Mississippi" was expanded when Twain revisited a much tamer Mississippi in 1882. A passage on flatboating, the "raftsman" passage, was pulled out of the *Huck Finn* manuscript Twain had been working on. Later in the book, newspaper, encyclopedia, and historical accounts fill up pages so that the final volume would be big enough to sell door-to-door as a subscription book. Nostalgia was reflected in the local color reportage of Twain's cub pilot experiences. In a less nostalgic vein Twain also attacked the influence of Sir Walter Scott (the great English writer of medieval romances such as *Ivanhoe*), on the South, especially in relation to ladies' finishing schools and false notions of chivalry. Twain returns to these themes in the "Walter Scott" episode in *Huck Finn*, in the character Sally Sellers in *The American Claimant*, and in *Pudd'nhead Wilson*. Twain also wrote a passage denouncing southern lynch law that he allowed to be removed before publication. Part of it is given to the maniac on the roof in *Huck Finn*, Colonel Sherburn. It was also rewritten as "The United States of Lyncherdom," which was not published during Twain's life; and parts of it show up in the "Slade" chapters of *Roughing It*.

Setting and Characters

The setting is partly the river—as shown particularly in the descriptions of the scenery and of "reading" the scenery, but actually the pilot house is the center of riverboat life in the early chapters. This work is a nostalgic chronicle of a booming time when captains and pilots were a law unto themselves. Chapters on the pilots association and the economic changes it brought about transform the setting into a reflection of business practice rather than local color. The association regularized life on the river and subdued its colorfulness to some extent. The country is only partly seen in terms of the civilizations that have occupied it, and the riverboat culture is the most recent, the gaudiest, the most "American." Later, the whole South as a culture comes under examination, influenced by Sir Walter Scott's romanticism to a cultural pretentiousness that, to Twain, lacked realistic perspective. The business interests of the region blend with its legendry to provide a sense of the South "after the waw." Yet the Civil War is the event that dates all things in this culture, and Chapter Forty-five, "Southern Sports," identifies it as the topic that ultimately intrudes into and dominates all conversations.

Two characters are important; the cub pilot—presumably the author, now Mr. "Mark Twain"—and the master-pilot and mentor, Horace Bixby. Together they encompass what it means to become a responsible professional person. Those characteristics involve energized knowledge set against lazy and uninformed ignorance. Toughness and courage balance the fearful hesitancy of untrained youth. Gruff competence is the adult mode, compared to the innocent's braggy admiration for hollow show. As the pilot trains his cub, traits mature, leaving a more competent professional, one who returns to the river later to record its changes from a gaudy frontier spectacle to a mundane commercial carrier. Mean men like the pilot Brown are foils to the matured cub pilot's steady and decent professionalism.

The later part of the document shows a world that has become safer but more commonplace. The river is now well marked, the risks and hazards clearly identified. The mature author and social critic, no longer in the role of cub, criticizes southern chauvinism in the later chapters and recounts varied stories and reportorial observations of life through Baton Rouge, Louisiana, where he criticizes "Castles and Culture," and New Orleans, where he notes how the high cost of burial above ground can ruin a black man. Even stories of a gambler's trip to California get tossed in, along with Joe Twichell's quip referring to Heaven and Hell which ends Chapter Forty-three in response to Twain's idea that he might get cremated: "I wouldn't worry about that, if I had your chances." The professional pilots of *Life on the Mississippi* are the clearest and most optimistic portraits Twain offers, and aspects of their attitudes and training appear in Twain's later heroes.

Plot and Thematic Issues

The first twenty chapters of *Life on the Mississippi* trace the experience of Mark Twain through his earliest perception of piloting and steamboats, gorgeous and gaudy objects of boyhood ambition. The first three chapters present the history of the region as "the body of the nation," but Chapter Four introduces the perceptions of river life as colored by boyhood naivete and the yearning for grandeur, a constant theme in Twain's works. Chapters Five and Six introduce a boy to the grownup responsibilities of piloting through a series of comic sequences. Twain burlesques the naivete of the narrator recollected in humility as he encounters the working reality of piloting (the romantics would have presented this as moments of beauty recollected in tranquility—not so Twain). Realizing that "I don't know" is not an acceptable answer to a piloting question on 1,000 miles of river enforces maturity. The cub's ignorance has to be overcome by extended hard work, part of a strong motif of gaining knowledge to enter a professional fraternity. Special knowledge and values of service come to be closely identified with this work in the "lightning pilot" episode of Chapter Seven, wherein Bixby gains the admiration of other pilots by means of a death-defying act of professional skill. The cub's experiences, however, by themselves, continue to be intellectual slapstick, a genre Twain develops to a high art.

The comedy of ignorance, work, learning, and growing reaches its climax at the end of Chapter Eight when Bixby says he will "learn" Twain the river . . . or kill him. The poignancy of Twain's actually learning the river is revealed in Chapter Nine. This chapter starts with more comedy on learning but climaxes in one of Twain's most "sublime" idealizations of Romance and Beauty, sometimes anthologized as an example of comparison and contrast: "Two Ways of Seeing the River." First, the cub is frightened by a wind reef, a false marker of danger on the surface of the water. This comic episode leads Twain to describe what scenery really means. The realist interprets the sentimental appearance of a gorgeous sunset, first finding beauty but then seeing a pilot's list of dangerous indicators, adding "a professional view." Here the working 1880s meet the idealized 1840s. This theme is continued in other works where Twain comments on what he perceives as the literary offenses of James Fenimore Cooper in "Fenimore Cooper's Literary Offenses" in 1895.

Chapters Ten and Eleven describe flatboats and backwoods planters in comic detail, more for the viewpoint of the educated pilots than for pictorial realism. Twain is an impressionist writing here for a middle-class audience, capturing the sense of backwoods life, vulgar profanity, and colorful events of working life in the rapidly changing kaleidoscope of the frontier Mississippi. The last line of the chapter is a typical "capper": after a pilot clears a difficult river passage while walking in his sleep, another pilot wonders how great his piloting would be if he were dead. The air of comic wonder is enhanced by these comic responses.

Chapters Twelve through Twenty-one continue to develop the qualities of life involved in piloting, with Twain stressing in Chapter Thirteen the requirements for courage and judgment over mere encyclopedic memory. The "quarter twain" fake shallow water story ending the chapter shows the cub being initiated into absolute confidence in his own knowledge, a requirement of all professional disciplines. By Chapter Fifteen, Twain has already narrated the history of piloting steamboats to its conclusion with the Civil War, and he completes the story with anecdotes of racing days, episodes of disasters, and finally a challenge to the pilot Brown and the death of his own brother Henry. This is the climax of the book, in many ways. Chapter Twenty-one provides a summary of twenty-one years of life in fewer than twenty-one lines.

Chapter Twenty-two begins with the words "After twenty years' absence." The reader now revisits the river after its glory days. Amusing episodes and the more modest life of the river provide interesting experiences, including the mystery story of "A Thumbprint and What Came of It," a fore-study of the use of fingerprints as employed by Pudd'nhead Wilson in the novel Twain would write a decade later. After stories of Vicksburg during the war and a gambling fraud, the narrative turns more literary, describing the "house beautiful" through the eyes of Charles Dickens and Natchez, Mississippi, by quoting the earlier English traveler, author of *The Domestic Manners of the Americans*, Mrs. Frances Trollope, among other reporters; but false rumors about cottonseed oil are the subject of the most revelation, substituting for butter and olive oil according to a conversation overheard in Chapter Thirty-nine. The riverboat by now has become a vehicle of selling and commercial profit, like the rest of America in the 1880s.

Chapter Forty introduces "Castles and Culture," wherein Twain launches an assault on southern chauvinism with criticism of southern women's finishing schools. Chapters on New Orleans discuss the burial of the dead and the financial disaster it represents for a poor Negro, but the sympathy developed by this information is given comic counterpoint when Twain reports that his minister had told him not to worry about cremation, considering his slim chances of going to heaven. Chapter Forty-six returns directly to Sir Walter Scott, whose writing is taken as symbolic of much that Twain hates about aristocracy generally; Twain goes so far as to blame him for the Civil War, accusing him of being a purveyor of an ideology breeding authoritarianism, inflated social pretensions and dishonesty. The next chapter focuses on Uncle Remus, the fictional narrator of Joel Chandler Harris's stories: Harris, being white, destroyed his credibility with the young audience described in the chapter; they thought he must be black like his narrator.

Twain goes on to offer a variety of reminiscent experiences, interwoven with jokes that are true-seeming myths, such as one about a farm expert who agreed to farm for two of every three shares of the crop and at the end of the season told the owner of the farm, who was a pilot, that they had only raised two shares so the pilot wouldn't get his "third." Even in Chapter Forty-nine, Twain continues to build the myth of the professional pilot, claiming in italics that there is no instance of a pilot deserting his post to save his own life when others' lives were at stake. Another kind of revelation in Chapter Fifty explains the "Mark Twain" name as originating with Captain Isaiah Sellers, whom Twain burlesqued in the New Orleans *True Delta* while he was a cub pilot.

Stories of Twain's childhood as well as tall tales complete the volume. The panorama is brought to present-day reality by means of anecdotal trips into the past. The volume has introduced the reader to a vanished world through the eye of a mature humorist; the framing of this world by the intellectual capacity of the critic has preserved its gaudiness.

OTHER TRAVEL BOOKS

A Tramp Abroad (1880) and *Following the Equator* (1897) are the two other most notable of Twain's travel writings. Both are rich in his unique style and humor, but they do not have the coherence of the three volumes treated in detail earlier in this chapter. One critic, Russell Banks, has argued in his introduction to the "Oxford Mark Twain" volume (1996) that *A Tramp Abroad* is a fore-study for *Adventures of Huckleberry Finn* in the raft voyage down the Neckar River. At least, it is a burlesque of the European walking tour many of Twain's readers were hearing about. In the book burlesque mountain tramps and climbs are punctuated with wry comments on European culture, of which the most enjoyable is the claim that Wagner's music is better than it sounds. The mock ascent of the Riffleberg is Twain's self-deprecating caricature of mountaineering adventures, a burlesque of the travel narrative genre that he expands in the ascent of Mont Blanc. He ends up endorsing life in America.

Following the Equator was the product of Twain's financial collapse; chapters were headed with a new series of Pudd'nhead Wilson's mottoes. Anecdotes and commentary reported on Twain's around-the-world trip to pay off his debts from the failed investment in the Paige typesetter. The bulk of the book describes travel experiences and the attendant personal reminiscences from Twain's own past, mostly focused in Australia and India. Unlike *The Innocents Abroad*, this book is respectful of places, accepting them at face value even while criticizing their cleanliness. It is more descriptive and reportorial, although still characterized by Twain's intellect—as in the first chapter, where he comments on the poor woman who had neglected to develop her vices and perished from an illness because she had no bad habits to reform for a cure.

HISTORICAL BACKGROUND

The post–Civil War period was a time of affluence in which urban centers and a rising middle class became much more prominent in America than they had been previously. This audience was hungry for new experience, as in the grand tour of Europe that formerly had been possible only for the wealthy and venturesome. The western and Mississippi River experiences highlighted the changing commercial activity and geographic center of a nation whose "manifest destiny" in the 1840s was quickly leading to a manifest reality of extended geographic boundaries.

To some extent, Americans recognized that change was a major theme of the late nineteenth century. Twain's travel books, especially *Roughing It* and *Life on the Mississippi*, are about change. They take up the issues—personal, economic, moral, and ethical—of new businesses; opportunities to buy new things; and cultural conflict between middle-class Americans and foreigners, frontiersmen, and natives. They offer an ironic reporter's perspective on established customs that run counter to the ethical norms that Twain's democratic and progressive readers endorsed and expected to see portrayed in written works. Most of Twain's books, including his fiction, followed the travel format, which reflected these social and cultural changes well and offered Twain what one critic called a "narrative plank" on which he could provide burlesque patterns to amuse his readers even while instructing them. After the Civil War, America was no longer isolated either geographically or economically, and Twain's travel writings reflect this important change.

ALTERNATE READING: ECO-CRITICISM

Eco-criticism starts with geography and looks at the text in terms of the land. The land is not merely considered the text's "setting." Rather, the land is taken as the primary point of reference; the eco-critic examines the life of the novel or story to see how cultural values are superimposed on the permanent features of landscape. Eco-critics do not assume that the land was made for humankind but that the landscape represents a broad platform on which many behaviors and ideologies can be played out. The treatment of the land by characters is one aspect of this critical approach. The attitude toward the land suggested by the author is another. Twain's travel narratives are deeply invested in portraying his changing expectations and attitudes and measuring them against real experience. Thus, eco-criticism offers an interesting avenue into his works.

The Innocents Abroad as a travel book is intended to view Europe and the Holy Land directly, but most of the landscape of Europe is subordinated to manmade objects and stories. Only in *A Tramp Abroad* does Twain actually treat European geography as such, and then it is employed heavily in a burlesque context as a target for human beings to overcome through walking, climbing, or rafting. The target shrugs man off, emphasizing his puniness. Geography in the later work is a personal challenge, largely external and not particularly productive. It is static and visual, except in the case of an avalanche. In *The Innocents Abroad*, the Holy Land and the Atlantic Ocean are more formidable and more directly involved in the experience and growth of the characters. The Atlantic turns the *Quaker City* passengers into semi-invalids with a spell of rough weather—reality dominates expectation. One after another, the pilgrims come on deck to vomit over the rail as Twain watches. But even here, the pilgrims pray for favorable weather at the expense of all others; their interaction with their environment is an index of their self-centeredness. After the group arrives in the Holy Land, Twain's sarcastic descriptions of the country and native people expand on his reportorial realism. His descriptions of geography are often comically exaggerated by his sense of unexpected heat, harsh terrain, and ugly people out to make a dollar by cheating him or abusing animals. The land is, in the reporter's skeptical view, unworthy of the sentiment lavished on it in the guidebooks. Further, Twain's comparisons to the American West, including Lake Tahoe, show the Holy Land unscenic at best and at worst pestilential, populated by abused animals and exploitive Arabs and vermin. The sentimentalism that other writers invest in the land is critiqued through this realistic view of its harshness as an imposition on a potential visitor. The built-up nature of Jerusalem, as well as the contentiousness surrounding holy sites, mirrors the harshness of the setting. The most "sublime" spectacle from this area of the world is a man-made object—the Sphinx in Egypt—rather than a natural feature of the geography. The surroundings are possessed and dominated by humankind, and not for the better, according to the narrator.

Roughing It takes the reader first to the American West and then to Hawaii. The journey leaves many critics unsettled at the seeming lack of integration, but from an eco-critical perspective the lessons learned in the Washoe mining country are further expanded and developed in Hawaii. The first reality of the plains is the jackass rabbit, a natural creature like the coyote fitted to an unsupportive world of alkali and sagebrush. These elements correspond to each other, unprepossessing though they are. Narrator Twain is a greater threat to the environment, setting a forest fire on the shore of Lake Tahoe. Exploitation of mines shows the setting as a lure for the greedy and an astounding source of wealth. The enterprise, however, does not endorse hard work as much as it does flukes, luck, and absurd coincidences, bolstered and made worse by man-made law. The natural features of the world exist for humankind's benefit solely, but only conceptually; in the concrete, one piece of land is as likely as not to slide down on another and the new owner claim both. Finally, Hawaii reflects the dominance of Christianity over the integrated life of the natives in a paradise well provisioned for their original way of life, even if an occasional ancestor had to be fooled away to propitiate native gods. In this view western culture as an overlay makes a primitive paradise absurd, although conventionally moral according to the newly dominant culture.

Life on the Mississippi represents a vision superimposed on a landscape. The river and the surrounding flood plains and riverbanks are subsumed within a richly embroidered economic and social framework of piloting. For the most part, the river is a vehicle of a shifting array of enterprise and memory. Humanity imposes perceptions on an unbridled force, capable of destroying towns or making people abandon them. Chapter Seven's "lightning pilot" episode is a high point in the book that shows the river generating challenges to skilled pilots. Twain here defines a community of knowledgeable men united to serve through special courage and ability. Risking a lot of people's lives to satisfy the pilot Horace Bixby's ego, as the chapter suggests, might actually be bragging and stupidity; but this is probably not what Twain intended readers to extract here. The vision is of man's heroism in overcoming nature rather than integrating himself within it. However, as Twain describes himself "learning" the river, he also describes a poignant process of maturation and recognition of mortality. The justly famous passage in which he describes "two ways of seeing the river"—one romantic and sentimental, aware primarily of the pictorial; the other educated, professional, and realistic, highly aware of the mortal dangers lurking beneath the river's surface—is one of the high points of the Twain canon. Its beauty as a natural artifact comes into play as a crucial moment of perception. Naturally beautiful features contrast with an alternate perception of their hidden dangers inherently opposed to human enterprise. Geography becomes a means to personal insight. Twain himself is in many ways an eco-critic, seeing the histories of the river at various times as layers of social perception impressed on the landscape and causing a variety of social outcomes more or less divorced from the river itself.

5

The Adventures of
Tom Sawyer
(1876)

Despite the high standing of *Adventures of Huckleberry Finn* in American critical circles and its place in many anthologies of American literature, *The Adventures of Tom Sawyer* is the most widely known of Twain's books around the world. Lecturing outside the United States in 1998, this author asked a number of English-language scholars who were not Twain specialists if they had read *Huck Finn*; they responded that they had, and they had especially enjoyed the part where the fence is whitewashed. Specialists in Twain, whether foreign or American, immediately identify this as the signature scene in *Tom Sawyer*, one that has been used in national advertising campaigns for paint companies and is re-enacted in Twain festivals wherever they are held. As with the "Jumping Frog" story ten years earlier, Twain brought into literature a scene that resonated in the hearts of American readers and identified a special component of American culture to outsiders. A critical reader should ask why the whitewashing scene, the cat and the painkiller, the lifting of the schoolmaster's wig, and the discovery of Injun Joe's stolen treasure provide such memorable moments. They project important attitudes and provide substantial insight into American culture

The Adventures of Tom Sawyer is cunningly labeled a "boys' book" for children of all ages, a sufficiently broad warning from a humorist to let the reader know of a possible serious side. Twain writes, "most of the adventures in this book really occurred; one or two were experiences of my own, the rest those of boys who were schoolmates of mine." More important, though, the adventures are colored by feelings of suppression and repression, both of physical acts and of expressed emotions. This emotional coloring represents a very important aspect of the book. One dimension of the power of this book lies in its nature as a psychological portrait of the American village of the nineteenth century. Embodying this dimension are the pranks, practical jokes, shrewd dealings, and general boyishness of the hero and his Aunt Polly; such incidents bring the material alive in images. Twain's openly sentimental intrusions and his ability to write sheer melodrama and build to climaxes in the action give the book great power as a work of fiction. It was his first solo novel, and it further refined his place as an American author with an ability to realistically portray life and bring to it the freshness of a new character, a genuine boy of the Southwest. As one reviewer wrote, "Those who regard Mark Twain as only 'a funny man' greatly underestimate his power." [(Hartford, CT) *Christian Secretary* for 17 May 1877].

SETTING

Tom Sawyer is very much a boy in a village. Indeed, the village setting dominates every aspect of the story Twain tells. The varieties of characters represented are those of the village: a doctor, a petty tyrant schoolteacher, an important judge who comes from the county seat, schoolboys and schoolgirls. The streets are dirt, and cottages and houses are surrounded by traditional whitewashed fences. School, church, the kitchen, and dusty streets in front of picket fences and houses provide the details of village life.

In place of the old swimming hole Tom and his comrades have the Mississippi River, with its invitation to afternoons spent playing hookey from school to go swimming. Jackson's Island and McDougal's Cave offer secrets removed from the everyday life of the town. They provide special arenas where boy life and boy "business" can be transacted. Such business may be filled with emotional overtones that were unexpected, as the boys discover in experiencing loneliness when away from their homes; but, if anything, this potential enhances the book by adding emotional depth to the action. Other components of the setting include the graveyard and the deserted house, also presumably typical small-town artifacts.

In several cases, the settings add dimension to the plot by heightening the reader's sense of superstition in the boys. Varied hiding places and midnight escapades let events move beyond the commonplace limitations of daily village life, as another writer such as Twain's friend William Dean Howells might have shown it. The cave provides as many dimensions for heightened action as it has side passages where the incautious can become lost. Characters find moments of darkness, danger, and suspense not only in the graveyard, cave, and haunted house but even in the repressive violence of the schoolroom. As evil-doers employ remote scenes for their own purposes, setting and event magnify tension and provide Twain with the opportunity to build potent effects. A Sunday church service provides another example of how Twain uses local detail brilliantly to build effects. Twain shows this ability in unexpected, mundane places, such as the classroom where Tom discovers his own heroism or in the mysterious temperance hotel room "Number 2," which covers not only a crime but also small-town hypocrisy. Weather, time of day, and the feel of the country on a summer morning, as in Tom's perceptions of nature on Jackson's Island, provide moments that Twain develops as part of the special texture of this novel's experience.

PLOT DEVELOPMENT

Chapter One opens with Aunt Polly rousting Tom out of the kitchen closet covered with the jam he has been raiding. Tricked into looking behind her so that Tom can escape, she muses on discipline with enough traces of dialect to reveal herself to the reader as a southwesterner who is not formally educated. Her thoughts turn on religious responsibility, punishment, restriction, and "duty" so as not to be the "ruination of that child." Tom then plays hookey from school and is discovered only because his too-good half-brother Sid alerts Aunt Polly that Tom has circumvented her own tricks. She has sewed his shirt shut to catch him swimming, but he has resewn the collar, using the wrong color thread, as Sid points out. The chapter is a battle of wits, on local ground, taking place within a young boy's world—explicitly likened to a man's world. Tom goes out to practice his newly acquired art of whistling and finds a well-dressed new boy, later introduced as Alfred Temple, and the boys challenge each other until they fight. Tom wins and is soon chased off by the boy's mother. Crawling into his bedroom window he is caught by his aunt, waiting in ambush; as punishment she condemns him to whitewash the fence on Saturday morning. Chapter Two offers up the small-town spectacle of whitewashing the fence, one of the book's most memorable moments. After an attempt to get the slave-boy Jim to do the job, Tom has the "magnificent inspiration" to make the job exciting and thus induces various boys to trade him their treasures to do the job as he watches. The fence gets not one but three coats of whitewash, and Aunt Polly, amazed, rewards Tom with his second apple of the day—he has already gotten most of a first such prize in trade from Ben Rogers, who exchanged pretending to be a steamboat for a chance to be the first at the whitewash brush. Tom's world is heavily freighted with such innocent and seemingly trivial comic ironies.

Tom escapes the house, stealing a donut as he goes and throwing clods of dirt at Sid for revenge over his betrayal of Tom's earlier trick. He plays with other boys until he discovers the "new girl" in town—Becky Thatcher, with whom he falls in love, performing a variety of child antics to court her. Returning home, he is wrongly punished for Sid's breaking a sugar bowl and goes off to console himself with misery and yearnings for the new girl. Outside her house at night he is soaked when water is thrown out a second story window, and he then goes home to bed (without praying, as noted by Sid for future use). The next day, his lovely and kind older cousin Mary coaches him in his Bible lesson with the lure of a treasured "Barlow" knife, every village boy's desire. Mary then gets him washed and dressed in his "other" clothes, reserved for Sunday—he has only two sets, the reader is told, as Twain adds another piece of small-town detail. Mary is also identified as a typical character of many villages, if not a stereotype. Uncomfortable and restricted though Tom feels, he is soon at work trading for Bible recitation tickets to exchange for a new Bible. Mr. Walters, the Sunday-school superintendent, then commences showing off for important visitors from Corinth, twelve miles away, as does everyone else. As these characters perform for their visitors, the only needed climax is a Bible presentation, and Tom comes forward with his tickets for verses memorized. Unfortunately, when quizzed he can only guess that the first two disciples of Jesus were David and Goliath—a comic response line on which Twain closes the chapter, leaving the outcome to the reader's imagination. Clearly this village is close to misrule at any time when Tom Sawyer is on the loose.

Chapter Five carries on the detailed representation of a small-town Sunday by depicting the church service. Even typography (with slanting lines), is used to represent the hymn singing, followed by the Reverend Mr. Sprague's reading of notices. The boys' attention, not held by the boring formalities, turns first to flies, then to a "pinch bug" beetle that disrupts the sermon with smothered "unholy mirth" on the part of the congregation. It finally bites a dog on the behind, creating pandemonium. By Monday (Chapter Six), Tom has conceived of a hurt toe as his excuse to escape school, but he ends up instead with Aunt Polly pulling his loose tooth, making him a hero to the other boys because of the gap in his teeth—satisfying his need for attention. Huckleberry Finn is introduced as a boy hated by all mothers but loved and envied by other boys because he is free of the restraints of proper clothing and cleanliness. Tom and Huck believe that the town "witch" has told them how to cure warts by taking a dead cat to the graveyard at midnight; this detail establishes the basis for a trip there in Chapter Nine. By the end of this chapter, Tom has admired a tick and managed to get punished for consorting with Huck Finn, causing the schoolmaster to beat him and send him to sit among the girls—his objective—where he flirts with Becky Thatcher. Punished again, he is so excited by Becky's responses to his overtures that he loses various boy games and cannot even retain his pewter spelling medals he has worn for months.

A variety of events take the reader from the schoolyard romance— not without emotional overtones—to much deeper and more frightening events. At recess in Chapter Seven, Tom and Becky talk, but he unintentionally blurts out his relationship with Amy Lawrence, causing an emotional breach in their courtship that even his treasured brass and iron knob cannot repair as a love offering. Chapter Eight takes him to the woods to brood about running away and becoming a pirate, but he is soon joined by Joe Harper, and the two indulge in games of Robin Hood. Chapter Nine brings deeper melodrama, as Huck Finn appears late at night with a dead cat and Tom and Huck head for the graveyard. There they witness the revengeful murder of Dr. Robinson, who has come to rob a grave, by Injun Joe, who is smarting for charity denied him five years earlier at the Robinsons' back door. Joe rigs the murder so that the drunken Muff Potter thinks he did it, and in Chapter Ten the reader follows the boys' flight in terror back to the village. They recognize that if they tell on Injun Joe and he is not hung, he will think no more of killing them than of drowning a couple of cats. They vow in blood—because handshakes are for "gals" who "go back on you anyway"—not to reveal their secret knowledge in a scrawled document, which is reproduced in the text. In an agony of fear the boys, while hidden in the tannery, are confronted by a howling dog, meaning death, but the dog points to Muff Potter, snoring in a stupor. Tom returns home and is overcome with guilt and depression as Aunt Polly weeps over him, rather than punishing him for being out late (Sid has told on him again). Becky's return of his brass knob in school completes his misery.

The action of the novel seems to grow ever worse for Tom Sawyer; and if not for the mock seriousness with which the romance and Aunt Polly are treated, the book could hardly even be called comic. The murder revealed, Tom and Huck are shocked when Injun Joe places the blame on Muff Potter, who is arrested. Surprisingly, Heaven does not strike the murderous liar with lightning, and the boys' courage erodes. Sid tries to learn Tom's secret by eavesdropping on his troubled sleep-talk, demonstrating how evil a "good" boy can be in seeking to enhance himself by exploiting the minor vice of another. The villagers are too cowardly to tar and feather Injun Joe. All in all, Chapter Eleven marks several low points in the portrayal of human character, both individually and collectively. In Chapter Twelve, even Aunt Polly is shown to be self-aggrandizing: Tom's melancholy gives her an excuse to try out a number of ill-conceived medical frauds on him. Finally, the business is ended in a slapstick comic scene when Tom feeds his "Pain-Killer" to the luckless cat, who goes into wild gyrations and flees after doing much damage. Tom reasons with his aunt that the painkiller must be doing the cat as much good as it is to him to have his bowels "roasted out." Aunt and boy are shown in a sympathetic moment before Tom heads for school and more misery as Becky rejects his renewed antics.

Chapters Thirteen through Eighteen are devoted to scenes of boy life in natural settings, most notably in the adventures of Tom, Joe Harper, and Huck on Jackson's Island, to which they retreat to play pirate. Twain puts Tom and Joe's sense of being abused by the world into perspective with mock-heroic sentimental language. Stealing sufficient provisions from home, and a chunk of "fire" from a raft, and using appropriate pirate language, the boys ground their own raft on a sandbank just above the island and commence their version of a life of crime. Tom and Joe envy Huck's pipe smoking, a "majestic vice," establishing a basis for later trying it and making themselves horribly sick. Chapter Thirteen closes sentimentally and tenderly, with Huck easily falling asleep because he is well fed—which he is not, usually—and Joe and Tom being troubled in conscience at having stolen things and run away. Chapter Fourteen begins idyllically with Tom examining his natural surroundings and the boys cavorting in the water until a twinge of homesickness colors their thinking. A steamboat now appears, firing its canon to raise the corpses of the presumably drowned boys. The boys feel heroic because of this "dazzling notoriety," but it is not enough to keep Joe and Tom from feeling guilt about the distress others are undergoing at home on account of the boys' disappearance. Tom collects pieces of sycamore bark and writes on them, but Twain does not let the reader know what is written, and so Tom leaves his sleeping comrades late that night. Noteworthy about this chapter is Twain's foreshadowing of the later disappearance of Tom and Becky after the trip to the cave, also bringing great distress to their families and also to be resolved melodramatically by Tom.

Chapter Fifteen allows the reader to follow Tom in his flight across the river and through the darkened village streets to Aunt Polly's house, where the reader finds her and Sid, Mary, and Joe Harper's mother grieving. Copious tears flow from the story's participants—and from readers—as the two women repent their attempts to discipline boyish pranks, as Tom eavesdrops from under the bed, shedding his own tears over Aunt Polly's heartfelt prayers and love for him. Deciding not to leave one of his sycamore scrolls for Aunt Polly, he returns melodramatically to his two comrades on the island just in the nick of time for a grand entrance and a long nap, having promised his reappearance on the other scroll of bark left in camp. Chapter Sixteen follows the details of boy life with unsparingly sentimentalized detail. The boys find less joy in swimming when there's no one to say they can't, make themselves wretchedly ill in trying to master pipe smoking under Huck's tutoring, and are drenched by a thunderstorm. Heedless lads that they are, their fire is out, but the boys persevere against this problem and their incipient feelings of homesickness by deciding to become Indians. They discover that they can now at least get a whiff of a pipe without throwing up. Twain employs his language carefully throughout the narrative, and especially here, to suggest innocence, an amusedly genteel circumlocution in describing events, and a tone of bemused nostalgia. This is the heart of the book as a "boy book." The experience concludes in the following chapter when Tom and his comrades appear dramatically at their own mourning service. The service is something of a mockery of indulgently sentimental self-deception, climaxed by Tom's reappearance from the unused upper gallery and the minister's shouted command to sing "Old Hundred" in gratitude for their deliverance. The repressed love of the community for its incorrigible lads is now released; Tom, the center of all attention, considers this his finest moment.

Tom's relation to Aunt Polly is further considered when a discussion takes place the next morning concerning Tom's letting his family know he wasn't dead. Tom is made to feel mean and selfish when Aunt Polly finds out he was ashore and observed the family activities he had pretended to have dreamed. Sid responds skeptically to Tom's "dream" account of Polly's grieving with Mrs. Harper. The matter is resolved in another sentimental climax when Aunt Polly finds the sycamore bark in Tom's jacket that was to tell her he was alive. She realizes he loves her and has not lied to her. This revelation essentially concludes the development of this strand of the book's action at the end of Chapter Nineteen. The repressed love of family members for each other has been established.

The school experience provides an important alternative emotional line of action that leads through a variety of escapades over the next several chapters to the novel's conclusion at the cave. Tom now enjoys such "glittering notoriety" that he would not part with it for a circus—the ultimate statement of value in his small-village boy world. Swaggering now, with a group of small boys at his heels, he indulges all his "vicious vanity" by focusing attention on Amy Lawrence rather than on Becky, who is now sending signals of reconciliation. Becky, in revenge, plans a picnic, excluding Tom, and sits cozily with Alfred Temple, a sight that sears Tom's eyeballs with vexation. Tom soon escapes Amy, and Becky drives off Alfred, who sees how he has been used and spills ink on Tom's spelling book in revenge for his humiliation. Although Becky sees the act, she determines out of jealousy to let Tom bear the consequences.

The scene is thus set for another emotional climax in Chapter Twenty-one that exceeds even the stained spelling book intrigue. The chapter opens with Tom skipping up to Becky to apologize—credited to his emotional ease and openness—and being coldly rejected. Deeper matters are afoot, however. Schoolmaster Dobbins has the lowly status of country schoolteacher because of his unsatisfied ambition to be a doctor, and he broods secretly over an anatomy text, usually locked in his desk drawer, that Becky finds and, startled by Tom's entrance as she observes a naked figure, tears. Having damaged the forbidden book she is sure to be whipped, and Tom muses on the thin-skinned chicken-heartedness of girls, letting her "sweat it out." When the schoolmaster discovers the tear, he seeks out the culprit; Becky now looks like a "hunted and helpless rabbit" to Tom. As Becky is about to crumble under interrogation, Tom springs up to take the blame—an act of folly and nobility that earns him a ferocious flogging from the repressed schoolmaster and the heartfelt admiration of and reconciliation with Becky, which is "lingering in his ear" as he falls asleep that night. Even Tom is depicted as not having planned his intervention, an artful contrivance by Twain to intensify the reader's appreciation of Tom's essential, but as yet not fully developed, decency; nonetheless, Tom plans vengeance against Alfred Temple.

At this point readers will expect the schoolmaster to receive retribution for his harshness, and Twain sets out to satisfy this need through another great moment built around the boys' practical jokes. The master's vindictive tyranny will be avenged on "examination evening," the climax of the school year. On this night terrified little boys recite mechanically; Tom fails yet another recitation miserably—because the recitation requires real academic discipline, which he lacks; and a variety of trite copy-book themes are presented by squirmy students. A model essay on life and a poem entitled "A Missouri Maiden's Farewell to Alabama" are followed by an even more dreadful ten-page composition entitled "A Vision"—all to be found in a real book, a footnote at the end of the chapter tells the reader. Scholar Hamlin Hill has identified the book, close in title to the name given in Twain's text, and verified the claim ("The Composition and Structure of *Tom Sawyer*," *American Literature* 32 [January 1961: 379–92]). The great event follows this "nightmare," as the master, now almost mellow because he is somewhat fuddled with drink, attempts and fails to draw a map on the blackboard for his geography students. A frantic blindfolded cat is lowered on a string from the garret above and claws off his wig before being pulled up again. The sign-painter's boy has gilded the schoolmaster's bald head: the meeting is broken up and the boys are avenged in the climax. So much emotional business has been completed at this point that Twain could easily have added a chapter or two and finished the book here, but the matter of Dr. Robinson's murder remains to be resolved, and the demands of the "subscription book" trade required Twain to write a longer text to sell door-to-door even had this not been the case. The institutional life of the town has been exposed as trivial, banal, and somewhat ugly, and the wily boy pranks have punished its chief representative, the schoolmaster.

Chapter Twenty-two provides a brief interlude in which Tom joins the "Cadets of Temperance," copies a passing minstrel show, and otherwise inches through the dullness of a village summer, interrupted by two weeks of the measles. The other boys in the village, including Huck, are captured by the religious revival and even Huck quotes scripture to Tom. Fear of Injun Joe remains a troubling undercurrent, and after this chapter concludes with the boys re-lapsing to normal ways, the novel takes up the plight of Muff Potter, falsely ac-cused of murder.

The murder trial returns to the center of the action in Chapter Twenty-three with Tom and Huck discussing how Potter had been no worse than a preacher, loafing and fishing, and he has done them other good turns such as fixing fish-ing lines. Muff himself is grateful to the boys for small favors, thinking himself guilty of the murder while drunk, but the boys are guilt-ridden. After the sec-ond day of the trial Tom stays out late and is highly excited, Injun Joe is as stolid as ever, and readers are ready for a dramatic turning point, which Twain holds back. As circumstances tighten around Potter, the defense attorney surprises all present by calling and swearing in Tom Sawyer, who retells the story of his night in the graveyard. Though he is badly scared, even the detail of the dead cat is brought in as evidence, providing the jury and audience with comic counterpoint to the action. Injun Joe crashes out of the courtroom window and escapes as Tom reveals him to be the real murderer, ending one of a series of great trial scenes in Twain's novels from *The Gilded Age* through *Pudd'nhead Wilson* and beyond. Tom is once again a hero to young and old alike, but Injun Joe cannot be found despite the hiring of a detective, and Tom's nights are terri-fying to him in fear of retribution from Injun Joe. Huck has lost faith in hu-mankind on account of Tom's violation of their oath. The matter remains open until Injun Joe is found dead and Tom has "seen the corpse."

Sharing "every rightly constructed boy's life" in Chapter Twenty-five, Tom advances to new endeavors focused on digging for hidden treasure and recruits Huck again, other boys being unavailable. Funny dialogue revealing the boys' prejudices against kings and women follows, and the boys work through the night digging. Huck declares he wouldn't want a single given name, as kings have, because it would be "like a nigger"—one of the few moments in the book where Twain indicates the casual racism of this historical environment for peo-ple of Huck's low class. Cautious of dead bodies buried with treasure and eager to avoid the haunted house nearby, the boys end their night of treasure hunting around the woods at the rear of Cardiff Hill—locations that will figure promi-nently in the coming events. Two days later the boys, continuing their search for treasure, timorously enter the haunted house and are trapped there when two ruffians enter. One, appearing as a deaf and dumb Spaniard, speaks, reveal-ing himself to be Injun Joe in disguise. Too frightened to flee, the boys remain hidden above stairs as Injun Joe, awakening after a long nap, attempts to hide $600 in silver only to discover an iron box filled with gold coins. Although he is urged by his partner to leave with the money, Joe now declares that his purpose is also revenge and that he will remain in the town to carry it out, an evil inten-tion that will lead to his horrible death.

The action now turns to detective work. Injun Joe is puzzled by the fresh dirt on a pick he finds in the house, but he is prevented from discovering the boys hidden on the upper floor when the rotten stairs collapse underneath him. Tom's turn to play detective now arrives. A mystery arises when the villains decide to hide the money in the otherwise undefined hiding place "Number Two" rather than "Number One." Tom is agonized to think the "revenge" might have him as a target, but the sight of the treasure spurs him to find out the location of the money and get it for himself and Huck. He talks Huck into following Injun Joe at night, but it is Tom who almost steps on the drunken Indian's hand as he enters room number 2 in the local temperance hotel, discovering the Indian's hiding place. The boys speculate that all temperance hotels might have such rooms (Twain's sarcasm). They decide against returning because Joe has only one bottle beside him and is not drunk enough for the boys to safely pass. They will watch for an opportunity, with Huck sleeping nearby in Ben Rogers's hayloft, which he is allowed to do by Uncle Jake, "a mighty good nigger" who likes Huck because Huck acts as if they were equals, although Huck wouldn't want to do that as a "steady thing."

Summer passes along and Becky Thatcher returns to town, arranging for the picnic planned earlier in the novel, and Tom soon convinces her to go with him to the Widow Douglas's for ice cream instead of going to Susy Harper's to stay overnight after the event. "Boy like," he forgets his arrangement with Huck Finn to watch for Injun Joe. The children then enter a vast and dangerous labyrinth three miles below town known as McDougal's Cave. The steamboat returns the tired children as Huck, unaware of the adventure, watches for the conspirators. Joe and his accomplice soon pass him, carrying the box and heading up Cardiff Hill, where they pause outside the gate to the Widow Douglas's house. The widow is the target of Joe's pathologically evil revenge; her husband as justice of the peace once had Joe whipped in front of the jail "like a nigger" and he now proposes to disfigure the widow—and possibly more, tying her to the bed and letting her bleed to death. However, in the climactic Chapter Thirty, Huck tells an honest Scotsman of the plot and Joe is chased off during the night. Huck is, for the first time in his life, "welcome" at a decent family's door because of his intervention—a poignant moment. The Scotsman sets his "three negro men" to watch and protect the widow's house and in the morning dispatches his stalwart sons to join the posse to catch the villain. Huck, seriously frightened, is an unacknowledged hero; but he soon falls ill and is cared for by the Scotsman and the Widow Douglas, who recognize in him the good that God puts in all His creatures. Huck's worries about the treasure and Tom Sawyer lead the reader into even more exciting concerns. Tom Sawyer and Becky Thatcher are discovered missing and presumed lost in the cave. Chapter Thirty ends by revealing that even the news that the temperance hotel served liquor paled beside the plight of Tom and Becky, as three days pass with no word of their situation and hope turns to desperation.

The reader returns in Chapter Thirty-one to Tom and Becky, at first exploring with other picnicking children, but soon lost by themselves, in McDougal's Cave. The natural beauty of the place lures the two children deeper into unexplored territory, where, frightened by bats, they become finally and fully separated from their group. Attempting to find a way out, Tom sees Injun Joe also lurking in the cave. Soon, however, Tom's candles burn out and he and Becky are left alone, terrified, in the dark. After three days Tom is able to glimpse daylight and urges the despairing Becky to escape through a small outlet, five miles from their original entrance point. They are returned to town in a sort of universal village triumph in Chapter Thirty-two, and Judge Thatcher, not knowing that Injun Joe is also in the cave, has it sealed with a heavy door sheathed in boiler iron. Joe is discovered in the following chapter dead at the door, having starved to death after eating the few bats he could catch, a grisly end to a terrifying figure.

An echo of the concerns of *The Gilded Age* occurs as Twain records that Joe's death stops a "committee of sappy women" from petitioning the governor for his pardon. It also frees Tom and Huck to search for the money, which they realize is hidden in the cave. "Borrowing" a small skiff, they return to Tom's hidden entryway to the cave and soon discover a cross marked in the cave designating the treasure spot. Tom overpowers Huck's superstitious desire to flee, and they find the gold. Leaving Joe's guns and other trappings behind for later robber "orgies," the boys remove the gold in bags. On their way to hide the treasure they meet the Scotsman, Mr. Jones, and are brought to the widow's house. Most of the village has assembled to wish them well, and two new suits of clothes have been bought for Huck Finn. Sid is hit and kicked by Tom for revealing, with mean intentions, that Huck was the one who exposed Injun Joe's designs. In response to the discussion of Huck being poor and living at the widow's, Tom brings the celebration to a crescendo by unveiling the $12,000 in gold treasure and dumping it on the table, to the amazement of all. It is the grandest of his ever-grander effects building throughout the novel. As a result, echoing the get-rich-quick attitudes of the "gilded age," sober grown men turn to tearing up every derelict house in the country, hoping to find more hidden treasure.

Chapter Thirty-five and an abrupt two-paragraph "Conclusion" finish the story. Tom and Huck are both "rich," of course. Becky tells her father of Tom's sparing her whipping, and he determines to reward the "noble lie" by seeing that Tom goes to military academy and law school to be groomed for a great occupation. Huck is "dragged" into a society that turns his language insipid and shackles him with "civilization." After three weeks he flees to his pipe and rags, living in an old barrel, "free and happy," until Tom convinces him to return and become a robber. Huck says he can't stand everything being so regular because the widow eats and sleeps "by the bell" and prays "all the time," and his own "grub comes too easy." Huck and Tom will initiate their gang at midnight with an oath in blood (but not in a haunted house because the haunted houses have all been torn up in search of more treasure). Twain concludes the action by reminding the reader that this is the story of boys and it could not go much further without becoming the story of "men," a story left for a later time.

CHARACTER DEVELOPMENT

Tom Sawyer is the title character and dominant figure in the book. Twain immediately tells the reader, "He was not the Model Boy of the village. He knew the model boy very well though—and loathed him." Tom is a new creation in American literature, a truly unfettered free spirit. In many ways he is also an elaboration of the already fictionalized would-be cub pilot of "Old Times on the Mississippi." The reader does not follow Tom through the pilot's cycle of education and growth, however, for *The Adventures of Tom Sawyer* ends very abruptly with the discovery of the gold and the return of Huck Finn to the Widow Douglas through the lure of membership in Tom Sawyer's gang. Tom plays the role of a boy, not a man, not an artist in development, and certainly not an adult moralist scaled down and forced into the character of a child for the purposes of an author's moralizing. The other characters in the book, particularly the children, are part of a panorama of childhood rather than full-blown protagonists. Huck Finn is an exception, and he later became Mark Twain's most finely realized creation. Adults loom large in this world because of their power to control children, and their authority seems absolute, even though consistently subverted by the pranks of Tom Sawyer. Varied and conflicting psychological currents drive these characters, and Twain identifies those drives in his narration.

Tom is a richly realized character depicting a "real" boy rather than a moral exemplum. Thomas Bailey Aldrich's "Tom Bailey" in *The Story of a Bad Boy* (1869) provided a model for a boy who is mischievous and human, as seen from an adult perspective; but Tom is more detailed than the earlier portrait. He is full of surprises for the reader and even, so Twain makes it appear, for himself—as when he brilliantly, at the last possible moment, conceives of the method by which he can save Becky Thatcher from a caning for tearing the schoolmaster's anatomy text. However, Tom is also driven by the need for glory, whether earned or unearned. He trades for Bible recitation tickets to win a Bible although he has not done the memorization—it is the "moment" of the award he covets. He behaves similarly in courting Becky and in staging his own disappearance. He is driven by a need for "Romance" of the melodramatic adventure sort. As a result, he seems somewhat in opposition to others, and his doings amaze the community. Within limits he is subversive to order, but only in a comic sense; although he hurts others emotionally, he would not commit a crime in reality. His sudden recognition of Becky's "danger" of getting a caning at school is managed by Twain to be melodramatic; the author withholds evidence of Tom's thinking. The character revealed is soundly chivalric and the capacity for action makes Tom admirable, if somewhat sentimentalized. He lives by a social code that others accept. Even though he seems at variance with society, he is more at variance with the adult bullies within it. His discovery in Chapter Two that "work consists of whatever a body is *obliged* to do" is presented as news to Tom and as a new truth to readers. With the reader, Tom discovers how life works; treasure is his reward for persevering in that series of discoveries and dominating the situation through his inventiveness.

Aunt Polly is introduced by means of description of the vanity she expresses through her glasses "for 'style,' not service." She wants to express love for Tom but is torn by her sense of needing to train him by punishment and control. Readers understand her to be a representative parent in a small town, although no conventional husband-wife relationship is portrayed. Thwarted by what she perceives as her duty, she becomes the butt of many of Tom's escapades. Yet she feels and expresses to herself her affection for him, to which he, later in the novel, responds. In fact, she yearns for signs of his love so much that the discovery of a piece of bark confirming that he intended to spare her grief is an important emotional climax in the novel. She is one of many characters who suggest the emotional repressions of the small village, its petty piety, and the warfare between adults and boys over disruptive and unruly, but natural, boyish pranks.

Injun Joe is a half-breed Indian who haunts the area around St. Petersburg. The most frightening character in the novel, his role is murderous—motivated by vengeance as well as greed. He describes himself as having been mistreated by various people. He is first seen as part of a grave robbing expedition, during which he murders Dr. Robinson when the young doctor refuses his extortion of more money for the ugly task. Joe then places the blame for the murder on Muff Potter, a drunken innocent. Later, Joe plans to disfigure the Widow Douglas, but his plans are disrupted by Huck Finn. Joe finally starves to death walled up within the cave, an ugly retribution for a fearsome existence. Questions might be raised about Twain's negative depiction of Joe as an Indian: Is Joe evil by the necessity of characterization, or because of anti-Indian bias that Twain may have held in common with mainstream American society in 1875?

Other boys figure in the action, but mostly as foils for Tom. His closest friend is Joe Harper—at the outset more a sidekick to Tom than Huck Finn.

They play as opposing generals. Two other boys get Tom in trouble—Alfred Temple and Sid, the "good" boy who is actually motivated by jealousy and is really quite mean-spirited. Both boys, with a touch of reality, play tricks on Tom or tell tales on him that bring him punishments; they are Twain's attack on hypocrites to be, yet they are also "real" children. Huckleberry Finn, introduced in Chapter Six, is most important because he represents a spirit of freedom from restraint that other boys yearn for; he is a "romantic outcast" in social terms, but a much admired one by the boys. His superstitiousness joins with Tom's to bring them into melodramatic events where Huck is characteristically cautious and realistic, making him the foil for Tom's enthusiastic romanticism. Of tremendous significance is Huck's statement about Uncle Jake, at the end of Chapter Twenty-eight in which he displays the racial assumptions of his time, place, *and* class, foreshadowing the later book that will bear his name. Huck is a truly rounded character, capable of courageous action even in the face of his own fear and recognized by the Scotsman and the Widow Douglas as having good qualities.

The cast of girls—or "gals," as Huck calls them—holds only three significant figures: Becky Thatcher, Amy Lawrence, and Mary (Tom's older cousin). The few other girls such as those at the school examination night are merely carriers of burlesque material. Mary is the image of kindness and piety, able to coax even Tom into proper behavior; her presence in the novel is minimal. Amy is the victim of Tom's change of affection toward Becky and is likewise a flat figure, a victim of the passivity of her role as a "girl." Becky, on the other hand, although a victim of the passive role, is also an active manipulator of it, filled with spirit and determined to assert her emotional dignity. Huck thinks she might "comb," or subdue, Tom in the manner of women everywhere, for she shares some of his traits, inquisitive over the anatomy book and willing to risk a night out for courting and adventure, leading finally to her entrapment with Tom in the cave. In the cave she becomes completely passive, submissive, and dependent on Tom.

A variety of other adults round out the gallery of village types who hold authority over boy life in the town. The Sunday-school superintendent, Mr. Watson, the Reverend Mr. Sprague, and the schoolmaster, Mr. Dobbins, are all petty tyrants who enjoy using their position for emotional, if not economic, self-aggrandizement. They appear in this setting as boring and stilted human beings whose need for glory seems to be the driving purpose behind their restrictiveness, uncreativeness, and unpleasantness. They fawn on those they perceive to be socially above them and are willing to brutalize the children under them in order to show off for outsiders. Each is, in turn, shown up comically by events that prove them not to have real control of the situations they presume to control. Young Dr. Robinson is a grave robber, which puts his ethics somewhat in doubt. In terms of mature positive models of behavior, readers are left with the Scotsman and his stalwart boys, seen very briefly, and possibly the rather pompous Judge Thatcher. Tom's dominance is all the more evident in a world almost without true men.

THEMATIC ISSUES

One of the most notable thematic issues of this novel is the consistent reversal of the reader's sense of social organization and control. Again and again, the figures that should provide leadership in the best sense represent it in the worst sense. As a result, emotional repression on an adult level dominates the book in a way that is threatening. As Twain suggested in a letter to William Dean Howells (his friend, literary mentor, and confidant), it was not a children's book; it would be read by adults. In fact, it is read by adults to children, but different shades of meaning and reader recognition may significantly affect how it is received. Adults such as Aunt Polly are caught in a web of self-imposed emotional restraints that consistently bring them great pain. When their pain is released it is often as a secret joy, unshared in a personal sense with their children. Tom Sawyer's fantastic social displays and dramatizations make him the center of attention and admiration, but the admiration is at his show and not at his emotional substance. In many ways, an astute reader will find the world Twain depicts as a troubling commentary on relations among people who care for one another.

Punishment for social pretension is a long-standing use of comedy going back to the times of Greek and Roman theater. *The Adventures of Tom Sawyer* punishes social pretension through boy pranks and practical jokes. In some cases the punishment is inadvertent and unexpected, as in Tom Sawyer's failed response to the quiz on disciples in Chapter Four. In others it can be chance, as with the pinch-bug and poodle disrupting the sermon in Chapter Five. In Chapter Twenty-one, with the painting of the schoolmaster's head and the pulling off of his wig by the suspended cat, the comic revenge against folly is completely premeditated. In this case, the "fool" characters scourge social falsity, bringing the reader to a more honest evaluation of the world. With the cat and the painkiller a somewhat deeper level is reached, as Tom visits on a hapless animal a torture that Aunt Polly has visited on him out of well-intentioned ignorance. The comedy here responds to her abuse of authority. Twain lets the reader laugh at the lesson being taught through the slapstick action, but he leaves out explicit moralizing. Tom, rather, makes a slyly ironic comment that causes Aunt Polly to reproach herself instead.

The theme of repression of boy life is reiterated in comic events and in characters' attitudes. Swimming is to be prevented by Aunt Polly sewing Tom's shirt closed with colored thread. At the end of Chapter Six, Tom identifies himself to Becky Thatcher with a statement about the name Thomas Sawyer: "That's the name they lick me by. I'm Tom, when I'm good. You call me Tom, will you?" Village propriety denies naturalness. Readers would expect this conflict in a world where "Church ain't shucks to a circus," as proposed in Chapter Seven: few social institutions could pass the test of being set up in polarity with a circus in a child's perspective. The schoolmaster, even more than the minister, is the ultimate repressor, and he is punished by the boys' prank on examination night. Boys, not adults, however, break through the limitations of good behavior to provide a bolder, more exciting response to evil, which, as depicted in Injun Joe, townsmen consider too dangerous to try to arrest or punish.

The greatest and most fearful force in the book is the fear-invoking image of Injun Joe. A figure who lives outside acceptable society, his presence invokes fear in Tom and Huck as if he were a projection of its ultimate power to control and destroy. Without being explicitly linked, he too is an intimidator of boys, a physical threat and a power hovering over their lives—in one case literally dominating Tom's dreams. Readers experience Injun Joe and Muff Potter as the most fully realized adult men of the novel. Their behavior adds little to the readers' expectations of good from grown-ups.

Fear and danger are important thematic components of this book. Indeed, the melodrama of the plot carries the reader into a world full of psychological undertones. Emotional isolation is a substantial element in the boys' stay on Jackson's Island, where a fallen tree could have crushed them. Death is a real possibility for the boys and a vivid reality as Tom and Huck see Injun Joe stab Dr. Robinson. Tom's exposure of himself to death by intervening to save Muff Potter from wrongful conviction puts an important moral issue about courage and responsibility before young and adult readers in a way that is not preachy. The outcome seems to be in doubt as Tom agonizes over the danger and pledges with Huck never to tell about the murder they have witnessed, and the reader gets to review real problems of self-exposure in doing a brave deed that could ultimately be self-destructive. Feelings of vulnerability to evil are heightened as Injun Joe prepares to attack the widow later in the novel, and now Huck must act in haste while pleading that his identity not be disclosed. The planned torture of the widow as outlined by Joe in Chapter Twenty-nine is horrifying, and the details of brutal disfigurement are explicit whereas the suggestion of rape is implicit. Injun Joe is the most extreme of the outcasts, but the schoolmaster, Dobbins, shares some sense of his violence. Twain's world encompasses dangerous beings, both inside and outside social norms and controls, who can wreak tremendous havoc on the lives of the "innocent." The opening of the novel offers more inducements to superficial glory than to real heroism, which involves real risk. Late in the book lives are actually at stake. By focusing on the driving anger or personal psychology of his characters, Twain imbues the plot with energy, enhanced by his ability to melodramatize events. The negotiation between superficial and real heroism is the theme that Twain very likely felt to be the grown-up message making this more than a boy's book.

A note on race is appropriate. Twain inserts only two or three comments on race, one merely noting that Tom washed by Mary becomes a "man and brother," an allusion to the abolition motto "Am I not a man and a brother." However, two later asides by Huck Finn indicate a racist climate, even though the book is not about racism and the nostalgic context would seem substantially more ironic with a larger racist component. Huck comments in Chapter Twenty-five that he wouldn't want only one name, "like a nigger," and at the end of Chapter Twenty-eight he notes that he wouldn't want it known that he sat down and ate with a "nigger" as an equal: "A body's got to do things when he's awful hungry he wouldn't want to do as a steady thing." Without making the book a story about race, Twain has shown the world for what it is. Most of his characters are townspeople who do not have slaves, and the issue is down-played. The implications here will flower richly and repugnantly once the lower-class prejudice of Huck is expanded into a fully voiced character in *Adventures of Huckleberry Finn*. It is noteworthy that the Scotsman, Mr. Jones, designates his "three negro men" as watching the widow's cottage, making clear to readers that "nigger" is a word used by white trash, not by thoughtful people.

HISTORICAL BACKGROUND

The local color movement and nostalgia for childhood dominated the 1870s in the aftermath of the Civil War. Children's religious tracts were now supplemented with children's books that were still moralistic, but much less so than in the 1850s and 1860s. Thomas Bailey Aldrich's *Story of a Bad Boy*, featuring his own childhood memories of Portsmouth, New Hampshire, further opened up the genre of "boy's books" to tales that were less preachy and more natural and, incidentally, more amusing to read. A spreading secularization of American life may have nurtured this development; another factor may have been the growth of a true middle class, members of which favored stories relating to their own experience and expectations. Twain's sometimes gentle and sometimes sarcastic comments on religion, piety, and small-town hypocrisy provide evidence of the realistic movement in literature that sought to depict life through commonplace events and without the falsities of exotic events and overwrought sentimentality and romance. The latter two characteristics, however, remain richly ingrained in Twain's novel, suggesting how varied the literary forms in this era were.

The place of children in the family was a matter of consideration during this period, and family values, as now, were a prominent topic. Thirty years earlier Mrs. Partington's "plaguey boy Ike," the irrepressible 1840s "bad boy" created by B. P. Shillaber, provided the model "scapegrace" youth who was actually good-hearted but challenged the adult world through his behavior. The closing illustration of *The Adventures of Tom Sawyer*, in fact, shows an illustration of Dame Partington, so aligning Tom with Ike is reasonable. Villages and village boys offered to Americans, then as now, an opportunity to indulge in nostalgia for the "simple" fun of childhood. Aldrich's fictional New England town, Rivermouth, was a forerunner of this local color domestic portrait, and authors other than Twain tried to place real families and individuals in context in regional settings.

American politics was mixed, and neither immigration nor imperialism had yet become preoccupations. The timing was perfect for a book about boy life that adults could read with their children, and Mark Twain, now a family man, was just the one to write it. The Civil War was completed, but the social and economic position of the free Negro was not good, and the few indications evident in this novel implicate racism directly, as in Huck's scattering of comments. The frontier was still to be tamed, and, as Kent Rasmussen notes, Custer's Last Stand at Little Big Horn was one of the centennial year's most prominent events (*Mark Twain A to Z*, New York: Facts on File, 1995, p. 459). Indians were considered to be dangerous, and Injun Joe is no exception to this prevailing belief, fostered by dime novels and similar forms of popular literature. The freed slaves in the South were being forced back into invisibility and social and economic deprivation, heightened by increasing violence, but those themes did not bear on this book although they became central in the sequel. The need to adapt to village life spoke to small-town America and brought a picture of American life to English and European readers. Twain successfully represented broad psychological realities dressed up in a semi-rural setting that could easily have been a throwback to the 1840s and 1850s, as suggested by the author's "Preface."

American entrepreneurialism was a centennial motif. Commerce and invention flourished in the 1870s, and Mark Twain himself patented a self-pasting scrapbook and a suspender. After publication of *The Adventures of Tom Sawyer*, in fact, Twain licensed the name "Tom Sawyer" to a shirt company to sell shirts under the hero's label. In the North and Midwest, urban centers were growing; but the country remained largely rural, and many people thought to make better lives by farming. Tom's ambitiousness and adventuresomeness mirror the progressive ideals of the culture. A character like Tom Sawyer bridged those worlds, showing the spirit of enterprise, a need for glory, and a child's yearning for acceptance. At the same time Tom is by turns shrewdly manipulative, aggressive, and noble. The mix of elements reflects the spirit of American capitalism, money-driven and moralistic. The age of the robber barons, who manipulated industries and markets with increasing power, and political corruption, the growth of railroads and manufacturing, would bring about the modern industrial complex; Tom well represents his changing era.

ALTERNATE READING: FEMINIST CRITICISM

Feminist criticism emerged in the 1970s in an attempt to identify the consequences of gender-based ideology as influencing (1) the types of literature that are valued, and (2) the ways in which values are projected in literature. "Gender" in this context represents the cultural manifestations of differences in biological sex, so lifestyle and ideology have become more central to this analysis than emphasis on the female body as the determining influence in developing the terminology for a female "poetics"; but biological, hormonal, and physiological issues, which were central to early discussions of men's and women's sexuality, might also come to bear on broader areas of masculinity and femininity in present feminist criticism.

Feminist critics look for gender-based emotional and psychological traits within characters and in the author's concepts that cause certain actions (often male-oriented social and political behavior), to be valued over other behavior more closely identified with female gender, such as domestic activity and nurturing. Feminist critics are particularly wary of sexual stereotyping based on a so-called politics of self-interest by authors who are men. Typical stereotypes include women as passive, irrational, subjective, domestically oriented, and spiritual, whereas men are seen as active, rational, objective, workmanlike, and practical. In particular, the role of women in the action of a novel such as *The Adventures of Tom Sawyer* offers an opportunity to understand how a society's cultural expectations influence behavior and how an author who is a man might portray such a role on the basis of gender. Recent feminist criticism has advanced beyond assigning traits to male and female genders and sought to use the more complex social values of the whole culture to see how actions and characters are weighted by sex or gender role assumptions.

Twain's women are assigned motherly roles and emotions, whereas his boys are seen as irrepressibly active and aggressive. His men are somewhat or largely absent, or seen mostly as villains. This gender portrayal may suit the needs of the story-teller, but it also assigns passive roles to women. For example, Aunt Polly is both passive and repressed. Does she represent the society of the 1870s? Twain and his readers apparently felt that she did. After all, she is emotionally constricted and vulnerable. No role is posited for her that involves any commercial experience or activity beyond the strictly domestic. Discipline of a boy child leaves her distraught and uncertain, but it is the only activity allotted to her in the reader's sight. Her reliance on religion is strictly circumscribed to conventional-seeming pieties; the reader does not see her in the context of school, village meeting, or any location other than that of the parlor. Her shrewdness, in fact, is usually inferior to Tom's and is bent solely on restraining him (as by sewing his shirt closed to prevent him from playing hookey from school to go swimming) or ascertaining if he loves her (by discovering the bark scroll in his pocket that contains his message). In fact, the reader does not even see her in domestic tasks as such, so the idea of her actively cooking, making the jam that Tom steals, or even procuring the apples she gives him seems foreign to her role. Such an inactive role would not be likely for a woman in a village setting, so it is reasonable to assume that this portraiture does indeed show Twain assigning her an especially passive place in Tom's world.

The younger girls in the story, Amy Lawrence and Becky Thatcher, are seen wholly in terms of their roles as objects of a boy's budding love interest. Only the slightly older Mary seems to approach what might be called young womanhood, and she is explicitly identified as being a type of saintly young woman often found in small towns of the period, busying herself with kindly tasks and good works. Amy and Becky tease and attempt to use boys as part of a childish mating ritual. Amy, when she speaks more or less directly to Tom, is described as "artless." The art she lacks is used by Becky to heighten Tom's jealousy, with Alfred Temple as an unwitting agent. Becky is prideful and melancholy by turns, pushed this way and that by her emotions. Ultimately, when Tom spares her a whipping because she has always appeared to be the good girl in school, he becomes her hero and she devotes herself to him, so much so that she allows him to arrange for her to escape chaperonage with him. When they are lost in McDougal's Cave, she places her reliance in him, is treated chivalrously by him, and allows herself to become apathetic so that he must overcome her own despair to save her. Attributed a weaker physiology than Tom, it takes her longer to recover from the cave ordeal.

The role of women in *The Adventures of Tom Sawyer* is circumscribed so completely that the reader would be surprised to find men's roles more flexible, and they are not. Tom as the central male figure is motivated by glory even to ignore Becky's attempts at reconciliation: "Glory was sufficient." Money is a subcomponent of glory. Desiring to possess Becky's affection, he easily abandons a commitment to Amy. Desiring to play pirate or gain the excitement of getting her alone, he readily ignores Becky herself or Becky's own best interests. In saving her from a whipping, he is motivated by the pity of a hunter for a trapped rabbit—a sincere emotion, but one that suggests dominance or power over a pet as much as it represents a sacrifice by an equal of one interest in favor of another. To construe Tom's actions in this way is not to say that Twain meant to show, or Tom represents, a negative quality. Rather, the constellation of values represented by the various sexual roles makes stereotypes of loving relationships along exaggerated sentimental lines and deprives them—if one were to take them as real role models—of dimensions that would provide a richer range of behaviors and personal fulfillment. Roles are limited by sexual identities. It is possible that Aunt Polly and Tom, as well as Becky in her flirtatious behavior, are all engaged in a sort of "bad faith," as critic Forrest Robinson has argued (*In Bad Faith*, Cambridge, MA: Harvard University Press, 1986), in that they play "games," manipulating each other through emotional indirectness and collaborating in a sort of rejection of social expectations to gain dominance over each other. Feminist critics might argue that more direct and open negotiations would lead to a mutually wholesome set of relationships that would make life less stressful for all involved.

Sid as a model of the bad "good" boy, and Huck Finn as the free spirit, fill out the spectrum of young men. Sid is mean-spirited and tricky. He intends to use his capacity to spy to get Tom in trouble because his own ego demands satisfaction. Huck, on the other hand, experiences women as wanting to "comb me all to thunder"—"Hell" in the original manuscript—and subject him to stultifying and insipid "civilization." "Good" though women may be to him, they are also a restricting force that deprive his life of freedom, fun, spontaneity, and the accompanying dirt and raffishness that seem to be preconditions for a satisfactory boy life. The boys' realm is one of "action"; they trigger events rather than waiting for others to manufacture an event to participate in. As a result, there is little room for emotional growth in the lives depicted; and Tom, Joe Harper, and Huck are restricted in their play on Jackson's Island by their need to appear courageous. Their homesickness is fully identified, in this case, as a component of their emotional lives that they must neither admit nor act on. They victimize themselves according to their standards of masculine behavior .

The portraits offered by Twain do not fully represent his world. His wife, Livy, although intellectually her husband's equal and capable of heavily editing his manuscripts, was often ill. However, not only Livy but his own mother and other women in his life (such as "Mother" Fairbanks, who befriended him with personal and editorial advice for a long period after the *Quaker City* voyage), were intellectually strong and active. Assigning passive roles to women provided Tom with foils for his personal aggrandizement. Twain may have derived from this assignment some sense of security that his plot was contained in a manageable envelope of childhood. External relations between characters are based in action rather than in intellectual/psychological maturation. The real complexity of personal relationships can thus be subordinated to role playing, and the novelist is freed from the anxiety of constructing a plot in which characters must grow through verbal negotiation. A social satirist seeing the world from outside can practice this sort of art; a non-humorous and less distanced view of the same material might have resulted in a different kind of character and action.

6

The Prince and the Pauper
(1881)

The Prince and the Pauper represents a combination of Twain's ability to write "boy books" and reminiscences of the Southwest with his desire to find higher toned subjects for a more genteel northeastern and midwestern readership. Some of Twain's western friends and colleagues from the Nevada days thought the novelist should not abandon his native materials for medieval history and romance. On the other hand, his wife, Livy, and his children adored the book; the family even made a play out of it for themselves, manufacturing their own tickets and improvising costumes, with Twain playing Miles Hendon. The idea motivating the work is to show how changes in social condition can humanize thinking.

In order to do this Twain offers three central characters, two of whom are close to identical twins—the prince and the pauper, both boys roughly thirteen years of age. The two boys experience the problems associated with each other's roles, thereby developing themes present throughout the Twain canon: (1) appearance determines identity, (2) humanity is learned through training or experience, including suffering, and (3) people's status in life is the result of chance. Miles Hendon, the third major figure in the novel, embodies all three thematic elements. He is a kindly and well-disposed, but displaced, soldier of fortune who helps the prince. Some readers have found this book an odd but pleasant mix of elements, but the theme of switched places and boy adventures and fears is true to Twain's major interests; moreover his narrative style, embellished with supposedly accurate dialect touches of sixteenth-century England, remains breezy and informally "American." For example, at one point in Chapter Six the author mentions the pauper traversing the "snags and sand-bars" of social conventions—this is language from the Mississippi River, not London's River Thames.

HISTORICAL SETTING

The setting is late medieval England, 1547, the year in which King Henry VIII died and was succeeded by his son Edward VI, the "prince" of the title. English documents and coins are depicted at the front of the text, providing verisimilitude to make the comic novel one of historical fiction with some mystery and romance. "Offal Court," where pauper Tom Canty is born, and London Bridge, where the prince escapes from the wicked father, John Canty, in Chapter Twelve, are really small towns on the American model, as Twain conceived of all villages as essentially the same. People on London Bridge talk "bridgy" talk and live according to their own customs. Hendon lodges there in a sparely furnished room appropriate to his own poverty. The bridge also features the "object lessons" of decapitated heads of renowned men impaled on pikes, evidence of the cruelty of the age. In Offal Court, crowded tenements house poverty-stricken drunks and criminals preying on the gentry and on their own vulnerable wives and children. Later, readers are introduced to a vast barn that houses a vagabond gang, a hermit's hut, a small farm, and the manor and prisons associated with Hendon Hall, where Miles attempts to take up his former identity. Violence is widespread, and criminality and insanity are a threat to the young prince's well-being from almost every corner—except from certain women, his mother and sisters and a kindly farm wife, and Miles Hendon, an almost androgynous father/mother in his tenderness toward the boy he believes to be mad.

In counterpoint, the royal court shows the gilded spectacle of royal wealth. Social practice and legal custom here are formal and parliamentary, making the great seal an important artifact needed to sign a death warrant (although Tom Canty uses it to crack nuts). This world, with its opulence and formality, is presented largely through the experience of Tom Canty, the pauper, and thus is experienced as Huck Finn experiences his world. Customs are restrictive; clothes define status, and status changes if people are stripped naked and exchange clothes; knowledge of forms and formality represents social sanity. Politics is a constant threat to well-being and requires free speech to be suppressed. Such a setting provides an ideal platform for the naive pauper to discredit absurd laws in making innovative "practical" dispositions of legal cases. The final "dream" effect of the gorgeous royal setting allows Twain to integrate the thematic issue of doubt/insanity into the setting of riches and wealth, realizing a satisfying climax to the adventures of the three main figures but casting a romantic haze on the outcome.

PLOT DEVELOPMENT

The novel opens with the juxtaposed births of Tom Canty, unwanted by his poor family in Offal Court, and Edward Tudor, son of Henry VIII, wanted by all of England. With the scant protection of his self-sacrificing mother and sisters from the drunken fiends John Canty, his thieving father, and his grandmother, Tom is educated to read by Father Andrew, a kindly priest. Desiring to see a real prince, Tom, wise beyond his years, goes through the motions of begging while dreaming of the royal court. In Chapter Three, Tom, in his rags, watches the court and its splendid carriages. He is brushed away by a guard, which draws the prince's attention, and soon the two boys are chatting. The prince muses that it would be worth his father's kingdom to see popular entertainment like Punch and Judy shows and other "boy life" experiences of the poor. They exchange clothes, and are astonished at their likenesses, after which the prince says, "Fared we forth naked, there is none could say which was you and which the Prince of Wales." Pausing only to hide the royal scepter, known also as the Great Seal, the prince impetuously rushes outside the castle to reprimand a guard for his harsh treatment of Tom and is ejected from the palace. The roles of prince and pauper are suddenly reversed.

In Chapter Four, "The Prince's Troubles Begin," the prince is beaten up by the young boys at Christ's Hospital, an orphanage, and realizes that a full belly is worth little if the mind and heart are starved. He finally makes his way to Offal Court, where John Canty thinks him to be his own son, Tom, gone stark mad. Tom, back at the palace, wonders what will happen if he is discovered to be an imposter: "Might they not hang him first and inquire into his case afterwards?" (in American lynch law fashion). After a trying audience with the king in which he is thought to be the prince now deranged by over-study, his former dreams of royal riches, once so pleasant, become a dreary reality, punctuated by visions of the severed head of the Duke of Norfolk reproaching him for murder. Tom is instructed by the lord St. John to conceal his illness, and a difficult interview with Jane Grey and Elizabeth, the real prince's royal cousins, follows. After this interview he tries to rest, watched over by uncomfortable servants whom he does not know how to dismiss, to both his regret and theirs. He wonders if they would insist on breathing for him, so much is done for him. St. John suspects Tom is not the real prince but is frightened into silence by the idea that to say so would be treasonous. Retreating to his chambers, Tom plays with armor, cracks some nuts (neither he nor the reader knows he is using the royal seal of Britain to do this), finds a book on etiquette, and retires to study his new role as prince.

The actual prince is now removed from the palace, and melodramatic complications multiply. King Henry is near death and cries for his Seal, which he had given to the prince. But Tom as the prince cannot produce it. Chapter Nine offers readers the spectacle of the grand river pageant. In immediate counterpoint, John Canty drags the real prince back to Offal Court but murders Father Andrew on the way. The prince proclaims his royalty, frightening Tom's mother and sisters, who then attempt to shield him from the beating by "his" evil father and grandmother. The bathos (a sentimentalized and overdone form of pathos, or sympathetic sadness) is deepened as the mother creeps to him in the night and tests his reflexes to sudden light, determining that he may not be her son. The prince, as if waking from a bad dream, now realizes that he has indeed changed places and is an outcast in a filthy den among beggars and thieves rather than the subject of an adoring multitude. The family must flee for their lives as John Canty must escape the penalty of his murder of Father Andrew, but they are engulfed in drunken revelry celebrating the Prince of Wales—the imposter pauper—and Edward escapes from Tom's father, who, like everyone else, presumes him merely Tom Canty, gone mad.

Miles Hendon, the book's hero, appears in Chapter Eleven. He values the gallantry of the prince, who he finds defying a taunting mob that mocks his claims of royalty. Hendon thinks, like everyone else, that the boy is mad. They make their escape from a mob only because messengers bearing news of the king's death ride through the crowd. Tom's first act is to spare the life of the Duke of Norfolk, causing the royal crowd to cheer that the reign of blood has ended. Readers are now introduced to the village life of London Bridge and Miles Hendon's quarters. Hendon refuses to yield the boy to the ruffian John Canty and decides to teach and cure him because of the "soldier-like" way in which he faced the "smutty rabble." Hendon recounts his own story at the bidding of the prince, who now identifies himself as king and insists that Hendon treat him appropriately, leading to several comic moments. Hendon has been banished from his home, and he hopes to return after years of hard times and adventure to see if he can claim his beloved Edith, object of his wicked younger brother Hugh's plotting for her wealth. The king now offers Hendon a reward for his service. Hendon, inspired by practicality, claims the right to *sit* in the presence of the kings of England and is thus inducted into a knighthood in the "Kingdom of Dreams and Shadows." The machinations of his wicked younger brother Hugh become important later in the story.

The next three chapters play heavily on the juxtapositions of life. The image of Hendon sewing is domestic comedy, but the description of how to hold needle and thread is verisimilitude—a pretense to truthful detail. On learning that the dead King Henry will not be buried for three days, the pauper, now both "captive and king" in his royal role, muses, "'Tis a strange folly. Will he keep?" Tom is stunned by the indebtedness of the court but allows the bills to be paid while thinking he should let the servants go and take a small house in Billingsgate, a run down suburb of London. He meets Humphrey Marlow, the whipping-boy who earns his keep by being whipped for the king's scholarly failures, and promises to study so poorly that Humphrey's wages will go up due to expanded punishments. Meanwhile, Tom regrets his own removal from boy life and his mother. The Great Seal remains missing.

Chapter Fifteen separates for the reader the real, human meaning of the law from the evil that results from applying the letter of the law, as Twain does in other works. Tom educates himself to his elevated role and by chance, while staring out the window, makes an inquiry about a mob. His authority to command intervention compensates for his kingly restraints. "The Wise Fool," or naif, now disentangles practical truth from superstition and connivance. A series of false accusations of witchcraft are disputed by the boy from his Offal Court perspective, each incident being brought to a comic climax that endorses the boy's practical wisdom. Although he is the "false shadow" of a king rather than the substance, he nevertheless decrees an end to the practice of death by boiling in oil and angrily dismisses a case based on "idle, harebrained evidence." He thus represents a sort of practical "American" attitude toward law and is admired for his intelligence and spirit. He even begs a "witch" to fetch him a storm, a test of her powers, but finding she cannot, he frees her also. A royal dinner scene concludes the experience, with Twain noting that clothes make everyone appear graceful. Meanwhile, Tom is slowly getting used to his place in this world of power and authority.

"Foo-foo the First," Chapter Seventeen, introduces the reader to one of Twain's great portraits of outsiders: the band of tramps presided over by the Ruffler. John Canty, now "John Hobbs" in disguise to avoid capture as a murderer, has arranged for the king to be lured to the country, with Hendon following by chance in the same direction. A marvelous moment of description follows as Twain depicts the peasant spectacle of the Ruffler and his band. Seedy, disguised vagrants and thieves, they are pleased that one of their number has killed a priest and admire the swearing of women being burned for witchcraft: "There be base and weakling imitations left, but no true blasphemy," the Ruffler laments. One of Twain's most powerful social vignettes, however, illuminates how criminality might be justified in a world of harsh and unreasonable laws, including slavery. A minor character named Yokel indicts British law, which caused his mother to be murdered for the imputation of witchcraft and then had him whipped and enslaved for begging, leading to the death of his wife and children by starvation. Having been made a legal slave, he has run away from his master and will be hanged if caught. In his case the law has not served good ends. In startling counterpoint, the aroused young Edward responds, mirroring Tom's actions at court, by declaring the law void. He is soon declared "Foo-foo the First, King of the Mooncalves" in derision.

The king now experiences the underside of English life, ranging from crime by vagrants to monkish fanaticism and insanity in the wake of his father's destruction of the monasteries. The Ruffler mentors the king, as did Hendon, advising him to "make no threats against thy mates"; however, a mean young thief named Hugo warns Edward to start begging or take the consequences: "bone wrackings and bastings be plenty enow in this life." Hugo believes the elder Canty's claim that Edward is his son because lying is too good a commodity to waste and therefore Canty is probably truthful. The band, in the meantime, abuses and terrifies honest farmers and their families, but Edward escapes from Hugo when he upsets Hugo's plan to rob an old gentleman. After he flees, a moment of terror in the dark subsides into warmth and security from a ferocious storm as the king nestles with a calf in a deserted barn.

The king now learns humility when he is accepted by the girls and mother of a peasant family and put to work but burns the bread. He must flee this brief refuge and the self-complacency it has engendered; the challenge to prove himself by "showy menial heroisms" was a "boy" adventure, but John Canty and Hugo reappear. The boy ends up in a worse predicament, setting the stage for the most melodramatic sequence in a melodramatic book. A maddened monk, taking the boy's claim of royal standing to be as true as his own deluded standing as an archangel, welcomes the boy to his hermit's hut and decides to kill him in revenge for his father's destruction of the monasteries. The mad hermit is also a corrupt figure. Particularly annoying to the lunatic is that he is merely an archangel although he might have been Pope—a more politically powerful position in the eye of the ironist author Twain. The comic anticlimax, a comment on both economics and religion, is typical of Twain's social irony.

Miles Hendon continues the search for his protégé and finally finds him in distress. Hendon first reappears at the hermit's door in search of the king, but he is lured away as the gagged boy tries to signal him. Then John Canty and Hugo enter the hut, seize the boy, and return with him to the band of ruffians. He soon gains the admiration of all but John and Hugo by beating Hugo with a half-staff and is renamed "King of the Game-Cocks." Hugo decides to disfigure the king's leg with a "clime," or sore, and force him to beg; but as the villains fasten the ulcerating material on the boy, Yokel, the abused vagrant/slave, intervenes, bringing the case back to the band for resolution. The king is now "promoted" from begging to stealing, and Hugo arranges that the king will be caught as they try to steal a dressed pig from a woman going to market. In the hands of an angry mob the king is saved by Hendon's sword, the flat side of which falls convincingly on a burly blacksmith's arm as he prepares to thrash the boy. Thus, the stage is set for another court trial, one of many climactic ones in the Twain canon.

Chapter Twenty-three offers an impressive sequence of events depicting the root of much evil to be avarice, a constant theme in English literature since Chaucer's time. The king is educated about good citizenship, and the reader develops a sense of the importance of imagination and bold bluffing to achieve good outcomes—a somewhat morally ambiguous lesson. As a constable conducts the accused thief to court, Hendon counsels the feisty Edward to respect his own laws. His "theft," however, is valued at three shillings and eight pence, making the deed a hanging offense. A kind justice encourages the woman to revise the price to eight pence, which she does thankfully, escaping the guilt of putting a child to death for such a trivial offense; but the constable then extorts the pig from her by threatening to expose her as a perjurer. The king is sentenced to jail and flogging, but Hendon is able to silence him before he makes the matter worse by protesting; Hendon urges him sharply to keep peace and allow what God wills to happen before he complains or rejoices. The comic intensity escalates in the following chapter as Hendon, in turn, bluffs with fake Latin but accurate surveillance of the constable's injustice. He requires the man to restore the woman's property and the prince's freedom. Hendon and the king now make their way toward Hendon Hall, recounting their adventures to each other as they go.

The return to Hendon Hall is not joyous, for Hugh, who has seized control of the manor and married Edith (Hendon's beloved), has dismissed twenty-two loyal servants and retained only the five villains; he is master of the manor. Emotional roles are reversed as Hendon is denied his own reality by his scheming brother and the king expresses absolute trust in him, throwing the honest soldier into confusion by asking only in response, "Dost thou doubt *me?*" Hugh orchestrates a scene in which Edith is forced to deny her love's identity, and Hendon springs at his throat in anger. Edith visits Hendon in the night as the king busies himself writing a letter to the Earl of Hertford to gain back his throne in the face of Hendon's continuing incredulity; Hendon is now denied his identity and told to flee because Hugh's power over the people is so great that his word means life or death. The theme of tyranny versus the people is thus inserted into this medieval setting. As the interview ends, officers burst in and carry Hendon and Edward to prison.

Imprisonment and capture scenes always give Twain extraordinary scope in which to paint the atrocities of unbridled authority against the helpless, and Chapters Twenty-eight and Twenty-nine are fully exploited for this potential. Now all the novel's themes come together in melodrama. Kingdom of dreams, nobility, and sacrifice and suffering for another are drawn directly to the forefront. Thrust among an obscene and noisy crowd in prison, Hendon is covertly aided by old Andrews, a loyal former family servant, from whom he learns of the family betrayals engineered by his wicked brother. Two women befriend the king, now saddened by a sense that the pauper has displaced him, but they are Baptists and for this "little" crime are burned at the stake. The king, looking away in horror, declares that he will never forget the sight, and Hendon congratulates himself that Edward's insanity is mending because he is so subdued in his response. Hearing other stories of legal atrocities, the king declares that he will change the laws within the month.

Before the king can humanize his kingdom, however, Hendon's sacrifices on his behalf increase. He offers himself in place of the boy, who is about to be flogged for theft. His brother Hugh endorses the substitution with keen satisfaction, but the crowd now comes to admire Hendon for the sacrifice and Edward whispers to Hendon that his brave, good heart will not be forgotten. Hendon bears his whipping with soldierly fortitude, and the king picks up the bloody scourge and dubs him, for his "good, great soul," an earl. Hendon muses, "Now am I finely tinseled, indeed! The spectre-knight of the Kingdom of Dreams and Shadows is become a spectre-earl!" Nevertheless, he says he will value these "valueless" honors "for the love that doth bestow them." Released from the stocks and denied their identities, Hendon, like the king, is now recognized for his courage. The lack of abuse from the silent crowd is testimony to their altered feelings—a latecomer who ventures abuse is knocked down himself. The story has reached a climax, and the varied plots are drawn together as Hendon determines that his only chance is to return to London and seek help from the imposter king.

The concluding five chapters of the novel resolve the dream motif, returning the rightful king to his throne. However, Twain takes full advantage of the sentimental possibilities inherent in the families and supporting caste of characters, while indulging himself fully in the opportunity to describe the pageantry of a royal inauguration. Hendon and the king return to London Bridge and are once again separated by the riotous crowd, thrown into chaos as another severed noble head falls on them, "so evanescent and unstable are men's works, in this world." In Chapter Thirty, Twain abruptly shifts from the "roaring masses of humanity" to Tom's progress in the royal court. With some help from Elizabeth and Lady Jane Grey, he doubles the pomp and ceremony of the court but moderates some of the harshness of current laws; however, he also gradually forgets the little king and his own mother and sisters, a source of guilt to him. As a sumptuous inauguration is initiated the former pauper scatters coins among the crowd during his triumphal parade, filled with excitement, but all his pleasure falls away and turns to "rotten rags" when his mother recognizes him and clutches at him, seeing the evidence of his fear of fireworks, but is turned away with the words, "I do not know you, woman!" Shame at his stolen royalty now causes him to collapse emotionally, and the Lord Protector, who has acted as his advisor, groans to himself that the king's madness has returned again. Dreaming and denial thus come together with familial love and affection as the clothing image reminds the reader of an important theme.

Chapter Thirty-two offers a gorgeous display of aristocratic wealth for the coronation, as well as one of the novel's most dramatic climaxes. At the moment of coronation, the rag-clad Edward forbids the lowering of the crown on Tom's head and Tom Canty also asserts his authority in reversing the exchange of the boys. The final identification rests on the location of the Great Seal, missing since early in the story. Twain plays with the allegiance of servitors to power by having crowds drift from Tom to Edward and back, as the proof of kingship shifts. At the last moment Twain intensifies the tension of Edward remembering the location of the great seal: "one single little elusive fact, found, would seat him on the throne—unfound, would leave him as he was, for good and all—a pauper and an outcast." The seal is finally discovered, as Tom prompts Edward to remember leaving it in a suit of armor; Tom had used it to crack nuts, causing all present to roar with laughter. The restored king cautions the Lord Protector that he will sue through Tom to him to maintain his dukedom, a statement demonstrating the authority and unity of boyish decency over self-interested power.

Miles Hendon, in the meantime, has been searching for his lost ward. Penniless and hungry, wearing tattered rags, he scours London Bridge and the slums, finally drifting toward Westminster in hope of aid from his old friend Sir Humphrey Marlow. The comedy of Hendon's appearance is heightened as he is discovered by the younger Humphrey Marlow, the king's whipping-boy, and saved from arrest for sedition so unexpectedly that he muses, "were I not travelling to death and judgment, and so must needs economize in sin, I would throttle this knave for his mock courtesy." However, upon entering the great hall, lined with respectful "flunkeys," Hendon sees "the lord of the Kingdom of Dreams and Shadows on his throne!" So stunned is he that the only test he can contrive is to seize a chair and sit, outraging bystanders until the king announces it is Hendon's right, earned by Hendon's service, as are his new estates and titles. As Hendon wishes he had a bag to hide his head in, Sir Hugh arrives and is promptly arrested at the king's order. Tom Canty reappears and is nominated head of Christ's Hospital, where he will improve hearts as well as bodies. The various details of the story are wrapped up, and characters such as Yokel are recompensed so much as is possible. Hendon and Edith are to be reunited. The "Conclusion" announces that Edward's reign was short but singularly merciful, stressing that no "gilded vassal" of the crown could argue against leniency without the king chiding him that he and his people knew more of suffering than did a member of the aristocracy.

CHARACTER DEVELOPMENT

Miles Hendon is the fulcrum of the story—all events balance on his character, a sterling if somewhat raffish one. He is a soldier of fortune, down at the heels and somewhat tattered and clownish but with a heart as true and manly as any sentimental novelist could create. He has been formed by involvement in the European wars, where he developed manliness by being in battle and prison, after his father banished him from England for three years—now stretched to ten. But the father's death left Miles an orphan of sorts, for, as the reader learns late in the book, his wicked brother Hugh has seized his estates and his prospective bride. The reasons for his adoption of the prince, however, are the best index to his personality. Seeing the prince's bravery in confronting a crowd of scoffers, Hendon decides to nurse him back to health because of his bravery. Hendon willingly sleeps on the floor and submits to the will of the small lad, whom he presumes he is nursing back to sanity. Hendon's matter-of-fact acceptance of discomfort is a soldierly quality, as is his pragmatism, which causes him later in the story to seek the boon of sitting in company with royalty when the prince offers him a reward of his choosing. Hendon describes himself as "matter-of-fact," but his idealism and bravery far exceed what modern readers might expect solely on the basis of practicality. Without the pride of technology that marks the Connecticut Yankee in Arthurian England in the later novel, Hendon is a model of professional decency and is almost motherly in his concern for his adopted charge, valuing the titles the prince confers on him (even though he thinks them valueless), for the "love" they represent.

The prince and the pauper are boys and share a boy's yearning for adventure, leading to the premise of the story—they switch clothes to see what it feels like, and the prince is ejected from the palace grounds as a pauper. The prince is courageous and determined, having been trained for his royal role, and although he may be beaten, he refuses to concede his identity, earning the respect first of Hendon and later of the Ruffler, head of the band of thieves. Twain notes that gruff King Henry VIII was kind to the prince, thereby instilling in the boy an affectionate but imperious nature that gives him pride and leads, also, through education, to a sound and well-grounded intellect. He and Tom Canty share an appealing thoughtfulness wedded to their naivete as boys, and both gain in wisdom as they gain in knowledge. The prince develops a mature wisdom through his struggles with various cruelties imposed by the monarchy's laws, but characteristically he accepts his protector, Miles Hendon, at face value. The dangers Hendon and others help him navigate deepen his humanity, as only interaction with the common people, away from the gilded finery and pretensions of the court, can do. He is taught humility to temper his royal privilege. By the end of the story he has developed a genuine wisdom that seems to place him above others of his time.

Tom Canty, the pauper, has been taught the rudiments of royal behavior and reading by kindly Father Andrew, who is subsequently murdered by Tom's father. Tom is so wise that even adults submit their disputes to him, so it is appropriate for him to exchange roles with the prince. When he does so, realizing his romantic notions proves frightening, but he overcomes various challenges of deportment much as a "green" American backwoodsman would adapt to on a Mississippi riverboat (Tom even drinks from his fingerbowl at one dinner, not knowing he is supposed to wash his hands in it—as did an American frontiersman in a popular story of the 1840s). When he has to try court cases, his wisdom and practicality lead to humane decisions. He rejects faulty evidence and rejects laws that seem to give to the devil rights that are withheld from Englishmen, which places him firmly on the side of human-centered action. He submits to his advisors, even when questioning royal practices, but in one case he learns that violence has a place: the royal whipping-boy takes punishments on behalf of the prince. A naif, an innocent lad, Tom misses his own freedom as a boy; he is not a profit-seeking usurper of the throne but honestly yearns to return it to Edward. Both boys are united in purpose by underlying decency and intelligence.

Not all the people outside the law in historical England were necessarily bad, but the book offers villains aplenty. John Canty, Gammer Canty, Hugo, and Hugh Hendon are melodramatized villains. Drink figures heavily in the elder Cantys' violence toward children, demonstrating Twain's awareness of a moral point about families that was coming to increasing prominence in Victorian America. Once the elder Canty seems defeated and Yokel has saved the boy from Hugo's attempt to maim him, the mad former monk/archangel expands the threat of evil to pathological insanity. The figure is developed as a maniac, and his reasoning out of injustice to himself is used by Twain as an opportunity for religious satire rather than character development. Significantly, the Ruffler and Yokel are "outsiders" to the law who are good men. The Ruffler, in Chapter Seventeen, counsels the prince to be king, if it suits his madness, but "be not harmful in it," a thematic message that informed all of Twain's views of politics. Yokel is a man driven by the law into "crimes" that derive from hardship and necessity; his family has been lost and he has been branded and enslaved by unfair laws. He subsequently saves the prince from disfigurement, proving his own decency. Various other minor characters reinforce the decency of common people, which deeply affects the youthful king. At variance with Yokel and loyal servants are (1) the likes of the jailor who extorts a pig from a kindly woman who did not wish to see a child hurt by the law, and (2) the boys at Christ's Hospital; Twain does not divide goodness or viciousness in his characters strictly along class lines or social strata. Moreover, the judge is notable for his compassion, saving Edward's life by bending the rules of evidence.

Tom's mother and sister, a farm wife, another woman who owns a pig that the prince refuses to steal, and Miles's fiancee, Edith, have special roles in this book as the source of sympathy and caring. Mother Canty shelters the prince from her husband's blows and by "mother instinct" determines that he is not Tom; humanity and insight—"kindness and devotion"—distinguish her in Chapter Ten from her husband and those like him in the lower class. The housewife of Chapter Nineteen is similar although perhaps a bit more businesslike, also poor, defined by her "womanly heart," and intent on discovering the prince's real identity. Most poignant in light of these characterizations, late in the book Tom's mother is rejected by him on his royal ride toward the coronation pageant, and the moment represents both the joy and despair inherent in the separation of a mother and child. Other children accept Edward when they are with their family. However, if they are in a gang, like Hugo, or an institution, they reject him or attempt to dominate him. Thus, Twain uses character in this novel to demonstrate the difference between kindliness in individuals and the authoritarian power of institutions and other constructed social forms. Gilded carriages and stiff guardsmen serve a royal class that institutes harsh laws. Edith, Hendon's fiancee, is the most obvious victim as the wicked usurper, Hugh Hendon, forces her to renounce Miles, whom she loves, or bring about his death, so she must sacrifice her happiness in order to save the man she loves. Also victimized are the two kind Baptist mothers being burned at the stake as their daughters run to them shrieking, in Chapter Twenty-seven. Such powerful vignettes convey Twain's major theme, the abuse of loving humanity by the abstract power of "the law" to punish infractions of rules without considering the human issues involved.

THEMATIC ISSUES

The central theme is the sternness of medieval law. Such laws abuse human beings by enforcing rigid standards without sympathy for individual cases. Decapitated heads on pikes are identified as a common historical lesson early in the book, and later a falling head illustrates man's fleeting power. In fact, Twain attacks all authoritarian power and aristocratic privilege in this novel and throughout his canon. Here, soldiers treat the poor roughly, and courtiers act out of fear and protect their political position. Tom finds himself not free to leave the court, realizing that he is "fettered by restrictions and ceremonious observances." Simply put, boy life is not fun at court. Courtly manners offer varied opportunities for joking about authority, and monarchical doings are the butt of Twain's humor, especially as Tom tries to grapple his way through complex and somewhat silly court customs. Gilded vassals, the halberdiers carrying long pikes, and officious constables symbolize the rigid authority which denies compassion to individuals. Most of the incidents in the novel play on the opposition of authority to common kindness: Tom's first act as king is to spare the Duke of Norfolk from being beheaded; only Tom can reverse laws that damn witches on the basis of nonsensical evidence; only a justice and a housewife can spare the prince's life by altering facts before they are put on the legal record —episode after episode elaborates this theme. Twain had already examined this issue in *The Gilded Age* in 1873 in terms of American politics, and he returned to it in *A Connecticut Yankee in King Arthur's Court* in 1889. *Personal Recollections of Joan of Arc*, a less readable book, idealized similar themes in 1896.

Social interchangeability and empathy are important thematic issues throughout the novel as well, in both action and images. Thomas Carlyle, the English writer-philosopher, in *Sartor Resartus* (1838) announced the "clothes philosophy" suggesting that clothes establish social status, as the prince and the pauper discover. Rags and gilded finery are external determiners of ethical condition— the better the clothes, the worse the wearer—throughout the novel, a philosophy that Twain advanced again in *A Connecticut Yankee*. Hendon's ragged dress and broken plume correspond to his personality; he is too practical and human—possibly too naive, as well, to copy its more ostentatious self-aggrandizing meanness. The children of Christ's Hospital have adequate clothes but no sympathy for others. Rank and privilege will be redressed when the dream world of the outsider Hendon is placed on the throne. The misapplication of the Great Seal as a nutcracker by Tom is the final symbolic representation of the falseness of symbols of authority despite their political importance.

Although the story is placed in a historical English setting, the humor and language retain a Twainian style. Although only one overt use of Mississippi terminology appears in the text, the jokes are often "American" in attitude. There is less interplay between vulgar slang and formal diction than in other Twain works and such short stories as "Scotty Biggs and the Parson," in which a gambler and a pastor work together to develop a funeral ceremony. Authorial diction in this novel tends to be flagrantly sentimental, as when Twain identifies the "little Prince of Poverty." The boy's talk is supposedly of the period, but it also reflects Twain's dry irony, as when Tom describes "a grandam likewise that is but indifferently precious to me."

As with other books by Twain, humor is important, although less so here than in some other volumes. Irony is developed around the roles of Miles Hendon and the prince. The expectations derived from aristocratic authority are comic when confined to Hendon's sparse room. Twain also develops social satire around the court in relation to Tom. Because he is presented as a comic naif, his pragmatism undermines the rigid application of laws based on prejudice, superstition, or overly harsh treatment of petty crimes. Moreover, jokes on the ways of royalty as interpreted by a lower-class vulgarian abound. And using a plumber as a poison-taster is a clear anachronism, for there were no plumbers in medieval England. Drinking from the finger bowl, as mentioned earlier, is an old southwestern humor story by which Twain draws in America as motif if not a literal presence.

Ferocity, inhumanity, and authority are closely linked in this novel, as in all Twain's works. The law crops people's ears and brands them; the law, rigidly enforced, burns harmless women at the stake; the law provides the wicked—like a jailor or Sir Hugh—the tools to carry out theft against decent and innocent people. Yokel, in a central vignette, makes the clearest statement against harsh laws driven by a lack of compassion for the poor. His situation and others are redressed at the conclusion of the novel, providing closure on these abuses for the reader.

The dream motif of social status and wealth develops into a major thematic issue by the end of the novel. Hendon identifies the prince as a dreamer, and the band of ruffians name him "Foo-foo the First, King of the Mooncalves." Hendon sees all the little king's offers of titles as dreams derived from madness. The final chapters reverse these characters' situations, and Hendon becomes a miracle of tatters so profound that Humphrey Marlow thinks making two of him would be "to cheapen miracles by wasteful repetition." Consequently, when Hendon is ushered into the great hall and makes his final recognition of the kingly claimant on a real throne, it is a climax both in the action and in a central motif, a powerful bringing together of a wistful consciousness in the face of real authority. The only way to achieve a larger effect is to cast the hero adrift in time, as Twain does in *A Connecticut Yankee*. A letter from Twain to his cousin Susan Crane from Italy in 1893 demonstrates that Twain sometimes wondered about his own life and career in similar terms to the dream motif expressed by Hendon at novel's end.

HISTORICAL BACKGROUND

The Prince and the Pauper is more responsive to its day than its medieval setting might at first suggest. Civil service reform and civic action were becoming issues of local and national importance in America in the 1870s, leading to major reforms in the years after the novel was published. In Connecticut, vagrancy and the status of tramps was a matter of social concern. Typically, tramps were seen as a criminal element, and harsh laws and workhouses were the proposed remedy with little thought to humanitarian alternatives. As

Twain's treatment of Yokel and other characters of the poorer classes suggests, however, he saw social and economic reasons why otherwise good people and potentially loyal subjects like the Ruffler were forced by circumstances into crime. In these cases Twain regarded society as avoiding responsibility and punishing its own victims unjustly, merely because they are too politically weak to seek redress. Thus, this novel, with its emphasis on the prince-as-tramp and Hendon and the band of thieves, is timely. It is not simplistic in treating the issue, pointing out that some of the members of the band of ruffians are victims of economic, social, and legal circumstances beyond their control—a point Twain makes even more forcefully in *A Connecticut Yankee*.

Twain himself was now as fully integrated into the life of Hartford as he would become. He had been one of the twenty members of Hartford's intellectual Monday Evening Club since 1873, giving a talk a year to its members. J. Hammond Trumbull was a founder and member, and Twain's use of his book on Connecticut blue laws is evidence of Twain's respect for his fellow citizen's understanding of comparative law. Twain comments in a "General Note" at the end of the book that over two hundred capital crimes in England were reduced to fourteen in Connecticut, information derived from Trumbull. Interest in things medieval was also a prominent Victorian trait, and Twain's depiction of chivalry and life in London gave him an opportunity to address that topic. Some English reviewers scoffed at Twain's materials, which were often closer to his readings of French historians than to actual English history, but few Americans would have cared about fine points of accuracy in such a medieval romance, especially from a humorist writing in a juvenile genre.

ALTERNATE READING: MARXIST CRITICISM

Marxist criticism is based on the economic theories of Karl Marx, a German political philosopher and socialist. Marx (1818–1883) spent his adult life developing a theory of socialism that regarded economic history as leading inevitably to the workers' control of production and enjoyment of the wealth that they created through production; these theories are most notably embodied in his work *Das Kapital* (1867, 1885, 1894). Marxism held that economics drove social experience. Feudalism, capitalism, and socialism represent a thesis (controlled merchantilism), antithesis (free and uncontrolled competitive trade), and synthesis (means of production and wealth controlled by workers) of economic growth leading from competition to collective welfare. Marxist critics look for representations of this philosophy in literature, finding many plots and characters to be based on the social and economic class that the author represents and to which he or she appeals. Marxism presumes that class conflicts—either violent or peaceful—are inevitable. Finally, a non-exploitive "synthesis" will remove the barriers of class. Marxist literary critics identify how plots and settings demonstrate the results of economic oppression of the poor by the rich and how class warfare appears in literary images. Marxist theory focuses on the impact of exploitive economic forces on those who are repressed. Proletarian heroes represent the highest possibilities of social reform or victimization, and their struggles with capitalism represent the need for unity of the working and producing classes to obtain fair compensation for their key place in the production of wealth.

The Prince and the Pauper is based on class polarities. A distinct upper class composed of royalty and a lower class of disenfranchised slum dwellers is clearly defined. Any contact between the two classes is impossible, as onlookers in the great hall, marveling at the similarities of the boys, attest. An agricultural middle class and a class of lawyers and judges dealing with their problems are depicted when Edward is accused of stealing a pig, but these classes are seen as fixed and static. Any idea of progression, improvement in economic status, or meaningful interaction between economic classes is foreign to the world portrayed. Intense and repressive physical punishment punctuates the personal experiences of a wide array of victims, including those at the top, such as the Duke of Norfolk, and those at the bottom, such as Yokel. In fact, Yokel is forced into crime by a mixture of superstition and economics, for it is "a crime to be hungry in England." The laws for theft of anything valued above thirteen pence, the basis of the trial during which Hendon saves the little king, are patently oppressive, and their economic basis is stressed. Arbitrary authority rules this world through a governing system that is largely corrupted and given to self-serving manipulation. One of Edward's significant acts of reversal is to chide the Lord Protector that he will have to sue for his titles *through* Tom Canty the pauper as their identities are sorted out. Class warfare would seem inevitable, except that the lower classes are divided and prey upon each other. Nonetheless the final episode holds out the slim possibility for a unity of upper and lower classes, even though it would likely take a miracle.

The ruling power seems to have imposed its concept of the world on those it rules. For example, the Ruffler and his gang express loyalty to a king whose laws they flout and are victims of—an expression of loyalty that makes little sense, gratifying though it is to "Foo-foo the First, King of the Mooncalves." The residents of London Bridge are glad to celebrate patriotic events drunkenly, even though at each event the author mentions the severed heads decorating pikes in full view of the crowds. Drink and revelry may, in fact, be the only possible outlets for the masses described here, evidence of their debasement by a system that denies them identity and participation in the society. Even the young king, late in the novel, orders Miles Hendon to carve the rabble to rags, speaking of them collectively; he still thinks in class terms. He may have learned sympathy for individuals, but he finds in the lower orders, as a class, antagonists who mock and persecute his own pretensions to being of another class. The way characters interact with each other holds out no hope of the broader recognitions that would lead to a peaceful fusion of goals, a meaningful surrendering of power across class lines, or a redefinition of social roles that would enhance the lives of all the characters. The poor of England are a conquered community overseen by a powerful economic authority that holds itself aloof, just as a foreign imperialist power would (and considering the Norman origins of power in England, perhaps this is understandable). Humphrey Marlow, the whipping- boy, is the symbol of this society, which irrationally punishes those not responsible for failures and even acquires the sufferer's gratitude for the compensation involved in being beaten. In terms of the Marxist concept of production, the novel provides only brief references to (1) the farmers' families abused by the Ruffler's gang, and (2) the peasants oppressed by the absolute power of Hugh Hendon.

The polarities between the classes are shown in *The Prince and the Pauper* to be all but unbridgeable, giving a certain irony to the London Bridge motif early and late in the novel. Anger at "the law," as expressed by Yokel illuminates for the reader the misshaped economic organization destroying individual lives. Worse, the king is seen as the source of reform but in fact his power is the arbitrary power of absolute authority—capricious, unreliable, and as likely unjust as just. Furthermore, the trappings of state as depicted by Twain, like those of the "gilded age" in America, are oriented toward show rather than substance, and government is not seen as a promoter of social equality as much as a source of unmerited profit and self-aggrandizement. When Twain returned to the medieval theme, a mature "Connecticut Yankee" was minded towards a peaceful industrial revolution. However, he creates havoc in a feudal system which is characterized by unenlightened repression, moderated only by isolated spots of individual caring. The oppressive lives of the poor, particularly as depicted in London, seem to confirm the presence of the proletariat, but Twain has not developed a plot that suggests social and economic reform is possible, except through individual action. Moreover his chief actor, as his "Conclusion" points out, was unusually merciful for his time, and his rule was a brief one. Thus, from a Marxist perspective the book is gloomy.

7

Adventures of
Huckleberry Finn
(1885)

Adventures of Huckleberry Finn is both praised and attacked as the "quintessential" American novel. Within its pages are found the great reaches of the Mississippi River and the heights and depths of the journey of the American democratic spirit toward its fullest expression, all presented in a slangy, colloquial language that is half regional dialect and half intellectual irony and literary humor. Twain probably knew, in the final stages of drafting, that he was writing a masterpiece. He complained at one point that he had had to go back through the manuscript and rewrite an entire character—an unusual degree of revision for an author who was often impatient with his manuscripts. If that character was Huck Finn, and the rewriting moved him from being the subject of a distant third-person narrator to being the center of his own seemingly guileless first-person colloquial narration, the rewriting had a profound influence on modern American fiction. If the character was Jim, the rewriting created a subtle and uncompromisingly realistic portrait of the plight of a Negro in American culture—one that continues to be a matter of controversy. If it was Tom Sawyer, Twain converted the "realistic" boy of the earlier novel, *The Adventures of Tom Sawyer*, into a symbol of self-aggrandizing white culture, feasting—vulturelike—on the suffering of Jim—mildly at first, grotesquely in conclusion.

Many readers are deceived into thinking that *Adventures of Huckleberry Finn* is "about" 1845, justifying harsh language, including the use of the word *nigger* 204 times, to depict the language usages of that time. *Adventures of Huckleberry*

Finn is not a historical novel, however. The novel is set in 1845, to be sure, but it is about racism in *any* time, and the language is chosen by the author for its effect on the reader. In 1885, when the novel was published in America, race relations were plummeting to a "nadir," a term often used by black historians today to describe the post–Civil War period. Lynchings of blacks by whites were abundant. The convict-lease system where convicts were leased out as laborers in the South reinvented a new form of slavery and oppression. Blacks were marginalized throughout the nation; subsequently, even baseball would be segregated along racial lines. America suffers from this reprehensible heritage to the present day. As the book demonstrates, many otherwise good people are unaware of their racist attitudes; and so the abuses continue. Twain's hope, as expressed through Huck Finn, is for a better understanding among racial groups. His expectation, as expressed in the last section of the novel, is that times and attitudes do not change much. The persistence of the awful word *nigger* in the mouths of white characters symbolizes Twain's pessimism regarding progress in race relations.

THE PREFACES AND THE ILLUSTRATIONS

The novel is initiated by two pictures. The first is of the character Huckleberry Finn. A reader might think he is a frontier boy, for he holds a dead rabbit and an old rifle. A small bite has been taken out of his large-brimmed straw hat. Although his pants are held up by one suspender, only one darkish area on the left knee hints at a patch. His clothes are mussed up but not as ragged as one might expect. Nor does his nose look too "Irishy," as Twain had required of the illustrator. Huck is to be seen as a generic boy; he could almost be a middle-class boy on a holiday in the backwoods. The signature "E. W. Kemble" and the date 1884 are prominent in the lower right corner of the illustration. Facing this frontispiece is a photograph of a formal bust of Mark Twain, seen from the side, underscored with the bold "Mark Twain" signature and the words "From the bust by Karl Gerhardt." For a "boy book" this is rather imposing, and the two illustrations alter the sense of the book. They imply something more formal than a competing book of humor or boys' adventures. The overall visual work of the experience has already begun, and its author and illustrator want the reader to notice.

The novel starts with two deceptively brief prefaces: a "Notice" and an "Explanatory," or note. Both are lies. Humorists do not have to be routinely truthful; that is part of their role as humorists. The "Notice" claims there is no motive in the work; yet the author harshly satirizes the villainous backwoods towns and life along the Mississippi. The "Notice" also claims there is no moral; yet in fact the novel is virtually a moral tract on social conscience. The

"Notice" even claims there is no plot; yet the impulse to achieve safety and free-dom dominates the book and its two protagonists. By mentioning these three points—motive, moral, and plot—Twain plants the ideas in the reader's mind. Before that moment, a reader of a "boy's book" would not have considered those factors as important.

The "Explanatory," or note, claims that the dialects are accurate. They may well be accurate renderings of aspects of the "South-Western" and "Pike-County" dialects. Such dialects had appeared in literature since John Hay's *Pike County Ballads* in 1871. Just because Hay had been Abraham Lincoln's secretary, one cannot conclude that such language was acceptable for educated authors. Twain suggests that there are different shadings of characters in the work's language. But, in fact, all written speech is a literary contrivance. Indeed, a number of Huck's speeches sound more like Twain as a literary comedian than they do a twelve- or fourteen-year-old boy. Moreover, choices of misspellings to render dialect are portrayals of a perception of character as well as an "accurate" transcription. Twain cannot even be said to accurately transcribe real speech because his characters are fictional— *all* their speech is made up. Huck's speech and verbal nuance may be modeled on "sociable Jimmy," a young Negro servant in a hotel, but Twain as editor changed the voice, as in the description of "pap" in Huck's voice, changed from "drunk" to "mellow." Such a change is literary in nature, making the comment ironic understatement; it is not likely the verbal choice of a Mississippi roughneck boy of 1845. The significance of the "Explanatory" is that it establishes the book as truthful local color and realism, elevating the reader's expectations that it is documentary fiction, not merely a comic "boy book." Thus, the book takes on the guise of "literature."

HISTORICAL SETTING

The setting is a Mississippi river town of "forty to fifty years ago," a rich locus of frontier American life. To this setting Twain brought the reportorial voice of apparent objectivity and the eye for detail of a local color writer. The small towns along the Mississippi River were partly small-town America and partly southwestern frontier. The influence of the old South with its slave-holding plantations was strong, but the beginnings of small-town local mercantilism were present as well. Insularity made the citizenry vulnerable to various frauds. The religious culture of the time and place made the people narrow in moral behavior, even when kindly intentioned as individuals. Rough-hewn raftsmen and village loafers mixed with local aristocrats and professional men. Camp meetings, revivals, circuses, tent shows, and traveling thespians—as the duke and king impersonate—constituted the vulgar culture of a place and time that reverenced the Bible and John Bunyan's *Pilgrim's Progress* but also adored grossly sentimental poetry and maudlin popular songs.

Beyond that, the region was rich in moral issues: (1) of slavery—and the abuse of freedom and dignity within it—as worked out in Huck and Jim's discovery of each other as human beings, on the raft, with the duke and king, and at the Phelps farm; and, (2) more broadly, of humanity—the requirement that one bless rather than harm others, an issue posed in this book politically (pap's "call this a gov'ment" speech), socially (the Walter Scott episode), dramatically (the shooting of Boggs), intellectually and psychologically (the Wilks episode), psychologically (Huck's interior debates with himself), and historically (Huck and Jim's debates on King Sollermun).

Twain took various opportunities to describe the "world" of his novel's events. For example, Huck's voice is particularly apt in describing the banks of the Mississippi, including rotting fish and distant conversations, in a realistic manner (appropriate, that is, to the objective-seeming practice of realist writers). Twain also provides views of raftsmen on the river, the life of a village, the homes of wealthy and somewhat pretentious planters (the Grangerfords' sitting room and Emily's bedroom), and the Silas Phelps farm. The latter reflects Twain's youthful experience on his uncle John Quarles's farm. Descriptions of steamboats, circuses, churches, and slaves mix with images of small towns to give a sense of mid-nineteenth-century America that exudes energy and dynamism.

PLOT DEVELOPMENT

The story introduces the slangy, antisocial son of an alcoholic low-life and child-beater. Huck Finn has earned six thousand dollars with Tom Sawyer by discovering the money in a cave, and his "pap" wants the money and kidnaps Huck from the home of two well-intentioned but narrowly pious old women who have tried to "sivilize" him. Miss Watson and the Widow Douglas have lectured and wept over Huck and constricted him by moral lectures, forced schooling, and confining formal clothes. Tom Sawyer has involved Huck in his "gang" with its childish re-enactments of Tom's reading of romances of captivity, which he imposes on the other boys; Huck carries his admiration of Tom Sawyer's "style" with him throughout the novel as his ideal of imaginative behavior. Pap returns the boy to his rags, beats the boy, and nearly kills him; returning drunk to their isolated cabin, he denounces a "gov'ment" that would deprive him of Huck's money and let a "nigger" vote. His murderous rage—soon delirium tremens, causing him to identify Huck as the Angel of Death—drives Huck to fake his own murder and flee to Jackson's Island in the middle of the Mississippi River outside the town of St. Petersburg. On the island he meets the Negro slave of Miss Watson, Jim, on whom he and Tom have previously played tricks. Now, however, the action turns serious as Jim reveals to Huck that he has run away and Huck agrees to keep his secret. This pledge makes Huck an abolitionist—a dirty word in that part of Missouri in that time.

Huck and Jim undergo various adventures on Jackson's Island that cement their friendship. Huck's attempt to play a joke on Jim in Chapter Ten backfires when a snakebite almost kills the Negro. This first practical joke leads to an increasingly dramatic series of jokes on Jim, which finally cause Jim to use the word "trash" in relation to the young white man's sense of humor and adventure. Huck visits the cottage of Mrs. Judith Loftus, where he is mistaken for a runaway apprentice. Mrs. Loftus, kindly toward the white Huck, is eager for her husband to get the bounty for capturing the runaway black, Jim. Huck and Jim flee together on a raft down the river—deeper into slave country—to escape bounty hunters. Nominally, their hope is to catch the inlet of the Ohio River at Cairo, Illinois, and canoe up that river to free territory, but so compelling is the journey that develops, it little matters what direction they are going in; the real power of the novel is in developing the relationship between the white boy and the kindly and increasingly humanized Jim.

A series of episodes marks the development of Huck's character and his growing relationship with Jim. At the outset of the book Huck is seen in the context of the town, the constricting environment of the Widow Douglas and Miss Watson. He is childish in Tom Sawyer's gang, cooperating with Sawyer's pranks on others; Twain has Tom rely on literary models of adventure, often enacting parodies of those models. In pap's cabin Huck is revealed as extraordinarily resourceful, able to evade death at the hands of a bigoted psychopath and brilliantly faking his own murder to cover up his escape. On Jackson's Island both Jim and Huck are portrayed as naturalists, comfortable outside of the town society they have escaped.

In flight, the boy and slave take to the raft. Throughout the first few days they begin to form a new ethic of cooperation, tinged with comic irony, as when Huck "borrows" things in Chapter Twelve: "Pap always said, take a chicken when you get a chance, because if you don't want him yourself you can easy find somebody that does, and a good deed ain't ever forgot." Also in Chapter Twelve, Huck unwisely insists that they land the raft for a Tom Sawyer–style adventure on a wrecked steamboat, the *Walter Scott,* where two thieves are plotting the death of a third under the pretense of their "rights," "sense," and "good morals." Huck subsequently tries to save them from drowning when the wreck breaks up by impersonating a wealthy man's child, one of his many disguises, but fails.

Huck and Jim soon develop a series of interactions that initiate Huck's re-education about Jim. In a fog and storm in Chapter Fifteen, Huck is separated from the raft and pretends on his return that Jim dreamed the event. Jim subsequently lectures Huck on how friends should not make each other ashamed. Deeply offended, he likens Huck to "trash" for shaming a "friend," a compelling assertion of the values of friendship and Jim's own rights as a person which comes about because of the series of practical jokes initiated in Chapter Ten. Huck realizes that he can "humble myself to a nigger" because feelings are more important than "mean tricks." As Jim eagerly anticipates fleeing to freedom at Cairo, Illinois, Huck agonizes over becoming an abolitionist; nevertheless he convinces two bounty hunters that Jim is his father with smallpox, gaining two twenty-dollar gold pieces and a conscience torn between bad and good. Climaxing Chapter Sixteen, almost immediately a steamboat runs over the raft, and Huck re-enters the shore world, washing up at the foot of the Grangerford plantation, where he is introduced to southern gentility and, more fearful, the realities of irresolvably bitter and violent southern feuds.

Huck is almost shot as a Sheperdson, so he knows immediately that the Sheperdson-Grangerford feud dominates the life of the aristocratic Colonel Grangerford and his family. Young Buck Grangerford befriends Huck, who develops sympathy for the family while describing to the reader their life in detail, including the fact that no one even knows why the feud started. Their trip to church is marked by "ornery" preaching, and the men take their guns in case fighting breaks out. Emmeline Grangerford, who had died young, left behind "crayons" and sentimental poetry that is a caricature of the sentimental art and literature of the old South, and Huck is impressed by its morbid seriousness. When Miss Charlotte runs off with Harney Sheperdson in a Romeo-Juliet affair that precipitates murderous violence, Buck is killed while Huck hides in a tree and watches. Huck then escapes to the swamp and rejoins Jim, who has recovered the raft, and the two head to the river again, experiencing in Chapter Nineteen the most idyllic moments of the majesty of the Mississippi River. At this point the raft is truly a haven of safety for both. However, it is a vulnerable world, almost immediately taken over by fraudulent aristocracy when the duke and king assume control of the raft and its passengers, Huck and Jim.

Chapters Nineteen through Thirty-one involve a fraudulent duke and king—two scalawags, "low-down humbugs and frauds," whom Huck accepts because "what you want, above all things, on a raft, is for everybody to be satisfied, and feel right and kind towards the others." Relying on past frauds, the two fakes devise a Shakespearean play that caricatures literature. Other diversions include a camp meeting revival at which the king impersonates a reformed pirate-preacher and fleeces the gullible audience. Huck next describes their visit to a town where the aristocratic—and psychopathic—Colonel Sherburn murders a harmless old drunk named Boggs as Boggs's daughter rushes to save him; a huge Bible is placed on the dying man's chest as the crowd re-enacts the murder. A lynch mob, however, is chased away by the Colonel, who declares that he knows both North and South and despises the cowardice of men in the mass—that is, mobs. Huck cannot respond to this experience, so he goes to a circus, where the crowd is fooled by the acts. The king and duke then post bills for their own fraudulent act, "The Royal Nonesuch," "Ladies and Children Not Admitted." The king dances around naked, painted with stripes; the crowd, defrauded, decides to keep silent and let others be similarly cheated so that they will not be humiliated. The king and duke outsmart the townspeople and escape.

In Chapter Twenty-four, Jim is dressed up in King Lear's outfit from the Shakespearean production and painted blue to resemble a sick Arab rather than having to lie tied up all day on the raft pretending to be a recaptured slave. Just before this, however, he has revealed to Huck that he once struck his own daughter, who had become deaf from scarlet fever, and that he will never forgive himself for that act of cruelty. By now the reader knows he is a very different father from pap Finn, as does Huck. Also in Chapter Twenty-four, the duke and king happen upon a better fraudulent scheme than their risky theatricals. They discover that a well-to-do farmer, Peter Wilks, has died and left cash, farm, and slaves in the keeping of his three daughters while his two brothers from England journey to the town. The duke and king present themselves as the brothers, take possession of the money, and immerse themselves in grotesque caricatures of what they think Englishmen would act like at Wilks's funeral and afterwards. Only a town doctor and lawyer protest their fraudulence. Chapters Twenty-four through Twenty-nine offer a confirmation of earlier satires on small-town thinking and life along the Mississippi. Huck says it was enough to make him ashamed of the human race.

As with Jim, Huck finds that Mary Jane Wilks's treatment of him calls for special loyalty. As Huck is discovered making wild lies by the younger sister Joanna, Mary Jane insists that he be treated "*kind,*" the same ethic that Huck and Jim had developed on the raft for themselves. Huck decides to steal back the money and rescue the girls' slaves, sold off by the rapacious duke. When the real brothers arrive from England, the crowd bears them to the Wilks's home in a procession which seems almost like a political campaign, laughing and carrying on, proclaiming, "*Here's* your opposition line! . . . you pays your money and you takes your choice!" The king and duke continue their bluff, the body of the dead man is disinterred, and Huck melodramatically escapes only as a flash of lightning reveals the bag of gold that he had hidden in the dead man's coffin to save it from the two frauds for Mary Jane and her sisters.

Chapters Thirty through Forty-three accomplish the final working out of the novel in burlesque action that profoundly troubles many readers and critics because of its treatment of Jim, who has gained in stature as a character and in Huck's affection throughout the story. Escaping from the town to the raft,

Huck and Jim immediately lose their freedom again as the duke and king, now infuriated at each other and suspicious of Huck, return as well. The king soon betrays Jim as a runaway slave for forty "dirty" dollars; and Huck, in the climactic moment of the novel, reprises all of Jim's kindnesses to him and determines to "*go* to Hell" to save his friend rather than turn him in to Miss Watson. He then separates from the duke and king, although he later tries—too late—to spare them from a well-deserved tar and feathering at the hands of another angry mob that they have tried to defraud. Huck again expresses his shame at the human race.

From Chapter Thirty-two onward, however, Huck has a different problem: freeing Jim. He soon discovers that Jim has been imprisoned as an escaped slave at the Silas Phelps plantation a couple of miles downriver. Huck goes to the plantation and is welcomed by Aunt Sally with open arms, for she mistakes him for none other than Tom Sawyer, her nephew, who is due for a visit and has been delayed. Huck slides into the role of Tom, attributing his lateness to a steamboat boiler explosion that "killed a nigger." To otherwise good-hearted Aunt Sally this is "lucky; because sometimes people do get hurt." When Tom appears, Huck is able to intercept him and tip him off to the deception, so Tom impersonates Sid Sawyer, his half-brother, and, inexplicably to Huck, agrees to become a low-down "*nigger stealer*" and join him in his plot to free Jim. As it turns out, Tom knows that Jim was already free under the terms of Miss Watson's will, but Huck does not know this. Tom is lowered in Huck's estimation because he will join Huck in freeing Jim.

Tom now takes control of the action and engineers an "evasion" involving a number of garish romantic inventions derived from his "intellectural" reading of historical melodramas. His fantasies, however, needlessly complicate for Huck and Jim the real problem of freeing Jim. Over various protests by Huck, and even by Jim, Tom foists on Jim the role which mirrors the prisoner of Zenda and other European romance literature. Because of these actions Aunt Sally is driven to distraction, the boys overwork themselves and Jim, and others in the plantation environment are confused and terrified. In the climax of this segment, armed locals convene at the Phelps farm to battle Tom's mythical "gang" as Huck realizes that they have "overdone this thing." Tom is shot in the leg, and Jim gives up his hiding place to help a local doctor get the now-delirious Tom back to safety. The doctor realizes that Jim, a runaway, has given up his own freedom to save Tom, and the doctor stops a potential lynch mob from cuffing and cursing Jim with the (ironically), ultimate compliment: "He ain't no bad nigger, gentlemen." Tom is cured and declares Jim "as free as any cretur that walks this earth!" The deceptions are now revealed; Jim reports that Huck's pap was dead in a derelict house they had encountered at the start of the raft journey; and the three—Tom, Huck, and Jim—although not necessarily returning to St. Petersburg on a steamboat in triumph as Tom had planned, do consider further adventures. Jim is forty dollars richer for being a patient prisoner. Huck declares in closing that "I reckon I got to light out for the Territory ahead of the rest, because Aunt Sally she's going to adopt me and sivilize me and I can't stand it. I been there before."

CHARACTER DEVELOPMENT

Huck Finn is the narrator of the book, and he confides at the end that if he had known how much trouble it was to make a book he never would have started—a comment that can be related more to the action of the novel than to any literary process. Huck's "voice"—innocent, naive, often a noncommittal dead-pan—may owe much to Twain's observation of a young black boy as recorded in a piece entitled "Sociable Jimmy," published in 1874. Huck always presents himself as subordinate to Tom Sawyer, even though he far outstrips Tom in his ability to relate to another human being, to mature as a person, and to reach serious objectives as opposed to childish ones. The story traces Huck's initiation from boyhood into maturity as a humane individual. The Widow Douglas almost "sivilizes" Huck before events force his flight to the river, and he is never a mean person, but her concept of civilization is to impose on him the requirement to wear constricting clothes, sit quietly, and be lectured on religious subjects by the intolerant Miss Watson. Huck is one of the least judgmental characters imaginable. He is willing to try praying for fish-line as Miss Watson implies he should and is even interested in Solomon until he learns that he is dead: Huck the practical boy "don't take no stock in dead people." However, he loves variety, whether in enjoying a barrel of chowder with the tastes all mixed up or in participating in the adventures of a friend like Tom Sawyer or visiting different towns.

Huck and Jim's escape encompasses a variety of adventures and discussions that deepen and enrich Huck's understanding and appreciation of Jim, whom he always thinks of as a "nigger" lower on the social scale than himself. However, he discovers that Jim does have significant human feelings, an important realization that breaks him loose from his racist background. When he plays a practical joke on Jim after a foggy storm, he discovers that Jim does have feelings and dignity as a man; subsequently he humbles himself "to a nigger" and admits that he never feels sorry for it afterwards. Huck grows even more when Jim bemoans mistreating his daughter; Huck is surprised that contrary to his white racist expectations, Jim actually cares as much about his children as a white man would. Finally, his understanding brings him to action when he realizes how many sacrifices Jim has made on his behalf, justifying his decision to "*go* to Hell" in return.

Tom Sawyer's role in this book allows Twain to satirize false ideals of romance. Tom has read romantic melodramas, which he introduces into the play of his gang of boys, using his knowledge to control them, sometimes manipulatively. His first gang plans to "ransom" maidens, even though he doesn't know what the word means, and act out fantasies from pirate literature, but he only ends up spoiling a Sunday school picnic. Huck's repeated refrain that he wishes Tom Sawyer were there to put the "fine touches" on various adventures indicates that Huck admires Tom's "style." Tom's style at the end of the novel, however, when it turns Jim's imprisonment into an "intellectural" caricature of romance novels, is the opposite of Huck's "heart" knowledge that has learned to treat Jim as a human being on the raft journey down the river. Tom repeatedly argues for imposing hardships like vermin in Jim's cabin because it is the way things are done in books: "intellectural" fun. Through Tom, Twain shows how instinctive humanity (such as the good relationship that develops) between Jim and Huck can be overcome by false and inaccurate ideas based on romantic models. Tom is centered on his own fun; even being shot in the leg adds to his pleasure because it glorifies him, although it costs Jim his freedom. Huck tells the reader in the last paragraph of the novel that Tom wears the bullet around his neck and shows it off; Tom never loses his self-centered "show off" quality.

The character Jim has become increasingly prominent in discussions of the book, most notably in *The Jim Dilemma* (1998) by scholar-critic Jocelyn Chadwick-Joshua, where his character is interpreted as an attack on racism. Jim is treated as a somewhat childlike slave early in the novel. He asserts logic in comic arguments with Huck, but his character has the flavor of a minstrel-show figure. However, his personality is considerably more mature as the Jackson's Island experience and the raft trip alter his relationship with Huck; he expresses grief over mistreating his child, he gives up his own safety to protect both Tom and Huck, and he is patient under Tom's abuse. His character is ultimately very strong. For example, being led in by a lynch mob after Tom's injury, he gives no sign of knowing Huck even though his own life is in danger. Jim comes into his own as a fully formed parent/father/man in the novel, making his condition at the end all the more grotesque. Reduced to absurdity by Tom's antics, he is a model of patience and, perhaps in Twain's view, an emblem of black experience in America, embodying a fundamental decency that is denied by the social characterizations of him as a "nigger." Finally, though, he is paid off with forty dollars (an echo of the "forty acres and a mule" once promised to freedmen after the Civil War), but little more. The trappings of the novel's comic ending should not disguise the fact that Jim, although "free," is not much improved in his lot otherwise.

The duke and king (Twain did not accord capital letters to these two frauds and was bemused that others would do so) are fairly well rounded as characters. The duke is capable of a small degree of guilt over selling Jim, but he is also thoroughly self-interested. The king, on the other hand, is ignorant, wily, and greedy. The fact that they can so easily defraud the Wilks girls, a camp meeting, and various townspeople is Twain's harsh comment on the level of intelligence of villagers in this society. Wily and full of guile, the duke and king are pitiless in their rapacity, but they are also small-time—this may explain how Huck can feel sympathy for them when they are tarred and feathered. The reader experiences them as preying on the weaknesses of others, especially the credulity of small-town locals about bad art and foreigners. Twain never likes parochialism, and these two scourge it, as does the murderer Colonel Sherburn in his speech facing down the lynch mob.

It might seem odd to discuss Miss Watson, the Widow Douglas, and pap in a single paragraph, but they are in agreement on society. They are all believers in a social hierarchy. Pap may be at the low end, sleeping with the hogs in the tan-yard, but he knows that others are still lower: "niggers," even if they are college professors. Miss Watson and the Widow Douglas have "two Providences," one violent and punishing, the other welcoming. The very first use of "nigger" occurs when they have prayers; Twain intended the ironic juxtaposition. Their world holds profound ambiguities in the treatment of Negroes that free Huck to seek his own course, as he does with Jim on the raft. Huck and Jim refer to pap and the two women and borrow from each one in creating a more workable ethic for getting along on the river.

A host of minor characters suggest that human beings can be both kindly and unaware of doing unkind things. Mrs. Judith Loftus helps the white "runaway apprentice" as her husband hunts the runaway slave. Flatboatmen, about to paint Huck blue, release him because he is "nothing but a cub." The Grangerfords welcome Huck once they determine he is not a blood enemy. Huck himself is convinced to help the Wilks girls because even though he is obviously not a British servant, they wish to treat him kindly as a stranger. Yet they reject their friends' good counsel and place their money in the hands of frauds through misguided social impulse. Finally, the Phelpses are kind to all, including slaves, even giving Jim tobacco; but it does not occur to them that there is anything wrong with the institution of slavery itself, and they live unquestioningly within its conventions.

The Phelpses are more important figures in the book than is usually thought. They are the satiric butts of Twain's demonstration that the supposedly "good" people are actually the origin of much evil through their deadened humanity. Of his mother and the townsfolk of Hannibal, Missouri, Twain later wrote that he thought slavery "stupefied everybody's humanity, as regarded the slave." (*Mark Twain's Hannibal, Hack & Tom,* Blair, ed., p. 50). He had not even seen the vicious brutality of more southern plantations, as he recognized. However, the point of his satire was this stupefaction. The Phelpses are kindly, but Aunt Sally worries over the steamboat explosion and thanks goodness to Huck's fictitious report that "only a nigger" was hurt. Uncle Silas is simply stupefied. The farmers are foreshadowed by the flatboatmen in the now-restored chapter of the novel in the University of California Press edition.

The doctor, unlike the farmers, as a professional should have a broader vision, and thus he becomes one of Twain's most pointed but least noticed satires. He is "good," as Huck tells us. Yet he, too, is an example of humanity stupefied by slavery. All he does, in the light of Jim's self-sacrifice, is prevent Jim's being beaten. He tells of Jim's heroism and concludes with a classic line of human deprecation, "he ain't no bad nigger." The outrageous undervaluing of Jim, the disproportionate indifference to the rights of a human being, undercut the man who should be the reader's model of deportment. Such is the duplicitous nature of satire that many readers miss this point.

THEMATIC ISSUES

Major themes of the novel include the narrow-minded viciousness of the townspeople along the Mississippi River; the humane sympathy Huck and Jim develop on the isolated raft; the social, literary, and religious constrictions of and distortions of humanity; and, finally, the ability of individual "heart" understanding to overcome the socially trained "conscience" of racism and race.

Most interpretations of *Adventures of Huckleberry Finn* through the 1960s addressed (1) its satire of the heartland of American civilization, seen especially in situations like the Bricksville loafers who torture dogs, and (2) whether, despite its flawed structure with the last fifth of the novel given over to Tom Sawyer's "evasion," it was a candidate for the title of Great American Novel. An entire casebook was developed on this topic by Barry A. Marks in 1959, including landmark essays by Leo Marx and major critics at mid-century, and also Lionel Trilling's "The Greatness of *Huckleberry Finn,*" which is often put forth as the finest example of American critical writing in the short essay form. These readings focused on the satire of the small towns and the racist mentality that Huck Finn had to overcome through his friendship with Jim. Alternatively, the great river provided a natural setting of thematic import—an implied natural or native America that was a true heartland of ideal democracy and equality between Huck and Jim. As such, the river has become one of the great motifs of American literature, a mid-American icon that matches the East's Niagara Falls as a symbol of natural abundance and freshness. Soviet readers during the cold war between America and the Soviet Union were directed to the book as an attack on American capitalism, overlooking Twain's own ardent pursuit of the capitalist dream, and the novel was widely read behind the "iron curtain" during this period because it showed the flaws of the system that competed with Soviet socialism and the worker's state; the focus here was on the towns, not the river.

The Bricksville loafers, foreshadowed by pap Finn, are the most obvious example of small-town degeneracy. Trading chaws of tobacco, their chief pleasure is in setting fire to stray dogs. (A chapter on raftsmen foreshadowing them appears in some editions, but not in those of Twain's own lifetime because he had put the material in print in *Life on the Mississippi* and it would have made *Huckleberry Finn* longer than *Tom Sawyer*, to which it was a sequel.) The raftsmen, unlike another lowlife—pap Finn—are rather kindly roughnecks. The lynch mob faced down by Colonel Sherburn is another example of mob cowardice. Twain was certainly thinking of the plight of Negroes in the South, but he avoided depicting the lynching of a Negro because doing so would have taken the book out of the realm of humor and boy adventure. Had he included an interracial scene such as this, the book's appeal to a wide audience would have been considerably narrowed. The yokels at the end of the book complete the satiric spectrum of lower-class southern life.

Twain intended to burlesque romanticism. His theme was that intellectual impositions on natural knowledge hurt people. The theme dominates those portions of the novel where Tom Sawyer seems in command of the action. The derelict steamboat *Walter Scott* attaches a real author's name to southern abuses of the romantic tradition, which Twain had previously critiqued in *Life on the Mississippi*, finding that the tradition led to false social pretensions. When Huck and Jim board the wreck in search of adventure, they almost lose their lives—a testimony to the danger of intruding romantic notions into real-life situations. Huck never fully rejects Tom's style, however, although he abandons it in terms of Jim, an important human recognition. Tom remains annoyingly energetic in imposing his naive yet bookish romanticism, first on Huck and Jim with the excitement of candle-stealing, then with his gang and their overblown slogans, and finally with Jim and Huck at the end of the novel in creating hidden rope pies, "case knife" picks, and other wild improvisations to make difficult and torturous an escape that could have been undertaken in a few minutes. As Huck attempts to adopt Tom's style throughout his own adventures, he always runs into trouble. The final segment of the novel, however, where Tom is in his glory engineering a fake escape for the already free Negro, Jim, provides the most extended caricatures of the tradition of escape literature. Jim is told by Tom to weep and water his potted flower, but he protests that he doesn't cry much. The boys get intense stomach cramps from trying to eat up sawdust manufactured in unnecessary preparations for escape. The romantic coat-of-arms for Jim as a "state prisoner" shows "a runaway nigger *sable*, with his bundle over his shoulder on a bar sinister; and a couple of gules for supporters, which is you and me." Each term is distorted just enough to make this a parody of real romance, but one that, given the cartoon likeness to handbills about runaway slaves, also suggests an ugly moment in American history.

Humanitarian concerns and thematic issues about race account for the book's ongoing power, for these constitute key concerns of American society. Huck is the abused child of an alcoholic. Jim is a slave—slavery being an institution Abraham Lincoln had dealt with compellingly in his Second Inaugural Address as an abuse for which the nation must atone in blood (i.e., Civil War). In scene after scene the sound hearts of kind people, overpowered by racism, accept slavery and venality as natural conditions without question. Even Huck does so, and at the end of the book, although he says he will "*go* to Hell" for Jim, the reader is not sure that he fully understands slavery to be wrong. However, Huck has clearly recognized that Jim "cared just as much for his people as white folks does for their'n,"—a statement of Twain's egalitarian humanism. The heart is right, and Huck will even try to help the duke and the king on the basis that "human beings *can* be awful cruel to one another." The great thematic message of the novel is that rightness and kindness should prevail. The persistence of the word *nigger,* however, is intended to remind readers that simple equality and humanity will be hard to win, for the language of hatred is embedded within society, present even in the speech of the best characters of the novel.

Novelists Ernest Hemingway as noted earlier, and E. L. Doctorow, in a talk at the Mark Twain House in 1997, have rejected the end of the book, calling it a dramatic failure, as have others. They are frustrated because the absence of a breakthrough in some sort of dramatic climax casts suspicion on the pride white men feel in their ability to fix problems—in this novel, a real fix is not accomplished. Jim's forty-dollar reward from Tom makes him happy but does not fully satisfy readers, nor should it. Most of the world, as Huck's final line implies, remains the same; both Huck and Jim have "been there before." In fact, a thoughtful reader can approach the book from many perspectives and find in it a wealth of material for analysis and discussion, both in itself and in terms of later interpretations and visions of American culture. *Adventures of Huckleberry Finn,* for this reason, continues to be a controversial book in American intellectual circles.

STYLISTIC AND LITERARY DEVICES

Huck and Jim's raft is the central symbol of the novel, unless the Mississippi River itself is assigned a separate category. The raft is a haven where an ideal interracial friendship can develop apart from the corrupting influence of "sivilization." It is a hidden world, running at night, but a world of absolute freedom where Huck can be "naked." It is also an observation post and a refuge. Huck and Jim develop their own ethical code on the raft. The raft ethic is a compound of Miss Watson, pap on chicken stealing, and the humanity of Jim and Huck, all coalescing to give Huck an enhanced appreciation of Jim, who treats him much better than does his own abusive father. At the beginning of Chapter Nineteen the raft is at its most idyllic, with the natural beauty of the river punctuated by real sounds and sights; and the natural symbolism of the shooting stars is a metaphor for Huck and Jim themselves. At the end of the chapter, now under the control of the duke and king, Huck makes the ultimate symbolic comment: "what you want, above all things, on a raft, is for everybody to be satisfied, and feel right and kind towards the others." Only later, as the yokels complain of the "raft" of troubles the "evasion" has created, will the reader remember this ultimate rule.

The Mississippi River is a locus for much of the story's action. On the river, two men who are slave hunters approach Huck but end up giving him money out of guilt for not helping him, convinced by his fraudulent story that Jim is his sick father. Steamboats on the river offer images of attack: first, as the townspeople are arrayed on deck looking for Huck's alleged corpse; second, as the steamboat looking like a hell-bound train sinks the raft. Finally, at the conclusion is a sort of pageant reaffirming the very values that the book overturned, envisioning in fantasy Tom, Huck, and Jim on deck, as Huck comments that "it was about as well the way it was." In between, much of the action is woven around the river and the towns along its banks.

The Bible and religion figure prominently, as does American politics. For example, religious doctrine is the source of various stories discounted by Huck because he "don't take no stock in dead people." Also, Jim and Huck's debate over "Sollermun" is a Bible-based concept. And in graphic detail, Huck describes how a heavy Bible is placed on the chest of the dying Boggs. The value of religion, however, is uncertain: As Huck notes of churches, most folks only go to church when they have to, but a hog is different. Religion is active both as symbol and motif, and the scrambled events of the book's conclusion cause Uncle Silas, a lay preacher, to give one of his most remarkable sermons ever. In terms of politics, "the Gov'ment," as attacked by pap Finn, is a distant source of rights, privilege, and rank. A source of self-aggrandizement only, "rights" are referred to by the thieves on the wrecked *Walter Scott*. Even the Grangerfords have an American eagle painted on their table covering and the speeches of Henry Clay, the great Kentucky spokesman for national improvements in the 1820s, among their books. Politics is an understated but persistent motif. For example, the crowd surrounding the dying Boggs seems like an election event, as does the entrance of the real Wilks brothers. Yet this world makes its own laws and elects its own courses of action, justice and retribution often lie in the hands of mobs and psychopathic individuals. For more obvious political satire, the reader must turn back to Twain's *The Gilded Age* or forward to "To the Person Sitting in Darkness."

It may seem odd to talk about Tom Sawyer as a symbol, but Tom is present in the apparatus of Huck's thinking even when he is absent from the action in the novel. His name represents a way of doing things that varies from Huck and Jim's. As such, he becomes a talisman for romance and the dangers of practical joking. When Tom re-enters the action, he expands his symbolic presence by realizing in the plot the actions of literary romances.

Huck's voice—a "Pike-County" dialect—is a major invention of this novel, and his humor is crucial in its success. Twain's voice frequently permeates Huck's naive "innocence." Wry irony permeates Huck's views of pap and others. The dialect in which Huck speaks, however, is important in providing a language that can be pungent, vulgar, direct, and shocking. He uses "ain't"; more important, he uses "nigger," expressing society's disregard for slaves as human beings; and he calls one of Tom's proposals a "jackass idea"—strong language for an adventure novel of the 1880s. When he talks about the Mississippi River, he mentions stinking fish. His is the voice of local color realism, and it has inspired many major writers to try to write in a voice unfettered by formal, elevated expectations for language. When Huck describes Hank Bunker getting flattened and buried stretched out, or comments dryly that he never saw pap when he didn't want a stolen chicken himself, the voice is that of the mature literary comedian masquerading as a Pike County twelve-year-old. Some critics were repelled by the voice, scenes, and actions of the novel as being too vulgar to provide good models for readers of "boy books"; they are right—this book was written for adults and barely masquerades as a "boy book." Yet that was what Twain's readers expected, so Twain wrote for them. Humor can carry a serious message; however, satire and burlesque can also often be misunderstood.

HISTORICAL BACKGROUND

The period after post–Civil War Reconstruction is described by many historians as the nadir of African American experience. The freeing of the slaves was often subverted by local Jim Crow laws, which covertly reimposed the standards of slavery on free Negroes, the rise of organizations like the Ku Klux Klan, and even the retreat of federal courts in 1882 from voting rights protections for black Americans. Twain was aware of the harsh climate for black Americans and regarded slavery as a debt for whites to repay to blacks. He did not see the nation repaying that debt, however. In "A True Story" he had already proposed that whites realize little of the suffering embedded in the black American experience, and indeed, few writers dealt with this subject. At the same time, America was undergoing a period of expansion and energy spent on growth and reform. Major writers grappled with the sense of possible reform unsatisfactorily. Possibly, egalitarian democracy favored the idea of an individual hero capable of ethical action; evil robber barons might be offset by beneficent kings of commerce and knights of labor, but they were not. Unfortunately, African Americans seldom figured in any of those pictures. Black writers were not sought out, and the market for black labor or culture, outside of domestic service and the realm of amusing folk culture, was not expanding.

America's regions were blending into a single federal system, perhaps accounting for the local color movement in literature that flourished in the 1870s and 1880s. Dialect was accepted in both short fiction and poetry as representing the lives of typical Americans and their practical idealism toward their lives as workers and citizens, but it was not accepted in the common "public" school movement, where social uniformity was developed and where many Negroes were excluded. In the 1880s, writer George Washington Cable took controversial stands on the status of black Americans, but his cause often infuriated Louisiana residents whereas northerners flattered themselves that their economically segregated communities were less mean-spirited than in the South. Segregation was a way of life. So-called foreign labor agitators would only become a threat after the middle of the decade, so that strand of developing American economic life did not press for expression in this book.

The Victorian "cult of the child" placed the child on a cultural pedestal to be admired for innocence and goodheartedness. Sentimentalism was extensive, even in expressions of the cult of the child such as Thomas Bailey Aldrich's *The Story of a Bad Boy* (1870), followed by the works of J. T. Trowbridge and others. Huck's voice marked a radical divergence from the juvenile tradition. Language was rougher and more colloquial and the naivete of the character could be exploited more fully for harsh satire; violence could be magnified and realism increased. Otherwise, however, even the size of the book was adjusted to match the size of *Tom Sawyer* so that it might be sold as a companion volume. The illustrations were intended to help position it as a humorous "boy book." E. W. Kemble's portraits of Negroes now seem extremely stereotypical, but they are typical of comic illustrations of the period. The book was intended to be a funny story and a picture of authentic American life, but with a conscience that reflected the mature Twain of the 1880s. The book was not a revolutionary undertaking. This was an era of business, and Twain the businessman-author sought to sell books.

A RACIAL READING OF *ADVENTURES OF HUCKLEBERRY FINN*

African American critics offer varying interpretations of the novel. Many are positive, but some see it as an evasion of the racial story in America as grotesque as the "evasion" sequence in the novel itself. In *Satire or Evasion? Black Perspectives on Huckleberry Finn* (1992), editors James S. Leonard, Thomas A. Tenney, and Thadious M. Davis have collected an important spectrum of views on this subject. Race as a focus of analysis in *Huck Finn* has emerged most strongly only since the middle 1980s, although Twain's own record makes clear that race, especially as manifested in slavery, was an important component of his thinking from the late 1860s onward. This alternate reading section examines the potentially negative racial aspects of the novel, inasmuch as the preceding discussion has indicated how Twain's satire of racism seems to this author to be a dominant theme within the book's overall humanity.

First, of course, the language itself is so hostile to people of color that the book represents an affront. The word "nigger" is used 204 times, or more. Some apologists argue that such usage is verisimilitude, that a real boy in 1845 would have talked that way. The racial viewpoint would challenge this position. Twain's choice in 1885 to perpetuate that talk was insensitive, while teachers' choice in 2000 to impose it on students is both anachronistic and wrong. It re-creates and perpetuates the divisive sense of superiority of whites over black children who are required to read the book. Thus, even in language, the evil is perpetuated. The emotional cost to young black readers of seeing themselves identified with a repugnant word does emotional violence to them. Books are emotional experiences first, and only later are they objectified; in the meantime, the word introduces the theme of race hate into varied educational situations where it might not otherwise occur. Because the book is endorsed by teachers and school systems, they undertake some complicity in this emotional damage. A variety of words could have been introduced, including *slave, hands,* or other less charged racial epithets. After all, although Twain used the word *drunk* in Chapter Two, he changed it to *mellow* in another instance.

Second, and more important, the image of Jim is degraded in the novel and he presents a bad role model. At the beginning of the story he is shown as the ignorant butt of Tom's pranks, manufacturing a fake witch-ride and profiting from it as a result. He is seen as naively superstitious. As well, he is consistently seen as thinking at Huck's childish level, and the comic arguments about Solomon and Frenchmen suggest that he is stupid and illogical. Huck openly demeans Jim by declaring "you can't teach a nigger to argue" at the end of Chapter Fourteen. Thus, Huck generalizes from Jim to all slaves and, by implication, to all people of African origin. Tom perpetuates the idea in Chapter Thirty-five when he declares that "Jim's a nigger and wouldn't understand," never mind that he is equally denying Huck's ability to think. Young African American readers may feel themselves especially implicated in this analysis. It may not be reasonable to expect them to have critical detachment. Kemble's illustrations also reduce the visual experience to racist stereotypes; in fact, he specialized in this area, later profiting from comic captioned pictures of "pickaninnies" in books such as *Kemble's Coons* (1896).

Third, the plot demeans Jim. He is a minstrel-show figure in the early chapters and again when he argues logically with Huck Finn. The lines of "Mr. Bones" in the minstrel-show tradition, usually acted in burnt-cork black-face by white musicians, are given to the comic end-man, while "Mr. Interlocutor" in the middle provides the "straight" lines. Jim has the role of the end-man. His folksy wisdom on Jackson's Island hardly compensates for Huck's dismissal of his logic. The sequences reduce him to a caricature, even if his nonsense, like some of Huck's, is "fool wisdom" and makes great sense. Foreshadowing a crucial moment of revelation, he criticizes the biblical Solomon as not valuing children when he offered to resolve a child's custody by cutting the baby in half for each of two claimants. He points out that if Solomon had had fewer children he would have valued them more. Later, Huck discovers Jim "mourning and moaning" over having struck his "deef and dumb" daughter Lizabeth. His remorse humanizes him and leads to his plea to God to forgive him, for he will never forgive himself. But an alternate view is also possible. Progressing from caricature to humanity and back to caricature weakens Jim and aligns him with the image of pap, reduced to groveling from delirium tremens, pursued by an avenging angel, and murderously threatening a child.

The last chapters reduce Jim yet again to a minstrel-show caricature, after a long journey in which he might have gained some stature. Even Jim admits at one point that Tom and Huck "was white folks and knowed better than him" (Chapter Thirty-six). Jim's role as an adult is compromised throughout this section of the novel; he is subordinated to Tom Sawyer at his most childish level. He is involved in the actions of the boys in such ways as make him part of the events. Just before the boys turn to befuddling and degrading the Negro slave Nat, when dogs find their way into the cabin, Tom goes so far as to say that he wished he could "leave Jim to our children to get out," all in the name of his idea of glory. Jim is a commodity for Tom's ego here, not a person with his own capacity for life. Jim seems to concur. In fact, Jim is looking fit and healthy when Tom and Huck first find him, but his condition is significantly worsened in terms of food, work, and stress by everything the boys do. This is backward progress with a vengeance.

The outcome of the novel involves Jim's subservience to white boys. He gets forty dollars and is "pleased most to death." What young African American reader could find this a role model or compelling statement of humanity to follow? Yet Jim is the only fully developed African American figure in the book. This is not a novel about slaves that shows them battling for freedom and dignity, as novels of the twentieth century such as Arna Bontemps' *Black Thunder* (1936) or William Melvin Kelley's *A Different Drummer* (1962) do. White American book buyers of the 1880s would have found such independent statements featuring a racial revolution too terrifying to contemplate. For modern black readers, the experience is potentially a distressingly reactionary model from a repressive time of intense racism in American history. Such an argument should caution readers and critics that many stories may be perceived differently depending on the different backgrounds and levels of experience of different readers.

8

A Connecticut Yankee in King Arthur's Court (1889)

A Connecticut Yankee in King Arthur's Court was a popular book in America, but it was less popular in Great Britain, where many critics were offended by its burlesque of ideals of King Arthur's Round Table, part of hallowed British tradition. Twain's advocacy of yankee democracy and technology gave the plot and his various jokes their zest, as he showed his hero combating all the institutionalized ignorance and viciousness of bygone ages. Scholar Louis Budd points out in his Afterword to *The Oxford Mark Twain* edition (1996) that Hank Morgan, the hero of the novel, was intended to "embody a natural rights democracy for all times and climes" and, further, was a preeminent exponent of free enterprise capitalism and the rights of labor to fair pay (pp. 3–4). However, the Connecticut yankee was also a vulgar factory foreman who frequently ignored fine points of custom or was insensitive to his surroundings, sometimes even bullying others who opposed him. Along with the power of monarchy, in this novel the medieval Catholic church is a target of Twain's mockery on account of its inhumanity and advocacy of ignorance—a theme he had broached in *The Innocents Abroad* twenty years earlier. Advocacy of freedom and antagonism to oppression are the hallmarks of Twain in his most powerful satire, and this novel shows those qualities.

Yet the book has complex aspects such as the violent ending, which is easy to read as a triumph for the yankee but is actually his total defeat. For some readers, the high ideals of the yankee are subsumed in his rudeness. Outside the novel itself, a problem arose from a charge of plagiarism by Max Adeler (the pseudonym of humorist Charles Heber Clark), who claimed that Twain had stolen the idea of an industrial-age hero traveling in a medieval realm from his own novella—a long short story—"The Fortunate Island," published in 1882 (originally in 1880 under a different title), in which a modern professor and his daughter must confront medieval life on an isolated island and vanquish it through modern knowledge. Twain was unaware of plagiarizing Adeler, but the argument that he did has been put forth strongly by David Ketterer in *Charles Heber Clark: A Family Memoir* (1995).

HISTORICAL SETTING

A Connecticut Yankee is set in medieval England, but it is a very special England—the England of a book "not being a history but only a tale," as the author tells the reader in an endnote citing "Lecky" as his source for incidents in Chapter Twenty-two. Twain's vision of history is more important in defining the world than accuracy of factual detail, although he used his sources extensively. W.E.H. Lecky was the author of *History of the Rise and Influence of the Spirit of Rationalism in Europe* (1884), *A History of England in the Eighteenth Century* (1887), and later works; copies owned by Twain's sister-in-law show Twain's marginalia, indicating his use of their information, according to an insightful study by Joe B. Fulton. These books defined a world dominated by religious superstition enforced by physical atrocities. When combined with Thomas Babington Macaulay's histories of England, Sir Thomas Malory's *Le Morte d'Arthur* (c. 1469, 1485), and Thomas Carlyle's *The French Revolution* (1837), they helped Twain create a mental landscape that was the opposite of pragmatic, republican America in many respects, but that echoed the need in America for a better situation for the lower orders of workers and the disenfranchised, including slaves. Twain borrowed from American slave narratives to flesh out the gruesome details of human mistreatment that dot the Arthurian landscape, most notably in the castle of Morgan le Fay and during Hank's journey through Arthur's kingdom as a slave. The world is one of repressive ignorance and superstition, dominated by a church and state that place all power in heredity and the past. Dirt and poverty are the lot of the poor. Hank Morgan's contribution to this setting is to inject a boldly political democratic rhetoric into his repeated descriptions of the hardships of the life of commoners and the repeated atrocities perpetrated by nobility who are little better than the swine into which they are, at one point, thought to have been transformed literally by the fair maiden Alisande (later Hank's traveling companion, and wife, "Sandy"). The setting is dominated by the life of castles, the Valley of Holiness, and, as interplay, the huts of commoners. Although Hank's "man factories" are often referred to, they remain unseen, a hidden threat to the feudal abuses that make up the foreground of the novel.

PLOT DEVELOPMENT

"A Word of Explanation" makes this a framed story in which one narrator in a brief scene introduces us to a story "inside" the story. A bullet hole is found in an exhibit of armor, and an elderly stranger remarks that he saw it done and gives to the story-teller a manuscript that tells his history. The manuscript, like _Adventures of Huckleberry Finn_, is really a picaresque novel, taking the reader along on the roguish adventures of a traveling hero, Hank Morgan. Many thematic issues arise when this "yankee of the yankees" unfolds his tale. Crowbarred back into history by a burly mechanic named Hercules in the Colt's East Hartford firearms factory, he immediately tells us that he recognizes that Camelot is not like America; however, the first town he sees is a wretched village—it could be just another town like those along the Mississippi River. Almost immediately he originates the idea of being a Robinson Crusoe with the thought of "improving" and imposing "democratic" authority on medieval chivalry. Stripped by captors of his "magic" clothes in Chapter Four, he recognizes that the medieval chivalry lack modesty but "were not aware that they were indecent," illustrating a gulf between the culture of New England and that of old England. He is in Chapter Six able to use his fortuitous knowledge of an eclipse to gain control of a threatening situation and save his own life while defeating the magician Merlin, who becomes a major antagonist at several later points in the novel. Throughout the next four chapters, lack of brains among the nobility is equated with false stories and licentiousness. Hank's ability to translate his knowledge from life in 1879 to events in the year 528 makes him the "Boss" of these intellectual children, and he quickly acquires a young page as sidekick, Clarence, to help him. Having the technological upper hand gives Hank the power to create change.

In Chapter Seven, Hank lays out his technological agenda as a critique. He notices that there are no windows, gas lights, pen and ink, or books. Explicitly identifying himself as a Robinson Crusoe, he determines to "invent, contrive, create; reorganize things; set brain and hand to work." This is the modern world of practicality set against Arthurian ignorance. To prove the point, Hank fixes a lightning rod to Merlin's tower and causes its destruction, which he calls "an effective miracle." In Chapter Eight, entitled "The Boss," Hank names himself the real "substance," identifying the king's power as only a shadow. Yet Hank's power is covert, and his desire to change things lays the groundwork for a road trip with the king later. He fears the established church as an antagonist, and Merlin is a dangerous representative of the power of superstition. "Inherited ideas" are attacked by the yankee in impassioned rhetoric that identifies "The Nation" as the most important thing, undermined by churchly "divine rights" among other pernicious doctrines.

Hank's skeptical tone dominates the action. The yankee complains that going holy grailing—that is, seeking the lost Holy Grail that Jesus was supposed to have drunk from, a quest often identified with medieval culture—has worlds of reputation in it but no money. From the beginning, Hank finds medieval armor comically uncomfortable. In fact, Twain said the idea of the novel started in slapstick comedy about Hank losing matches in his knight's helmet and not being able to scratch his nose. Only later does the journey in search of the grail turn serious. Meanwhile, Hank Morgan is busy training experts with "graded schools in full blast." The education and factory furnace themes are intertwined in Chapter Ten. Ironically, although Hank calls his civilization an "unassailable fact," inherited ideas and the church can assail it. This source of opposition will lead to dramatic tension and the final reversal of Hank's progressive development in the plot. With this tension in place, Hank's first road trip develops a comic contrast between Hank and Sandy—the fair Alisande, a medieval damsel who later becomes his wife. She represents a timeless flow of courtly language in the chivalric mode of Sir Thomas Malory's writing, opposite from Hank's slang. This is "gender" humor, modified by language humor, modified further by literary burlesque of Sir Thomas Malory's language describing King Arthur's Round Table in *Le Morte d'Arthur*. With all the caricature and burlesque mixed together, there is little personalization of Sandy as a love interest.

Hank is soon appalled at the servility and oppression of "Freemen!" by a "gilded minority" and lays out his philosophy of democracy in Chapter Thirteen. Identifying one of the humble crowd he talks to as having potential, he writes a note for Clarence to "Put him in the Man-Factory—." He intends to create a "New Deal" (reputedly the origin of Franklin D. Roosevelt's phrase during the Great Depression) by which a peaceful economic revolution would improve the lot of the "994" common people who do the work and earn the bread but are prevented from eating it by a self-elected board of direction of the "6" aristocrats out of 1,000 who expropriate the profits to themselves. In Chapter Fourteen, Hank captures knights by blowing smoke through his helmet's visor, appearing to be a dragon. Sandy negotiates their surrender and is now "a good person to have along on a raid" and a "daisy."

Sandy's tale, a droning burlesque of chivalry, puts Hank to sleep, and the couple soon arrives at the castle of the dreaded Morgan le Fay, the murderous sister of King Arthur. The yankee has mused, comically, that soap will undermine the Church by bringing habits of cleanliness and has knights on the road to promote it, but Morgan Le Fay is a sterner case of evil. She stabs an innocent young page to death and is cursed melodramatically by the mother; she imprisons people for frivolous reasons, interprets a request for "photographs" as an invitation to murder, and presides over an immoral Royal Banquet that is a feast of sexual license (referred to but not described, because the book is a nineteenth-century novel) and gluttony. In Chapter Seventeen, "The Queen's Banquet," a shriek brings Hank to another hidden side of evil: a husband is stretched on the rack for killing a deer to feed his family, a family that in Victorian American times would be ideal. Hank sees the wife as willing to sacrifice everything for her husband and the husband as an egalitarian, sacrificing entrepreneur and family man who will undergo torture rather than betray his family. In the next chapter Hank clears out the queen's dungeons, finding poor souls who have been tormented by false reports of the deaths of their loved ones and other actions of pure malevolence.

Hank and Sandy resume their adventure to save captured noblewomen, who Sandy has identified in slapstick comedy as enchanted pigs. Pilgrims appear on their way to the Valley of Holiness and are soon followed by a band of chained slaves. In Chapter Twenty-one, Hank describes the beating of a slave-mother and the violently forced separation of the family as she is sold away. Helpless to intervene, Hank says the picture remains in his mind to this day. In this section of text Twain portrays the Church as a target and an antagonist; the Valley of Holiness is described as a place where dirt is sacred and monks never wash. The band of slaves observed by Hank is a melodramatic expression of the cruelty of the authoritarian regime, the aristocracy over the common man.

Several extended episodes show the yankee overcoming superstition in the person of Merlin. Here, British stupidity blends with ignorance and the wiles of Merlin in opposition to the yankee technologist. The holy fountain has dried up and the monks are distressed because of the loss of business; they had stopped taking baths centuries earlier owing to ignorance and to superstition. The conflict to be resolved includes both the need to repair the fountain and to overcome Merlin as magician adversary. Hank approaches the well as an engineer; he gets lowered down on a rope and looks around. He then sends for supplies to correct the problem, but he also sends for fireworks to put on a great show of besting Merlin.

The technologist entrepreneur also succeeds economically by harnessing the pedal power of St. Simon Stylites, who stands on a tower bobbing in a repetitious pedal motion that is good for powering a belt system and running machines. Hank puts him to work making shirts for the nobility (paralleling the real Mark Twain's success in licensing the "Tom Sawyer" name for a brand of shirts). The incident not only spoofs ancient religious lore but subjects it to yankee money-making. The yankee goes a step further, however, when he notices that the saint is growing weak. He "stocks" the business and sells the worthless stock to knights, who then lose money. (Unlike Hank, Twain paid off his creditors when he went bankrupt in the mid-1890s, significantly enhancing his status as a moral spokesman.)

The yankee "showman" style is important in the Valley of Holiness as an alternative to false piety; it is, however, the opposite extreme of what he claims to be creating—a secret revolution. He is P. T. Barnum, the great showman, as technologist. But after Sandy is worn out with nursing him, he announces a second trip, this one in disguise with King Arthur to try to show the king the real suffering of his subjects. Now he and the king will have a genuine opportunity to play outsider.

In conflict with another rival over where the king is—at his palace or on a journey toward the Valley, as Hank knows—Hank's character at this point can be interpreted as a powerful and cautionary lesson on the changeability of the crowd and the human heart. A rival magician convinces the monks that the king is at home, although Hank knows by telephone that he is coming to the Valley. This experience suggests that fraud and credulity win out over science. The novel's ending is foreshadowed yet again—Hank merely poses the need of keeping his mystical "trademark" current, passing off the reversal in a joke and misdirecting the reader's attention to business. Indeed, readers have been primed for a final defeat of major proportions. After a brief vignette of a sweet young couple trying to escape *le droit de seigneur* (the right of a baron to have first sexual experience of a virgin bride), which is an ultimate perversion to Twain as a Victorian moralist, Hank continues his work.

Hank's attempt to develop a standing army based on a West Point model is defeated when hereditary titles are preferred over ability; the projected success crumbles into failure through enforced ignorant customs. His attempt to improve military roles with trained commoners is doomed from its inception. To Hank, knights have no knowledge, just brawn. The yankee is surprised that lineage from a family that has been brain-dead for four generations is the needed qualification to be an officer in a competitive examination under feudal judgment.

Chapter Twenty-six introduces the second journey and then turns to other topics. Clarence's new newspaper reflects good Arkansas journalism of the late nineteenth century, but it is also an index to softening changes in Hank. In the next chapter, the king and the Boss go on the road in disguise and unattended as simple yeomen, a dangerous undertaking. Comedy develops around the king's perilous inability to objectify his own role; he is always acting like a king pretending to be a commoner, and the yankee is in constant fear of discovery. Very shortly, the yankee must blow up some knights with a dynamite bomb to save the king and himself. Most of Chapter Twenty-eight is devoted to drilling the king in the weary and suffering demeanor that would derive from true commoner status, but such training goes against the king's natural bearing. Only in the chapter devoted to "The Small-Pox Hut" does the king come into his own as a human being. Ignoring his personal safety, the king unites a dying young girl with her dying mother, revealing to Hank lofty heroism that is sublimely great because it demonstrates genuine humanity, unarmed and not cheered by a multitude.

Great though he may be at that moment, at the beginning of Chapter Thirty, "The Tragedy of the Manor House," the king is in the same quandary as Huck Finn was concerning Jim's escape in *Adventures of Huckleberry Finn*. The sons of the dying woman have escaped from prison, and the king feels a duty to turn them in despite what readers recognize as the injustice of their original confinement, which caused the woman's demise. "Born so, educated so," like Huck, the king saw the unfair laws as just because it was part of his training. The issue is barely discussed, however, as another melodramatic event intervenes: the manor house where the lads were imprisoned is on fire. Hank immediately considers the insurance business he wants to start in opposition to the fatalism of the Church (according to which God wills everything), but in the dark his comical musings are interrupted as he runs into a hanging corpse. Now a mob is depicted lynching suspects, and it is the king who demonstrates a moment of sheer practicality when he prevents Hank from "doing useless courtesies unto dead folk . . . it is unprofitable to tarry here." They end up sequestered for a moment in a peasant cabin, where they gather details of the atrocities surrounding them—atrocities akin to those perpetrated by whites on blacks following the Civil War. In the concluding paragraph of the chapter, Hank restates his dream of a republican utopia in response to a peasant's revelation that he, too, senses the importance of an egalitarian democracy. Hank proclaims, "There it was, you see. A man *is* a man, at bottom. Whole ages of abuse and oppression cannot crush the manhood clear out of him." He then announces a whole agenda of democratic capitalist change in one of his most affirmative moments.

A lesson in political economy for some peasants follows, occupying Chapter Thirty-one through Thirty-three. Hank tries to educate Marco, a humble peasant, Dowley the blacksmith, and some other master mechanics to the relative value of money and the importance of free trade. Humiliating Dowley with his economic arguments, Hank is still unable to convert him as they share an enormous banquet that costs four dollars. Finally, the king's ignorance of farming and the yankee's behavior so frighten the people that they try to beat the pair up, ending by fighting themselves in blind rage while Hank and Arthur look on. The comic moment passes quickly, for Marco has gone for help, and they are soon chased by a mob and eventually seized and sold as slaves. The king's feelings are hurt by the low price he brings.

In Chapter Thirty-five, the king declares his intention to abolish slavery, which is music to Hank's ears. But the most pitiful incident of the book lies just ahead of them. A young woman's husband has been impressed into the British navy, and she has stolen a piece of cloth to buy food to feed her baby; now the law has condemned her to die. As her pitiful story is recorded, all are in sympathy, but the prosecutor argues that she should be punished to protect property from increasing theft. Hank declares, "—Oh, my God, is there no property in ruined homes, and orphaned babes, and broken hearts that British law holds precious!—and so he must require sentence." As she is about to be hung, a priest takes her baby and says he will raise it, gaining from her a look of divine gratitude. The chain of slaves, with Hank Morgan and King Arthur still in it, soon makes its way to London, where Morgan and the king escape, but the king is recaptured. Hank, working desperately to save him, calls Camelot by telephone; Sir Launcelot and his knights ride to the rescue, under the tutelage of Clarence, as the king is about to be hung. At the last minute, on bicycles, they save the king and Sir Boss.

The picaresque journey, in which Hank and Arthur have seen the underside of society as free agents, now ends, and the action returns to Camelot. Hank must enter into a chivalric contest, and a medieval joust is arranged. At first he uses a lariat to rope his opponents, but Merlin steals that, and Hank must resort to killing his opposition with heavy Civil War-style dragoon revolvers. He challenges all the knights to unequal combat, shooting nine before winning the day and, he thinks, "beginning the march of civilization by ending chivalry." Brother Merlin he declares defeated. (This chapter mixes many elements but also satisfies the reader's need to know how the bullet hole got in the armor, as recounted at the opening of the book.) Merlin is re-established as sneaky and dangerous; Hank kills knights and begins his battle with chivalry in earnest.

Chapter Forty skips ahead three years to a yankee utopia with slavery gone, telephones and sewing machines humming, and steamboats and railways just being developed. Hank is also planning to replace the Catholic Church with "go-as-you-please" Protestantism and, eventually, unlimited suffrage and a post-Arthurian republic. Hank and Sandy's baby, "Hello Central," becomes ill, however, and the Round Table turned stock market, a knightly baseball league, and all other interests are abandoned.

Hank has scored technological victories in battles, but can he win the war? He seems to, in Chapter Forty, which describes a utopian world; but in the next chapter his absence to nurse his sick child provides his enemy, the Church, with an opportunity. Civil war arises through the chaos surrounding the romance of Launcelot and Guenever. The Church exploits this opportunity with an "interdict" that isolates England, stops all trade, and arouses the feudal chivalry to take up arms against Sir Boss and his handful of loyal cadets. Hank travels homeward through a desolate landscape of empty railroad stations and deserted streets to find London, once fully electrically lighted, now a "blot upon darkness." As it turns out in Clarence's recounting, manipulations of the stock market triggered the actual events of industrial collapse, civil war, and the final battle, although the battle was inevitable; the outcome destroys Hank's plans for a new civilization.

The novel ends in violence. Superstition holds the upper hand, as only fifty-two brave boys go with Clarence and Hank to make their last stand in a cave, formerly Merlin's, surrounded by high-voltage electric wires, moats, and gatling guns. Initiating the final cataclysm, in a thrilling moment of melo drama a dead knight is discovered in the dark against an electric wire; the discovery is turned into comedy, but it is creepy nonetheless. Sir Boss and Clarence are funny in discussing the "report" of one church committee, blown up by a "torpedo." A futile "republic" is proclaimed, but a defensive sandbelt defines a constricted final refuge, where Hank engineers the electrocution, drowning, or shooting of twenty-five thousand knights by murderous fire from his gatling guns. Hank seems to win; but enclosed in walls of dead knights, his last great battle moment is tragicomic. Hank does not succeed. Stabbed by a knight and dominated by Merlin's magic for the last time, he is put to sleep for twelve centuries. A dream world and the movement through time engineered by his enemies, Hercules in Hartford and Merlin in Arthurian England, defeat him and separate him twice from those he loves. The final moments are the conclusion of his story by Clarence, who completes the tale in the old manuscript entombed with him. The narrator witnesses his death, separated by "an abyss of thirteen centuries" from his wife and child, in the modern castle in a "remote unborn age."

CHARACTER DEVELOPMENT

A Connecticut Yankee in King Arthur's Court could be characterized as a "one character" book, for the primary emphasis is on Hank Morgan, the Connecticut yankee who appears in Arthurian England and tries to convert it into a modern industrial capitalist democracy. Hank dominates all events both dramatically and by virtue of his strongly stated personal ideals. Other characters are his foils.

When Hanks says, "I am an American . . . I am a Yankee of the Yankees—practical . . . ," he defines himself as an archetypal American egalitarian entrepreneur drawn out of everything portrayed in Daniel Boorstin's *The Americans* (1973) and as a classic "go ahead" commercial pioneer in the spirit of the frontiersman Davy Crockett. Connecticut was populated with such figures in the first half of the nineteenth century: the yankee inventor-entrepreneurs such as Samuel Colt in Hartford, maker of Colt pistols, Eli Whitney, maker of cotton gins and rifles, and the other creators of the industrial revolution in America. Their driving ethos was making machine tools that would allow any yankee farm-boy to manufacture goods that only trained artisans could have handcrafted previously. This democratizing of production accompanied the broadening of the franchise, or right to vote, throughout the spectrum of white, male Americans (women were excluded, although Hank proposes to include them). Hank is closely identified with this franchise in his talk about democracy, his belief in manufacture, his concept of a new deal for the oppressed workers, and his broad humanism.

A further dimension of his personality is initiated with a seemingly silly joke when Hank sees Camelot's castles and says, "Bridgeport?" The reference is to P. T. Barnum's "Iranistan," an ornately turreted castle in Bridgeport, Connecticut, where Barnum sometimes harnessed an elephant to till his fields in sight of tourists. Irrepressible optimism and showmanship are the yankee's hallmarks, as they were Barnum's. As the novel progresses, the yankee strives for ever greater effects that would "be the making of me." He is a commercial phenomenon; like Barnum, he glories in "branding" his product. Barnum, yankees, and Americanness define the collision shaped by the yankee with Arthurian England, even in the preface before the action begins. Hank sees things from a Connecticut perspective, almost in isolation from other cultural considerations. Twain saw Hank Morgan much as he saw Colonel Sellers in *The Gilded Age* as having two sides; one a high and noble purpose, the other a vulgar go-getter spirit that was unbridled by considerations of the surrounding culture, or, in some cases, his responsibilities to his immediate family.

Hank's humanity is so entwined with the central motifs of the novel that it is hard to discuss one without the other. From the beginning he is an ardent champion of commercial enterprise. Soon he adds a dimension of political idealism when he sees the plight of commoners in feudal England. His desire to preserve "the one atom of me that is truly me" in some form extends this humanity to a personal desire for identity that generalizes to all humankind. Somehow, he avoids adopting a totally deterministic view of history and humankind, and he therefore persists in his expectation of massive change rather than accepting predetermined history as a given. He responds to the abuse of others and holds a code of his own that honors family—he marries Sandy so as not to compromise her according to yankee standards, but his attachment to her then becomes that of a truly devoted husband. Most readers relate to this idealism; Twain was conscious of its presence as one side of Hank's character, and it reflects his own life to a remarkable degree.

Clarence, who becomes Hank's page, is a supportive sounding board until the final chapter, when he offers the yankee a dose of reality in describing the nobility's ability to cooperate. The fair Alisande, or Sandy, develops from a medieval caricature into Hank's Victorian ideal mother. King Arthur and Morgan le Fay, in company with Merlin, provide the spectrum of feudal responses, in company with Marco and Dowley, commoners, and a handful of others. Yet such is Twain's skill as a writer that relatively few characters seem false, and many seem to have a convincing life, even as modern caricatures.

Sandy and Clarence are central supporters of the yankee. Both are depicted as being initially ignorant in the medieval way, but they are soon transformed by personal respect and affection. Sandy is the medium for various sexist jokes about women, including endless talk and vanity about her age, but her humanity and sympathy, even when mistaken in naming her child "Hello, Central" to remind Hank of his lost love, build the reader's affection for her. She shows strength in confronting knights, becoming, as Hank notes, a good person to have along on a raid. Confined to a conventionally stereotyped role, she deserves the reader's respect nonetheless. Clarence is likewise a realist more than a superstitious dolt. His workmanlike qualities enable him to develop into the Boss's right-hand man. He becomes "modern," free of medieval ignorance and superstition, and he even develops into a backwoods skeptical journalist, mocking the nobility. His part in the action, however, remains relatively small, as he never becomes Hank's traveling companion, a role which is allotted first to Sandy and second to King Arthur.

King Arthur, Morgan le Fay, and Merlin are representative of the spectrum of medieval society, and in fact they represent the spectrum of most societies. King Arthur is committed to medieval law and remains so, wrestling with his conscience, as did Huck Finn, about turning in law-breakers. His decision, however, is to seek law enforcement for the escaping sons who burned the manor house. (In this context the reader's attention is shifted to the lynch law characteristics of the commoners, which Twain is likely relating to "poor whites" of the American South.) Arthur's greatness lies in scattered moments of humanity, not in an ability to free himself from medieval ignorance. In the smallpox episode, Hank had felt the king's greatness of spirit in the kindness he showed to a dying mother regardless of his own safety, unarmed and without an admiring throng. In burlesque, Arthur had been shown to be brooding about the low price he commanded as a slave. His feelings as a king are dismissed in Chapter Thirty-five as "mere artificiality," but "as a man, he is a reality, and his feelings, as a man, are real." He is shamed to be valued below his own estimate. Of course, he had partly brought the trouble on himself by overacting his part and appearing to be a farmer turned madman, but that acting was also part of his overestimation of himself as a king. In danger, in the dark near the manor house, Arthur might have become a rounded character, but the opportunity is not developed; at most points he is a representation of the yankee's ideas about nobility, even though his actions in the plot make the reader accept his seeming reality.

Morgan le Fay and Merlin, being actively evil, are allowed some notable dramatic moments. The queen smoothly kills before the reader's eyes. She is psychopathic in wanting to do evil to her prisoners, and the boundlessness of her position in the feudal hierarchy makes her a representative of authority at its worst. Her character does not fully develop but in its awfulness fulfills the reader's need for a melodramatic villain. Merlin, likewise, is a foil for the yankee but shares many traits with Hank—so many, in fact, that Hank talks about allowing him to do his full act in the Valley of Holiness out of "professional courtesy." Merlin has the ability to work some kinds of magic and at the end puts the yankee to sleep for twelve centuries. For the yankee, however, he is a commercial opponent, someone to be out-advertised, out-sold, and overpowered by technology. Thus, Merlin carries the burden of representing economic and social ignorance in action. In this role, he first tries to get Hank burned at the stake, later provides competition in the Valley of Holiness, and still later steals Hank's lariat at the tournament, forcing him to kill. Yet Merlin is largely ineffectual. He and Hank never have a discussion in which viewpoints are argued or Merlin's personality develops. In this character Twain is not attempting to provide a study of psychopathology as much as a social critique. The reader knows Merlin from outside, for his wizardry that preys on the ignorance of his times to deliver a bad product and derive personal aggrandizement from it without helping others. He is the opposite of Sir Boss.

Finally, an array of commoners fills a variety of gaps. Various vignettes show individuals who are worthy to be sent to the "man factory" because they have initiative and are the stuff of a potential democracy because they think for themselves. Dowley and Marco, characters introduced late in the novel, are too frightened by or too impervious to the implications of free trade and democracy to see such ideas as anything other than traitorous. Like their peers (and like Americans later), they participate in lynchings out of fear of their community. Consequently the reader sees another class of pathetic sufferers, primarily women. The mother and daughter in the smallpox hut are sufferers of authoritarian abuse by feudal overlords with unbridled power. The young mother who is hung for minor theft, outraging Hank, is likewise a victim of the government's power to impress her husband into military service regardless of her own welfare. Throughout the novel, Hank finds the majority too afraid of his revolution to be promising, even though it is in their own best interests. At the end, only fifty-two youthful cadets, "pretty as girls," remain, symbolic that only the innocent and idealistic could be free of their training and environment.

THEMATIC ISSUES

As in *Adventures of Huckleberry Finn*, empathy with individual suffering is the primary thematic concern underlying the novel, but the immediacy of this empathy is often overshadowed by the technological entrepreneur. The individualism of the "atom that is truly me" is always trying to be free from the negative constraints placed upon it by social authorities. Hank is an ardent champion of democracy, a "new deal," and the building of individuals in the "man factory." He is also an entrepreneur in the style of P. T. Barnum and, later, Sinclair Lewis's character Elmer Gantry; he is competitive and boastful, but he also delivers real value. Nevertheless his emphasis on getting up "effects" may distract him and readers from the need for substantive reform, which presumably takes place in the "man factories" but never enters visibly into the main plot action. Barnum provided a model for much of the yankee's personality, arguing that if he used fraudulent advertising like a 32-foot banner to advertise a questionable 28-inch curiosity, the Feejee Mermaid, he made up for it by offering other curiosities that were both real and instructional. Barnum also advocated voting rights for African Americans in Connecticut in 1867, when such a stance was not popular, and he went to jail in 1832 for using the freedom of the press to attack unethical behavior. Nonetheless he wrote on the art of money-getting with relish and was an entrepreneur to the end. Twain complained in an 1890 letter to his daughter Clara that a stage production of *A Connecticut Yankee* showed the animal circus side of a rude man rather than his good intentions and heart; the theme of social responsibility complemented the persona of the entrepreneurial go-getter, vulgar and profit-oriented, but still egalitarian and kindly in intention, rather than conflicting with it.

Twain intended to show Hank Morgan developing from a self-centered vulgarian to an economic entrepreneur to an idealistic democratic creator of welfare for the mass of humanity. Although "chromos," for example, are cheaply printed, ugly and garish art to trained artists, they nevertheless could be hung on walls by people who would not have experienced art in any other way. Hank's appreciation of chromos shows him to be progressing culturally. However, Hank's philosophy is a constant: a man is only *part* of a man where there are ranks, castes, and control by lynch law and violence—Colonel Sherburn had spoken similarly in *Adventures of Huckleberry Finn*. The aristocracy opposing Hank are defined as white Indians—against progress, superstitious (Merlin, especially) and inhumane, as demonstrated by both Church and monarchy. But exceptions are noted by Hank in monks; in knights like Sir Launcelot, who loves Hank's child, "Hello, Central"; and in King Arthur in the smallpox hut. A complex theme revolves around Hank as liberated from medieval prejudices: he generalizes boldly on the ignorance of others without recognizing that he himself is not free of his own prejudices.

Twain attacks the authoritarian spirit throughout his canon, and this novel's central thematic issue is that of evil done by unrestricted, undemocratic power. At the outset, Hank is stripped naked and no one is embarrassed; sensitivity to individuals and the prevailing Victorian idea of decency is lacking. Technology and progress are unheard of and apparently unwanted; brutality rules, as conquered knights show by their condition. More to the point, the common people have no idea that skills and acquirements are more important than titles, as Hank declares in the chapter entitled "The Boss," where his own abilities have brought him the only appropriate title, "The Boss. Elected by the nation." Morgan le Fay jails people merely because they comment she has red hair instead of "auburn," a comic sequence that lightens a very sobering depiction of her dungeons. Others resist the sexual intrusion of *le droit de seigneur* and lose all. The logic of absolute caste and class power rules. Even Arthur, late in the novel, reasons from law rather than sympathy, although he is willing to abolish slavery after seeing the worst of its abuses through the eyes of a commoner and slave. On more than one occasion Hank makes analogies with modern America, and contemporary reviewers (such as Twain's friend William Dean Howells) pointed out that the novel moves elastically between the centuries. Slave drivers are the outstanding representatives of authoritarian evil, and they seem from the first episode of Hank's travels to be closely involved with the established Roman Catholic Church.

The Church is implicated at various points in the novel as the doer of great evil; against the innocence of individuals stands the religiously organized and sophisticated predatory evil. The original illustrator of the novel, Dan Beard, played up this theme in the varied political cartoons that add a significant dimension to the novel's "feel" (readers should definitely seek an illustrated edition of the book, several of which are available in paperback). Protestantism is portrayed as a variation of democracy, permitting multiple viewpoints. The Catholic Church is portrayed as a predatory capitalist monopoly that supports social oppression. Yet Hank occasionally finds a fatherly priest, as in the Valley of Holiness or at the hanging of the young mother, and grudgingly notes those exceptions. The Church is positioned as the author of the final downfall of the yankee democracy and the snuffing out of technological advance. Merlin, however, has been much more in evidence than any prelate. The "Interdict," in fact, sweeps Hank Morgan's enterprises to destruction through a carefully crafted plot that he and the reader learn of only through Clarence's retelling just before the final battles in the sandbelt around Merlin's cave. The Church and chivalry are united in their opposition to Hank's republic, but the Church is behind the scenes, accountable in the retelling more than in the plot action.

STYLISTIC AND LITERARY DEVICES

A Connecticut Yankee is a framed story (a narrator introduces readers to a story inside the story) wherein the detached narrator, presumably someone like Mr. Mark Twain visiting an English castle, meets a strange individual who provides an arcane manuscript—a palimpsest (that is, writing on vellum—sheepskin—over previously erased writing). The antique manuscript tells a wild tale in the voice of its author, the original "Connecticut yankee," now set adrift in time and place from those who had become his family in the sixth century. Because the narrator is at a remove from the reader, his exaggerations can be real to his story without pretending to be realism—the portrayal of everyday events. Twain is, more than most readers realize, a rather intellectual writer, concerned with how his hero's thinking plays out in the world of imagination. The framed story allows this fantasy full reign.

The yankee speaks in a slangy, colloquial voice of the lower-class or lower-middle-class American of the late 1880s. He labels a revered classical artist like Raphael "a bird" and describes his appreciation for bad art, or "chromos," as his idea of household decoration (Twain's own house in Hartford was a showplace with stenciling in the front hall and glass panels by Louis Comfort Tiffany). The racy, colloquial language of the yankee fully expresses his character. He is impatient with the rigid forms of church and state, although he seems to have a keen sense of moral values relating to marriage, the family, and the rights of the individual to economic reward. When he talks about something being "a daisy" or describes a knight looking like a victim of sunstroke being carried into a drugstore on a shutter, he presents life in the language of the lower classes; this is Twain's comic alternative to the chivalric language of Sir Thomas Malory's Arthurian tales.

Humor should be analyzed and enjoyed along with all the serious content. The book is a work of literary comedy, and it would be a distortion to miss enjoying its jokes and irony and using that understanding as a tool to identify its vision. Slapstick is involved in episodes including Sandy and the pigs, Hank's use of medieval armor, the fight with Dowley and his friends, and Sir Launcelot arriving on a bicycle to save the king. Comic action is ludicrous as well as murderous. Jokes occur in the mouth of Sir Dinadan the humorist, but Hank is also a humorist, and the redhead joke in the dungeon sequence was a typical joke of its period. Burlesques of Malory are obvious, but King Arthur's bungling attempt to pretend to know agriculture is modeled on Twain's earlier burlesque, "How I Edited an Agricultural Newspaper," a caricature of newspaper editor Horace Greeley. The attempt to sell soap to undermine the Church and the cleanliness of the monks in the Valley of Holiness represent satire. The satire turns bitter as pilgrims comment not on the whipping of slaves but rather on the technique with which the whip is used. Hank even shows traces of the dead-pan naivete of Huck Finn, and the comic dead-pan is both very American in its feel and also a good vehicle for irony. The tools in the comic writer's toolbox are numerous, and Twain uses most of them in this work. Sometimes they indict an evil; at other times they imply inappropriate naivete. Always they suggest that the work is partly fantasy, lightening horrible experience with comic detachment from the grim events.

Hank's "voice"—his narrative style in retelling his history—is a mix of sentimental, melodramatic, and realistic modes. For example, in Morgan le Fay's dungeons and elsewhere, Twain's sentimentalism runs amok: Hank is not merely a realist, and his outrage is fully displayed in Chapter Eighteen when he forces Morgan le Fay to free the prisoners from her dungeons. Hank delivers diatribes: he declares that if the nation were stripped naked one could not tell the royalty from the commoners and that all he wants is to preserve the one atom of himself that is truly himself—a poignant speech about identity and action. He attacks repression and demands reform without reserve. Hank expresses his viewpoint and his humanity forthrightly and tells the reader of his plans to implement his vision. In this work Twain accomplishes something that defeated almost every other writer of his era: he successfully combines the feeling of journalistic realism with the trappings and license of the romance. From this perspective, the incongruities of the writing style are actually the book's greatest achievement, allowing Twain to implicate modern life while seemingly distanced from it.

HISTORICAL BACKGROUND

American technology has been a boasting point of the nation's culture since 1818, when British industrialists first came to study what Europeans called the "American System of Manufacture" based on Eli Whitney's concept of using machine tools to make interchangeable parts. This system, the "Uniformity System" or "Whitney system," established the basis for American mass production.[1] By 1818, Chauncey Jerome, a yankee clockmaker, and others had perfected techniques that revolutionized manufacturing and led to a flood of cheap goods. Pride in these innovations, however, has led to some delusions among Americans about the strength of technology, as evidenced in Mark Twain's belief in the wealth he would amass from the Paige Typesetter experiment, whose failure bankrupted him in 1894. One of the most notable recent examples of this delusion occurred in 1986 when the *Challenger* rocket exploded. All seven astronauts aboard, including a civilian schoolteacher, died when the rocket's fuel seals leaked. The failure of the o-ring seals was an outcome of the national pride over technology. The head of the National Aeronautics and Space Administration (NASA) had put heavy pressure on Morton Thiokol Co. (the maker of the rocket fuel tanks) to sign off on the launch. Initially, they resisted, fearing the o-rings might leak fuel and cause an explosion at temperatures under 40 degrees; the temperature that night in Florida had been close to freezing. Nonetheless they did not postpone the launch. The pressure of NASA's and America's "prestige" (the Chinese would call it "face") being at risk should the space shuttle not launch on schedule was a central element in this drama.

The "Preface" to *The Yankee Enterprise, or The Two Millionaires and Other Thrilling Tales* (Boston: Wentworth & Co., 1855) states that the book was written to illustrate "the developments of the indomitable energy of the New Englander in every section of the globe, and to illustrate a verification of the saying that 'place a Yankee on an uninhabited island, with but a bunch of shingles and a jacknife, and he would construct a vessel to convey him home.'" These are ingrained American themes, but the claim was a joke— the book was made up of stories by British authors cribbed from other sources, and the yankee energy displayed was literary piracy.

To American readers, a democratic apologia seems to be naturally rooted in capitalism and production. Egalitarian democracy and empathy with human suffering are close to Hank's proposed technocracy for Arthurian England. When popular poet Will Carleton in "The Clang of the Yankee Reaper," published in his *Farm Ballads* in 1873, described himself as homesick in England he was solaced by the reaper's sound on Salisbury Plain, which he compared to the nation's flag. Patriotism, democracy, and capitalism seemed inherently linked as an incontrovertible truth. Americans also employed chivalric terminology as part of the capitalist myth in books with titles like *Kings of Capital and Knights of Labor* (1885), published during this era. In fact, Twain had used this language in speaking on the status of labor and capital in 1886, outlining to a labor union, the "Knights of Labor," at their annual convention a philosophy of civilization that the Connecticut yankee restated in the novel in 1889.[2] In *A Connecticut Yankee*, the yankee's thinking about freeing Russia from the autocracy of the czar is not merely an anomaly; it represents Twain's increasing concern with authoritarian regimes and imperialism in general. Such thematic issues would not emerge fully in his writing for another decade, but in this book the yankee's concerns show that Twain had become a world spokesman for democracy.

The political events of the 1880s also figured in the construction of *A Connecticut Yankee*. President Garfield had been assassinated in 1881, and General U.S. Grant had died in 1884, just after finishing his memoirs which were to be published by Twain's own publishing firm; great leaders were vanishing even as new leaders stepped up. Grover Cleveland's advocacy of free trade was a major issue in mid-decade, as he attempted to lower tariffs, sensing that lower tariffs would benefit consumers. Hank Morgan would echo his philosophy. Reform was a major theme in America in the 1880s; the Pendleton Act of 1883 established a merit system for civil appointments, as Hank attempts to do for Arthur's army, only to be defeated by feudal prejudice. One issue in the election of 1888 was hostility toward England, and the election itself was so close that Benjamin Harrison, the winner, actually polled fewer votes than the losing incumbent Cleveland. Clearly, these were shifting, uncertain times, and Twain's novel seems to reflect them.

ALTERNATE READING: A BAKHTINIAN READING

Russian literary philosopher Mikhail Bakhtin (1895–1975) and his colleagues promoted the idea that culture and language are continually redefining each other. Bakhtin argued that the clash of cultural definitions leads to social dislocation that is vibrant and stimulating but also chaotic. To view a work in a Bakhtinian way, readers need to regard the hero as objectifying an authorial moment in time, giving substance to a mood, which the character may come to control in the process of creating the story even more than the author himself. The author might not fully control a work's meaning, and the society represented in a novel like *A Connecticut Yankee* may become highly unstable as an outsider like Hank tries to force himself inside social organizations with an ill-fitting language. Bakhtinian readings examine the interactions of language and behavior to create events parallel to festivals or carnivals, celebrations of disorder that can be healthy *or* dangerous. Such a reading helps interpret comments by Henry Nash Smith in *Mark Twain's Fable of Progress* (1964), in which he complains about the contradictions and failures in the construction of *A Connecticut Yankee*, as have other formalist literary critics. Hank attempts to impose his language on medieval England from the start. In turn, the feudal ideology and the feudal institutions are not so much resistant as they are simply impervious to him. Consequently, the novel contradicts itself. One part involves Hank going outside the real world and creating a parallel one consistent with his imagination; the other part involves Hank interacting with people from the medieval world, leading to comic episodes and misunderstandings. When all these forms come into collision, the interactions are cataclysmic. The hero denies he is a revolutionary but creates a revolution because conflicting social ideals are beyond reconciliation. Humans can exert their wills and impose their visions of humankind, whether for good or ill, but confusion, misunderstanding, and chaos may result.

Comic interchanges are the most obvious superficial evidence of breaches in concept, beginning with the first correction: "Bridgeport?" . . . "Camelot." It is merely a step to the extended monologues of Sandy, in which the seemingly stilted language of Malory and the sense of the yankee that he is in the presence of the mother of the German language, with its complex syntax and extended backwards-seeming constructions, masks his greater distress with the "saharas of fact" based on concepts so completely different from his own that he cannot recognize them. Hank and Sandy have several go-arounds on language that show the yankee as a cultural ideologue who only recognizes his own language as sovereign. Therefore, it may be that Twain is creating some distance between the reader and the yankee. Hank is a male chauvinist who incorrectly identifies Sandy as an absurdity—an opinion he later revises. She has a lot of language and a lot of vocabulary that stamp her as smart.

Hank recognizes the variations between his practical culture and that of the fendal knights based on chivalry, but they cannot comprehend his concepts, so his interaction with the medieval society plays on his reputation as a magician rather than attempting to make his technology understandable. Noblemen are just "jackasses," he says in Chapter Fifteen, and worse, in the following chapters on Morgan le Fay. Even a prisoner named Hugo in le Fay's dungeon denies his own interests, as his wife denies hers, in charity for the other, creating utter confusion on Hank's part. Only when understood in terms of home and family does Hugo's willingness to suffer come to make sense to Hank in relation to his political agenda. From these contradictions come the wild festival experiences of the Valley of Holiness. Hank adds an overlay of superstitious mumbo-jumbo, burlesque German phrases, and dazzling pyrotechnics with hissing rockets and crowds first terrified and then shouting "hosannah with joy." Also, knights ride with sandwich boards selling soap while other knights are destroyed by a dynamite bomb. Hank translates peace into violence, reflecting that he does not want to lead a violent revolution, particularly a losing one like Wat Taylor's. As cultures clash, comedic energy is released; the novel reflects this energy in the wild array of effects that make readers laugh even as they see the clash of cultures and the failure to negotiate or mediate the values of the various participants.

More important, neither Hank Morgan nor the feudal culture he attacks seem aware that any values other than their own have real substance. Hank shows this most clearly when he denies the king's feelings because he regards a king as "a mere artificiality." Although the overall context affirms a man's feelings "as a man," the yankee misunderstands the effect of his own culture on himself in forging his definitions of manhood and humanity as much as he despises the feudal chivalric beliefs subsumed in Arthur's makeup. Regarding Twain as involved in a Bakhtinian journey, in fact, helps resolve one of the great problems of the novel. For all the yankee's advocacy of freedom and humanity, the closing scene is slaughter outside the cave that once belonged to Merlin.

Hank has changed places with the necromancer and produced an effect that is as murderous as any dungeon he has encountered, albeit more short-lived and immediate in its execution. If one understands the carnival of released energy, of tremendous effects, to be the most likely outcome of such clashes of strong and uncompromising language and culture, then *any* outcome of tremendous magnitude is predictable. The unleashing of the horror of all-out war is consistent with the forces elsewhere portrayed in the novel and easily conceptualized on the basis of European political history or that of modern Africa, among other historical examples. Language and any other form of social control have been invalidated in the conflict.

The yankee himself seems indifferent to the clash of cultures even though he acknowledges all the differences between himself as a "modern" man of the nineteenth century and what he regards as the ignorant medieval residents of Arthurian England. Consistently, as he plots his strategy, he fails to use his powers for altering perception except at a far remove, in the remote "man factories" that are supposed to create the stuff of democracy. Identifying the magician Merlin with his opposition, Hank in fact becomes Merlin by using his own techniques and claiming them as substance. Almost all values are contradicted at one time or another. Even affection for home and family can also be overcome by social dictates, as when Marco prepares to turn in his cousins or the yankee leaves his family to return to England and a final battle. Only his Merlin-like reputation gives him personal safety, not his real miracles of technical progress. Little sense is to be made of personal experience except to say that it is caught up in the flow of contradictory events. A festival of confusion and over-energized action overpowers his new order.

The Valley of Holiness is one of many indexes to the complexity of this process. The harnessing of St. Simon Stylites not only burlesques ancient religious lore but shows Hank subduing ignorant action to yankee productivity. The incorporated St. Simon machine is a caricature of Hank as well as of the Church. Its bizarre self-righteousness is a target, but so is the yankee's business practice. Hank defrauds knights by making the failing St. Simon into a stock corporation. The episode foreshadows the events that provide a trigger for the Church to pull at the end of the novel. The yankee machinations are not just a response to medieval ignorance and superstition; they are also a problem. Cultural conflict is thus the real story behind the novel. It pleases most readers to recognize the yankee's idealism as positive. But a broad view also recognizes that the belief system is arbitrary, capable of being highly punitive to those who don't understand or adapt to it. Technology is not a controlling metaphor for language and thought; nor can democracy replace medievalism in the sixth century as a permanent reality. The release of chaotic comic energy and disruptive social forces is an inevitable outcome.

NOTES

1. Daniel Boorstin, *The Americans* (New York: Vintage Books, 1974), 2:26, 31–34.

2. Paul J. Carter, Jr., "Mark Twain and the American Labor Movement," *New England Quarterly* 30 (September 1957):582–588 reprints the speech, titled "The New Dynasty."

9

Pudd'nhead Wilson
(1894)

Pudd'nhead Wilson has experienced a mixed reception, recognized in the later half of the twentieth century for its portrayal of American racism, especially after an appreciative foreword to the Bantam paperback edition by African American author and critic Langston Hughes in the 1950s. A very brief novel, it was propelled forward by Twain's need for money as the Paige typesetter, his major investment, began to fail, ultimately bankrupting him. The original extravaganza featured Siamese twins joined at the hip with two bodies and one pair of legs, but that manuscript was torn apart, leaving the Capello twins who are the characters in *Pudd'nhead Wilson*. The Siamese grotesques were consigned to a brief novel entitled *The Comedy of Those Extraordinary Twins*, corresponding to the other novel's longer title, *The Tragedy of Pudd'nhead Wilson*. The second piece attached to the first made a sufficiently large book to be sold door-to-door by subscription by the American Publishing Company, to which Twain had turned because his own publishing company, the Charles L. Webster Company, had no sales apparatus. However, Twain's joking description of himself as a "jack-leg" novelist in the introduction to the second segment has prompted a multitude of critics to assess all his works as structurally flawed, formal failures despite their emotional power.

In 1891 Twain closed his grand house in Hartford and moved with his family to Europe in hopes of improving his wife's health and to save money. He wrote to Webster's manager, Fred J. Hall, several times about the book, which he began as "Those Extraordinary Twins" in the summer of 1892 as a "howling farce."[1] By December he had two manuscripts under the two titles; only in July 1893 was he able to write to Hall, euphorically, that he had radically trimmed down the story, omitting descriptions of weather, scenery, and even a Mississippi steamboat sequence, and that it was "stripped for flight."[2] Once the novel was in print, critics hardly knew what to make of the book, recognizing its energy, irony, and unlikeness to any conventional novel. Frank Mayo, an old friend of Twain's, now an actor, created a play from the novel which was immediately popular. Some southerners, such as Martha McCullough Williams writing in the *Southern Magazine* (February 1894), hated the book for its "malicious and misleading" betrayal of Clemens's native South, where slaves, she thought, had been content and well treated. A scattering of recent critics have been even harsher, claiming Twain was unaware of his own racism in the portraiture of characters Tom and Roxy; but most critics, including Langston Hughes, recognize the book for the attack on prejudice and racism that it is.

PLOT DEVELOPMENT

Pudd'nhead Wilson is set in the small southern town of Dawson's Landing in the 1830s, "half a day's journey, per steamboat, below St. Louis." Cats recline on window sills, blissful in the sun, as steamboats pass on the great river. Dawson's Landing is soon identified as a slave-holding town backed by rich farmland, sleepy and contented. No sooner is this setting laid out, however, than Twain introduces a gallery of local grandees, the wealthy social upper crust of "F.F.V.'s"—"First Families of Virginia," "tide-water aristocracy" from the old South, who represent their aristocratic origins in names drawn from English heraldry: York, Leicester, Cecil, Essex, Northumberland and Pembroke among them. This is a very specialized setting where honor codes amount to religion, defended not only with high artillery but even with low-class "brad-awls." The seeds of violence are deeply ingrained within the culture, and its self-determined sense of importance is ironic. Two events folded within this setting begin the action of the story. First, two babies are born in the household of Percy Northumberland Driscoll, "one to him, the other to one of his slave girls." The mother of the first baby, Mrs. Percy Driscoll, dies within the week, and the father turns to his business speculations, leaving both babies in the care of the slave mother, Roxy. The second event is the arrival, "from an eastern law school," of a pleasant young man named David Wilson—not a Virginia grandee, just a youth of "Scottish" parentage.

The title event of Chapter One lies in the "fatal" moment when Wilson "gauges" himself in the eyes of a group of local yokels whose "verdict" confers on him the title of "Pudd'nhead," or "fool." Hearing a barking dog, he says he wishes he owned half the dog so that he could "kill my half." A panel of six locals tries to figure out the remark, missing its humor, and decides he is a "dam fool," hence his title, "Pudd'nhead." This incident causes him to remain on the margins of the town's life thereafter, never able to develop his law practice despite the varied evidence of his abilities. Even his interest in the new-fangled discovery of reading fingerprints, which he begins collecting, cements his reputation as an incomprehensible oddity. Actually, the misfired joke was itself a piece of American folklore. The Connecticut yankee showman P. T. Barnum had told it in his *Life of P. T. Barnum* (1855) of a circus owner named Bailey who was so incensed about being cheated out of his half of the profits from an elephant that he threatened to "shoot my half." In a later story, a southern preacher was reputed to have prayed for healing of "his half" of a slave. In other words, the locals in Twain's novel should have understood the joke; the fact that they did not is the first evidence of Twain's message that treating things by parts is unproductive and leads to injustice—the book's main theme.

Wilson hangs out his tin sign as a lawyer, gets no business, and turns to collecting fingerprints from all levels of society. Among others, he collects those of Roxy, a slave woman who is 15/16 white; those of her son, who is 31/32 white; and those of her master's almost identical son. In a terrifying moment, she and three other slaves are accused of stealing a small sum and are threatened with being sold "down" the river into the harshest conditions of slavery. Because of her near escape from this fate, she first contemplates killing her child and herself, in Chapter Three, and then decides to switch the two infants in their cradles, making her own slave-child the heir to the wealth of her master, Percy Driscoll. Her reasoning is a hysterical melange of historical precedent ("*white* folks has done it . . . *Kings!*") and religion ("it ain't no sin, case white folks done it"). Because Percy Driscoll is preoccupied with unwise investments, Roxy only fears detection by Pudd'nhead Wilson, who she knows is no fool although she thinks he may be a witch.

As they grow, the children exercise their prerogatives to act like children, except the changeling gets all the privileges. Roxy has made her own child her master "by the fiction created by herself." Tom, the changeling, cuffs the other child, Chambers, who would have been his master; and while Chambers grows strong on the coarse food and exercise of a slave, Tom grows vicious and weak, always jealous of Chambers and at one point stabbing him almost to death. Roxy notices herself sinking "from the sublime height of motherhood to the sombre deeps of unmodified slavery" owing to Tom's capricious temper and vicious nature. The awfulness of this debacle is hardly remedied at the end of Chapter Four by Driscoll setting Roxy free on his deathbed. Chambers, the reader is informed, was sold secretly to Judge Driscoll, Percy's brother, to prevent the scandal of his being sold down the river by the jealous Tom. When Percy's fortune collapses, the judge assures Tom that he will become his heir, a circumstance that later leads to his own murder. Wilson takes yet another set of fingerprints, now of the changelings under their new identities.

The Driscolls enjoy their new son, Tom, although the ironic language of the narrator undercuts any genuineness to this feeling, and Tom flunks out of Yale after two years, returning to Dawson's Landing with put-on airs that soon make him an object of ridicule. In Chapter Five, designated as twenty-three years after Pudd'nhead Wilson's entry into town, Judge Driscoll completes the destruction of Wilson's reputation by the well-meaning release of Wilson's "maxims," which have already served as amusing chapter headings for the reader. The townspeople do not have the mental capacity to understand the irony of his maxims any more than they could understand the "shoot my half" joke.

Now entering the story are two improbable Italian twins who take up residence at the Widow Cooper's, one a little fairer than the other but otherwise essentially identical—not unlike Tom and Chambers, one might imagine. They prove charming but soon reveal a checkered past, including the experience of slavery in a circus. Aunt Patsy Cooper, their new landlady, and her daughter Rowena are in their glory as the twins are introduced to the villagers and captivate everyone with a powerful piano "slam-banging."

Judge Driscoll introduces the strangers to the sights of the town and to Pudd'nhead Wilson, who has been wondering about his glimpse of a woman in Tom's bedroom—actually Tom himself practicing a disguise so that he can finance his gambling debts by robbing houses in town without detection. The twins and Pudd'nhead become friends as Tom carries on a ceaseless goading of the still clientless attorney. Roxy, in the meantime, has spent eight years as a chambermaid on steamboats, amassing a fortune of $400, which is lost when the bank she has entrusted with the money is broken. She returns to Dawson's Landing as a pauper to seek help from her changeling son, Tom. She is told by Chambers in an extended dialogue that Tom's gambling has caused him to be disinherited and that both Chambers and Roxy are only "imitation *white*" and don't amount to anything as "imitation *niggers*." Chambers is sent by Roxy to get Tom to see her, and Tom—the usurper of the family rights and name of the humbled and degraded Chambers—vents his anger by kicking the "pure-white slave" Chambers over the doorsill. Driven by his arrogant rejection of her pleas, Roxy takes revenge on Tom by threatening to reveal his secrets and have him disinherited. Neither one realizes that the secret she knows is different from, and worse than, the secret of his continuing gambling, which he thinks she knows about. When she forces him to beg on his knees, she is deeply satisfied to take revenge for two centuries of outrages perpetrated on blacks by whites; but the reader understands the grotesque irony of the situation, because Tom is her son.

For Tom, worse is to come. In Chapter Nine, Roxy reveals to him the ultimate problem of his personal history, that he "is a *nigger!—bawn* a nigger en a *slave!*" Tom, enraged, can do nothing other than brandish a billet of wood, which Roxy defies him to hit her with. Emotionally reduced to subservience, he now admits that he is stealing to keep his gambling creditors at bay and owes $300. Roxy reveals to Tom that Colonel Cecil Burleigh Essex, one of the most honored men in town by civic societies and churches, was actually his father. She has bluffed that she could actually prove Tom's history, but she knows him and is successful. Tom broods over the question, why were "niggers *and* whites" made? The revelation of his birth father has changed his "moral landscape." The "nigger" in him—Twain supplies the quotation marks at this crucial point—quails at exposure as a fraud—a Negro and slave who has supplanted a white master. Nevertheless, the now-united mother and son begin plotting together, as Tom continues to lose money gambling and has to continue to steal to pay his debts.

Twain now delivers the reader back to the point of the twins' arrival in town, and Tom baits and teases Wilson at the reception for them. As the very lengthy Chapter Eleven proceeds, Wilson reads the twins' palms and discovers that one has murdered a man; Tom snatches back his own hand when Wilson proposes to read it, foreshadowing the ending of the novel. As one of the twins, Angelo—a teetotaler who does not drink alcohol—is mistakenly inducted into a "wet" society opposed to temperance, Tom continues his nasty remarks, finally making one so publicly, under the stimulus of two drinks, that the other twin, Luigi, kicks him over the footlights of a stage and into a crowd. There he is manhandled until a fire breaks out and the whole fire company races out, the fire company representing more of a danger to the burning home than the fire itself.

The damage to Tom's reputation is immense, and in Chapter Twelve Judge Driscoll, an uncompromising F.F.V., is shocked and feels he must maintain his family's impeccable honor. When he questions Tom, however, he learns that Tom has merely retained Wilson to sue; Driscoll determines to challenge Luigi to a duel himself, disinheriting Tom as a coward. Even Wilson chides Tom for his degenerate cowardice, but another event soon overcomes this interest. Tom has burglarized many local homes, and the series of thefts has now been discovered. Among the items stolen are a valuable, ornately jeweled Indian dagger and case owned by the twins. Tom had planned to sell it to pay off his debts, and now he turns green as Wilson, constable Blake, and others discuss the reward they have secretly offered to pawnbrokers to catch the thief. Chapter Thirteen concludes with Wilson receiving his first recognition ever: he is offered the "humble" honor of running for mayor of the small town on the Democratic Party ticket.

In Chapter Fourteen, Judge Driscoll blames himself for indulging Tom instead of training and making a man of him, so he writes Tom back into his will on the eve of his duel with the twins. Tom, however, is a secret observer of the scene, and in deep depression he goes to confide in Roxy in secret. He is lectured on her honorable lineage from the Smith-Pocahontases (Twain's joke on Captain John Smith and Pocahontas) and a "nigger king outen Africa" and derided for his cowardice, which has tainted his soul by "de nigger in you." Roxy is, like Wilson, committed to the system that oppresses her, and her use of genealogy is fragmented and inconsistent. She, not he, has been in the duel herself and nicked by a bullet. Now, fearless of nothing, true to her Smith-Pocahontas genealogy, she demands a rigid standard of behavior that Tom must adhere to or be exposed. He claims to be reformed.

The town of Dawson's Landing takes both pride and glory in the duel. Tom Driscoll indulges his meanness, however, by teasing Blake and Wilson over the failure of their plan to catch the thief; he does his best to undermine confidence in the twins' truthfulness and sets in motion a plan to redeem himself with the judge, who, in response, decides he will ruin one of the twins and "not shoot him until after the election." Tom cannot hold off his creditors, however, because a "brother thief" on the steamboat to St. Louis has stolen Tom's plunder—now a new plan must be conceived. Roxy again rises above her woes, driven by the universal God-made power of motherhood; she conceives of a plan whereby Tom will sell her as a slave to pay off his debts; then he will buy her back in a year. She brushes off Tom's notice that she is free: "Much diffrence dat make! White folks ain't partickler"—which Twain could easily let serve as the motto for racial rights and equality stretching from the Civil War to the present time. "Luck," however, throws a man in Tom's way so that he can sell his mother *down* the river—the ultimate betrayal. He promptly and gratefully does so.

The story skips back again to Dawson's Landing, where Pudd'nhead Wilson is "elected" mayor and Judge Driscoll discloses his knowledge that one of the twins is an assassin. The twins are left forlorn and friendless by the fickle town. Melodrama, pathos, and historical horror now fuse in Chapter Eighteen when Roxy reappears in a rainstorm at Tom's door in St. Louis in disguise. She has beaten a brutal northern Yankee overseer. He had tried to work her to death and beaten a kindly child who slipped Roxy some food. When Roxy saw the child writhing in the dust like a crippled spider (such were the tales Twain had read in the true narratives of slaves), she lashed out in fury at the cruel Yankee overseer and made her getaway on the overseer's horse. Tom curses the overseer, not for the man's cruelty to his mother but for being the agent by which his mother once again enters his life. Such is the self-alienation of slavery that his own birth history is his greatest danger.

Once escaped, Roxy is fortunate to find her friends on the *Grand Mogul* steamboat where she had been a chambermaid, and they help her get to St. Louis. In disguise, she shrewdly penetrates Tom's weak lies and determines that he has not only helped to write the escaped slave warrant for her recapture but has even schemed to betray her again. Knowing Tom could "be Judas to yo' own mother," she forces on him the ultimate plan: that he confess his gambling debts, accepting disinheritance but once again freeing Roxy. He agrees, with one unspoken variation: he will not beg for the money, he concludes at the end of Chapter Eighteen that he will steal it.

Judge Driscoll has now become the implacable foe of the twin Luigi, whom he thinks he dueled with under the mistaken impression that Luigi was a gentleman. A murderous confrontation is projected within the next day or two. Wilson explains to Luigi that the judge is driven by the craving for affection from a worthless object—Tom (Roxy has acted similarly toward the same unworthy object, after all). The motif of clinging to that which is bad in the face of a more humane and broadened understanding is consistent with the larger racial theme of the novel. Now Driscoll is ready to shoot down the twins on sight, lawlessly, to fulfill his misguided code of honor. The "unwritten law of the region" governs his behavior, and Wilson is helpless to convince him otherwise, as he has been helpless to reverse his own fortunes over the course of two decades. Instead of a confrontation between duelists, however, Tom enters the judge's study, clothed as a woman, to steal money to pay off his debts. When the judge awakens, Tom plunges the stolen Indian dagger of Luigi into him, "and was free." The choice of language implicates slavery. The twins enter by the front door in answer to the judge's last cry for help as Tom exits by the rear, and they are soon placed under arrest for murder.

Wilson, although baffled, is not clueless; bloody fingerprints are visible on the knife-handle. Examining them, he is convinced that neither of the twins made the marks. His thoughts then turn, in detective fashion, to the "mysterious girl" he had seen in Tom's room. He studies his glass fingerprint records of the ladies and girls of the town without results. Chapter Nineteen ends with Wilson being perplexed. He thinks that Tom cannot be a suspect because of his cowardice; he could not murder anybody. As the trial approaches, the twins' case is desperate and continues to be so as Chapter Twenty takes the action into the courthouse. In the "nigger corner" sit Chambers and Roxy, she with her bill of sale in her pocket and a thirty-five-dollar-a-month pension from Tom. Roxy hates the twins for murdering Driscoll, who had been kind to her—an irony, considering the enormity of the wrongs of slavery inflicted on her throughout the book, yet absolute evidence of the intellectual alienation slavery worked on its victims. Wilson is a victim of the institution in another way, as his budding career as lawyer and politician seems about to founder on the obvious guilt of the twins whom he now defends against another representative F.F.V., lawyer Pembroke Howard. Tom, ever mean-spirited, decides to torture Pudd'nhead for the rest of his life with the nonexistent woman assassin. Dropping in to begin his teasing he inadvertently leaves a fingerprint on a glass slide, which betrays him.

Chapters Twenty, Twenty-one, and the "Conclusion" complete Tom's downfall and Pudd'nhead Wilson's dramatic, and ironic, redemption. The courtroom itself becomes a stage on which the drama of exchanged roles and scientific discovery is played out as a theatrical production, with the town providing the audience to which Wilson, as hero, plays. He recognizes Tom's fingerprint as identical with the bloody print on the dagger and, after twenty-three years, reveals that which no man has suspected: the babies were switched in their cradles. Roxy was right; the town was wrong; Wilson was no fool. Chapter Twenty-one is given over to building the drama of revelation to its highest pitch as Wilson plays the crowd, builds a net of evidence around Tom, and leads to Tom's final inevitable entrapment as the murderer, as Tom's eyes "are starting from their sockets." Shamelessly melodramatic in his presentation, Wilson reveals that the babies were switched in their cradles and that the real murderer is Tom, who faints dead away as Roxy falls to her knees and the clock strikes twelve. Her heart broken, she will never laugh again. The people of the town now declare themselves elected "pudd'nhead" after twenty years; the twins' reputation is restored; and Tom is sold "down the river" to satisfy his creditors, who would rather have the money than the lawful punishment of the murderer. The now unhappy Chambers takes his rightful place as a wealthy white man. The "nigger gallery" having been closed to him forever, he will remain encumbered with the manners and training of a slave for life, embarrassed and pathetic.

CHARACTER DEVELOPMENT

Pudd'nhead Wilson and Roxy would stand out in any novel, but Wilson stands out in an unusual way through his maxims and his absence from much of the action. Roxy represents an ultimate victim of slavery. Tom Driscoll and Valet de Chambres, or Chambers, are also victims. Only lesser characters, such as the Italian twins and the townspeople, escape the wreckage of their own lives. Taken as a group, the F.F.V.'s also bear much blame for the evil situation they perpetuate. Even Wilson's final redemption is at the cost of twenty lost years, and Chambers's restoration of his original identity is a torture.

Wilson's maxims establish his wit and his ironic detachment. Separated from the action of the novel, they appear as headnotes in italics at the start of each chapter. They were woven into the part of Wilson in Frank Mayo's play made from the novel so that Wilson could perform more of the action and take on the role of a folksy narrator. As they exist here, they shed an ironic light on some chapters. Without that centrality in the novel, Wilson is an anomalous outcast from the town. Popular with a freethinking judge only, his ruin as a lawyer is ensured by the judge's well-meaning circulation of his ironic maxims, as impenetrable to the town as his "shoot my half" remark, although his interest in collecting fingerprints is also a cause of the town's general conviction that he is a fool. His Scottish stubbornness is given as the reason he stays in Dawson's Landing, but the commitment he makes is also to a way of life, and that way of life includes slavery as an abuse in a democracy—as the reader is reminded by the occasional use of the word *election* in the text. Wilson is passive; he is verbally bullied by Tom on several occasions. Yet he is also always busy, and his business overturns an abuse of an abuse—a paradoxical victory that may seem ambiguous to modern readers because it is the "black" man who suffers punishment. His characteristic irony is well founded on his status in the plot. If he were folksier and Chambers more capable of resuming his "place," the novel might be simpler to interpret. It might also be more simplistic, as comparison to J. T. Trowbridge's early anti-slavery novel *Neighbor Jackwood* (1856), using similar themes, suggests.

Roxy is, like Wilson, a paradoxical product of the world of Dawson's Landing. Twain describes her as white in appearance, with only 1/16 of her genetic heritage designating her as a Negro and slave. Yet her manners and voice are those of the slave. Despite her sassy way and often proud demeanor, her language is a dialect. She is humble in the presence of whites, for she is a "slave and salable as such." But her ability to "chaff" others of her social class in verbal combat, as well as her vanity, join her, at the low end of the hierarchy, with her slave-masters at the top. Her fear for her child humanizes her, but it also demonstrates how slavery has confused her psyche. She is a richly rounded figure, but she is, in crucial ways, crazy, for her condition drives her to thoughts of murder and suicide. She is only prevented from drowning herself and her child through vanity early in the novel. In Chapter Eight, she looks upon her own son as if he were a slave-master atoning for centuries of insult and misery, but he is her son, a "Judas" that she created herself. The final outcome takes all joy and laughter from her life forever. Her planning and scheming with her real son, Tom, portray her as tough, shrewd, and competent. However, her suspicions of Tom—on whom she says at one point she has put shoes on to trample her with—and then her trust of him are paradoxes that can be explained only as examples of pure motherly sacrifice. To Twain, her sacrificial nature is consistent with what he understands as true motherhood, but the outcome in Tom's betrayal is thus all the more horrifying.

As a character, more than any other, Roxy demonstrates the destruction of the human psyche by the system that abuses all who participate in it, slave and master alike. Were there any doubt of this, Chapter Thirteen is a crucial point in the reader's understanding of Roxy's position, for she announces her own pride in the historical lineage she possesses—in this, Twain emphasizes the irony of slavery as a distortion of social reality. Roxy is proud to see herself as also inheriting special status through the patrimony she possesses. Her pride is to her a strength; the lineage, however, gives details of a historical abuse originating with white Europeans' rapid takeover of the American continent.

The F.F.V.'s share complicity in the abuse of humanity. Twain catalogues this group early on. His intent is to suggest a sort of group consciousness. The F.F.V.'s hold honor above religion. They will fight to the death with any low instrument, including brad-awls, a carpenter's tool. They even cross-breed with their slaves. Training for them is a dominant force; it gives them absolute power over their slaves and seems to invite indulgence of their own offspring, as Tom is spoiled. Few townspeople have meaningful roles in the story; the town, likewise, has only a collective personality. The culture is not a culture of alternatives. Nineteen-year-old Rowena and her mother, the Widow Cooper, represent its limited vanity, easily swayed by such glamour as the twins represent. The twins themselves are more pleasant characters than most other figures in the story and, like Wilson, are evidence of the fickle and visionless behavior of the community. The twins are not given a role to influence the action but are left somewhat dispossessed because the F.F.V.'s see in them a danger to their elevated culture; nonetheless the twins confront that culture with strength of character, accepting its challenges and entering into duels and politics.

Tom and Chambers are as much twins as are the Italians Luigi and Angelo, but they are chained together by hierarchical social abuse rather than by the close ties of kinship and mutual protection. The pairs make a marked contrast. Tom vents his animosity on Chambers for Chambers's natural superiority, and the miscegenation (that is, interbreeding of races) that seems to motivate Tom's meanness is actually a representation of the corruption of a corrupt system. Tom is indulged and his character is thus made mean-spirited, self-centered, and cowardly. He forces Chambers to fight his fights and soon sinks into false airs, gambling, and dissipation. Worse, he enjoys torturing others with words, bringing about his own downfall. Chambers, like Roxy, displays the vulgar dialect and foot-shuffling subservience that is trained into slaves—although he is a master. Notably, he has no speaking role in most of the novel. He is an anomalous object. The ending leaves him a miscast curiosity, doomed to a life of terror in a social role he cannot fulfill. The dismissal of Chambers with a mere line is stark indication that this is not a novel about his fate as a rounded character. Chambers is, rather, the miserable wreckage of a social and political evil.

THEMATIC ISSUES

The vicious concept of fractionalized humanity (1/16 of a person determining "race" and legal status) is the central thematic issue of *Pudd'nhead Wilson*. The opening anecdote of shooting "my half" of a dog characterizes Wilson and introduces the theme. The irony of Wilson's joke had appeared earlier in almost identical stories that Twain's readers were expected to recognize. As such, in the story the yokels' confusion is simple-minded; their contempt for Wilson is symbolic of the blindness of an entire society to an obvious absurdity: the fractionalizing of human beings through slavery. Detached amusement has no place in the small town of Dawson's Landing. Roxy is subject to the same kind of definition, for she is 1/16 Negro and thus, although essentially white, a slave and Negro by election; "the one-sixteenth of her which was black out-voted the other fifteen parts." Twain's insertion of the idea of election into this discussion identifies American democracy as bearing part of the responsibility for this abusive definition of human beings.

Fractionalized humanity may be a part of the broader problem of lineage and inheritance. The F.F.V.'s are certainly committed to a code of honor that seems dishonorable in its brutality, leading to duels and false pride. Even religion takes second place to this culture. Perhaps, then, honor as a social concept is another major theme. In Chapter Fourteen, Roxy finds in her own lineage a justification for her pride of place, without recognizing that the pride and social distinctions are also part of the system that enslaves her. She too sees the "nigger in you" making Tom a coward, evading his rightful place as a duelist.

A third thematic issue is the condition of slavery itself—an abuse of the rights of human beings that distorts and even perverts slaves' own perceptions of themselves.

In commenting on the stealing of things by slaves, the text explains that slaves had an "unfair" chance in the game of life because they had been subject to the ultimate theft: the theft of their own liberty. Tom's expansion of stealing throughout the town and into the homes of the F.F.V.'s themselves, leading finally to the murder of his uncle, expresses the infection of all levels of society by a social wrong that is not recognized and corrected. The ultimate theft is perpetrated by Roxy out of fear—the theft of the birthright of the baby who becomes Chambers the slave instead of taking his true place in the community as one of its leaders. Twain regarded the condition of black Americans at the end of the nineteenth century as unjust. In fact, he made this clear to his friend William Dean Howells in commenting on the expulsion of a Negro cadet from West Point (Johnson Chesnutt Whittaker in 1880–1881) on the basis of false accusations that he had staged his own abuse in a racial incident. Twain commented that the fraction of Negro blood "condemned" the man and allowed his conviction to proceed easily. Only during the presidency of Bill Clinton, on July 24, 1995, over a century later, was the case reopened and acknowledged as a fraud on the victim.[3]

Another thematic issue involves the scientific innovation of fingerprinting. Twain may have been the first writer to use this device in fiction, as the understanding of fingerprint variation was a new phenomenon in the early 1890s. Like other Twain heroes, Wilson has a "professional" status. He is an educated man who has a sense of community responsibility, however perverted by slavery as an institution. Because his training in law does him no good throughout most of the story, this curiosity at least allows the reader to see him as determined and systematic, although his hobby is also quirky and somewhat whimsical. To Roxy, furthermore, it is part of Wilson's witchcraft; for her, it becomes the instrument of undoing her switching of the babies.

Finally, humor is a key to the novel. Without an understanding and acceptance of satire, irony, burlesque, and caricature as Twain practices them, a distorted reading of the text is quite likely, as would also be the case with *Adventures of Huckleberry Finn* and, to a lesser extent, *A Connecticut Yankee in King Arthur's Court*. Even the foreword is an ironic burlesque in which Twain sits in Florence, Italy, among false ancestors contemplating Dante (an icon of stern literary inquiry into the ultimate secrets of reverence and behavior) and imagining Dante ogling girls. Twain will simply borrow fake Italian ancestors for himself, he claims, while checking the legal facts of his story with an incompetent drunk. The sense of witty reversal continues in the maxims heading each chapter that might—or might not—be glosses on the content that follows. Equally sarcastic about Columbus ("It was wonderful to find America but it would have been more wonderful to miss it") and cauliflower (simply "cabbage with a college education"), the maxims overturn the reader's schoolroom "copy-book" patriotism and platitudes. According to Chapter One's maxim, we may be more valued as an ass though less certain, socially, what it means to be called one. As for never putting all your eggs in one basket (Chapter Fifteen), the skeptic would be better just watching one basket than hedging bets. This world is ceaselessly antagonistic to simplicity and plain endeavor.

STYLISTIC AND LITERARY DEVICES

Throughout the text, humor as a device performs a massive amount of work in undercutting the characters' behaviors and their understandings of themselves. The humor is not light humor or verbal wit; rather, it performs the work of heavy sarcasm calling into question the supposedly homespun values that underlie the characters' psychology. Ugly universal ironies underpin much of the action. Why must Tom, in an evil mood, immediately feel better after kicking Chambers over his doorsill? First, a slave takes vengeance on a master for the fact of slavery—unknown to both characters, but clear to the reader; second, and even more subversive to non-ironic logic, the reader identifies with Chambers. He is "white" and the readers in many instances were white; Twain intended that they sense what it feels like to be humiliated unjustly. Similarly, Roxy, "the dupe of her own deceptions," is both pathetic and heroic. When she rises to assert herself in Chapters Eight and Fourteen, imposing her own pride on Tom, the reader experiences "cosmic irony," a reversal of the order of things that has distorted the characters' own perceptions to such an extent that no positive outcome is possible in the fictive world the author has created. This sort of irony continues in the discussion of starved parental instinct that causes Judge Driscoll to continue to forgive and indulge Tom. Only the driest and most laconic of Wilson's ironic maxims could match Wilson's explanation of the judge's behavior to the puzzled Luigi: "It is all a groping and ignorant effort to construct out of base metal and brass filings, so to speak, something to take the place of that golden treasure denied them by Nature, a child." The apparently inevitable outcome of this irony is the "Conclusion," in which Tom is quickly pardoned for his murder so that his creditors can sell him down the river. The social system is restored, but the money-motivation that drives the system is never questioned. Only the lives it ruined bear evidence to its evil. Such sarcasm is hardly "funny"; it is humor of the most serious sort.

Pudd'nhead Wilson as humorous literature satirizes villagy ignorance linked with natural human perversity, the only explanation of racism to Twain. Everyone in Dawson's Landing was infected with the delusion that the system was proper. Roxy, Pudd'nhead Wilson, the F.F.V.'s, the other townsfolk, and Tom and Chambers are equally its products. Only Tom, in his moment of vulnerable consciousness in Chapter Ten, questions it: "Why were niggers *and* whites made?" Both Tom and Chambers are rendered pathetic, finally; their lives are finished in a few ironic paragraphs. They fare no better than the Siamese twins, the slapstick grotesques pulled out of the original manuscript and made into the sequel "Those Extraordinary Twins." Much of their fate is mechanical comedy based on having too many body parts. It is unlikely to be improved by their own actions. The maxims are part of the village context, so too are the tragic rejection and self-hatred of the principle characters. The conflict of perspectives is a joke which turns grim because it was a grim joke to Twain, not because he didn't understand it. The episode in Chapter Two in which Driscoll decides only to sell his slaves locally—thereby seeing himself as a magnanimous savior of poor souls from Hell— shows the system at its worst. Twain's description of the humane Negro prowler stealing chickens is a clear use of irony, but the closing assertion that Driscoll had lifted a godlike hand and would move later generations to deeds of gentleness and humanity by the record in his diary is flagrant irony: no reasonable reader could miss Twain's sarcasm at the social system that breeds such self-delusion.

The recognition that Twain's vision was strong and clear seems to be demonstrated both in contemporary critics and also in the adaptation to drama by Frank Mayo. Mayo built up the part of Chambers and has him kick Tom, emphasizing the conflicting role reversals. The anti-slavery/racism message was heightened. Twain's message seemed unambiguous to those audiences. Overly complicated analysis may distort the equalitarian message. Such critics might seem to have an axe to grind were it not that critic Brander Matthews noted the same incapacity of understanding a century ago when he first analyzed the "penalty" that such a visionary humorist must pay, citing *Pudd'nhead Wilson* twice in a brief article; Twain having more humor, as Matthews said, has just paid more of a price in being misunderstood.[4] Twain's intention, high though it is, continues to be questioned, even though he knew that laughter, as he portrayed it in Roxy's laugh, belongs either to those who are angels or to those who have truly suffered.

HISTORICAL BACKGROUND

The 1890s constituted a period that many African American historians regard as the lowest point of black experience in American history. The Ku Klux Klan was strong in the South, and racial discrimination was prevalent and spreading nationally. Photographic historian Oliver Jensen, in *America's Yesterdays* (1978), notes that Atlanta, Georgia, newspaper editor Henry Grady reported "happily" that "the Negro as a political force has dropped out of serious consideration."[5] Jim Crow laws (the name derived from a song caricature of Negroes) had erected extensive barriers to African American participation in mainstream political or social life, so Grady's comment can be considered accurate. In 1896 the Supreme Court of the United States ruled in *Plessy vs. Ferguson* that "separate but equal" facilities satisfied the requirement of equality under the Constitution; the smokescreen created by this judgment obscured later practices of segregation and repression.

Where the law could not be used to repress former slaves and their offspring, violence could. Lynchings were on the rise. Documented lynchings in 1892 were approximately three times more numerous than in any year in the 1880s, scholar Shelley Fisher Fishkin has pointed out.[6] The national average of documented lynchings annually in the 1890s—not including the undocumented ones—was 110, a remarkable outbreak of lawless violence by whites against blacks in the South. Putting blacks under constraint with harsh penalties for minor crimes proved an effective tool as well. The convict lease system, which involved convicting black Americans for petty crimes and leasing them out for work—flourished. In 1882, a full decade before this novel appeared in print, the Supreme Court had invalidated much of the legislation put in place after the Civil War to ensure equal rights to freed slaves. The concept of miscegenation—that is, the intermarriage of people of supposedly pure races—also came into prominence at this time. Furthermore, some analysts have suggested a sexual basis for racism derived from white men's frustration at not being able to support their families in the harsh economic times of the early 1890s. Undoubtedly, racism involves a wide array of emotions involving resentment, frustration, and anger; many factors must have fueled the growing attacks on people of color.

ALTERNATE READING: NEW HISTORICISM

New historicism originated in the 1980s, particularly from seminal work by scholar-critic Stephen Greenblatt and others. It rejects formal boundaries of different types of formal, literary, and historical criticism and the idea that there is a "literary" canon distinct from other cultural artifacts. Instead, new historicism argues that all perspectives are enmeshed in social and political environments: politics, literature, economics, and culture are thoroughly intertwined, and conflicting issues of social control are more relevant than discriminations between texts on formal or generic grounds. Stephen Greenblatt identifies new historicism as welcoming a canon featuring "the painful, messy struggles over rights and values, the political and sexual and ethical dilemmas," rather than providing and analyzing a "shared and stable culture" which cements people together in a unified system of beliefs.[7] New historicists argue that literature represents social hegemonies—the controlling power and social beliefs of a given time—sometimes being influenced by accepted values and sometimes altering them as they are being brought into existence. Relating a work to its surrounding culture is a changing, fluid interaction between text, author, and reader. Seeing a work only as "art" misses important dimensions of its social significance, its reflection of cultural values and issues, and its support or questioning of accepted norms and values, sometimes unconsciously. On this basis, scholar Walter Benn Michaels reviews realist and naturalist fiction in America in *The Gold Standard and the Logic of Naturalism*, Stephen Greenblatt associates Shakespeare with questions of racism, colonialism, and Elizabethan social experience in *Shakespearean Negotiations: The Circulation of Social Energy in Renaissance England* (1988), and Twain scholar Forrest Robinson assesses the impact of painful emotional self-deceit and confusion of roles and identity among characters in Twain's novels in *In Bad Faith: The Dynamics of Deception in Mark Twain's America*.

"The Tragedy of Pudd'nhead Wilson and the Comedy of Those Extraordinary Twins" is the title of the book published in 1894 which Twain called "Pudd'nhead Wilson. A Tale." *Pudd'nhead Wilson*, treated by itself, as it often is in its publishing history, offers a comic world in which horrors may be spoken but not felt with the appropriate intensity. The tragedy of the novel is a tragedy of wasted lives—Pudd'nhead's, Tom's, and Chambers's, at least—and of a wasted sense of community both at the level of aristocracy and townspeople, all of whom adhere—as does Wilson—to a code of grotesque distortions far larger than the shenanigans woven around the Siamese duplicates in the second story. Finally, readers are satisfied that Tom, the greatest victim, gets the greatest punishment, but this cannot be true justice. The Siamese twins' story was appended to *Pudd'nhead Wilson*, even after being successfully separated from it as a novel, to serve the symbolic function of creating a bolder comic leer. But covering up one social disaster with another is scarcely comic to modern readers sensitized to the dismissive attitude of earlier times to disability as well as race. Or could it be that the publisher, determined to mute the message of the first tale, benefited by the pretense that the book had to be heavier to sell by subscription and thus the second slapstick comedy had to be added? The comic elements are an escape and dismissal of the message the book carried about cultural racism and superiorism even among those presumably well disposed toward the victims of such mistreatment.

Twain's wife, Livy, had made abundantly clear to him that he had to write the grotesque figures out of his novel centered on Pudd'nhead Wilson. A letter to his publisher commented, "Even Mrs. Clemens, the most difficult of critics, confesses it [the success of *Pudd'nhead Wilson*], and without reserve or qualifications. Formerly she would not consent that it be published either before or after my death. I have pulled the twins apart."[8] Although other critics point out that Olivia protested the sexual innuendoes surrounding Rowena's marriage to a Siamese twin, Olivia may have also rebelled at the treatment of Siamese twins as comic figures in the novel which dealt with slavery and the rights of Negroes to be treated equally. In insisting that the original not be published, she was demanding that the higher toned comedy be separated from the slapstick. But a further consequence was that the sexuality of Rowena and the voyeuristic sense of two men in bed with her was removed, thereby leaving the woman of color, Roxy, as the only person whose sexuality is part of the novel's concern. Isolating sexuality in the African American slave woman distances the action from a white reader, evidence of Twain's discomfort with sexuality and cultural and racial mixing except as something imposed on the person of color.

The positioning of persons of color below the standing of "white" characters is particularly notable. Tom, of course, is the primary victim; as a mulatto, he is given a bad character, while the "master," Chambers, is described as virtuous at least and perhaps even as saintly. Twain cannot seem to bring himself to make a heroic slave figure. Serious implications lie in the ambivalence and degradation of Tom, and a new historicist reader questions Twain's choice of this portrait. Twain personally knew heroic Negroes, such as John Lewis of Elmira, who risked his life to stop a runaway coach with young women of the Langdon family aboard. Twain knew of the incident and deleted a passage from *Pudd'nhead Wilson* in which the character Jasper performs such an act. Perhaps, elevating a Negro character to a position of strength would have undermined the novel's argument—that whites had imposed upon blacks and degraded them through white fictions of "law and custom." A heroic black figure would have made this point ambiguous. However, such a premise also bars Twain from displaying a positive model of color. In being unable to portray a heroic slave figure, Twain may have been succumbing to his own race's prejudices.

The Johnson C. Whittaker case at West Point provides evidence that Twain was sensitive to public debates about African American character. Historical background helps us understand that reading Tom as evil because of miscegenation goes against his comment on the "West Point" case to Howells. Twain sneered at reporters who claimed that it was the fraction of a "nigger" in the expelled cadet that accounted for his supposed crime. Yet, Howells also notes that Twain could order his Negro servant George about but couldn't bear to order a white man about, according to Twain's own admission, and the novel gives no evidence of any persons of color being superior to whites in any context.[9] The novel is studiedly "safe" in treating any issues that might have touched on the domestic economy of the Clemens family and their relations to people of color.

The novel depicts slavery's corrosive effects on human personality and community. Yet, what Twain chooses to dignify with careful treatment drives the imagery, and much of this focuses on the degrading comic side of Negro culture. Only the supposed slaves talk in dialect, whereas white characters seem to be reported only in standard spelling and pronunciation, although their pronunciations must have varied considerably from literary English. The book depicts a code, and the white upper-class users of that code are treated as the dominant southern "culture." Although black characters also have a culture, the reader's view of it is trivialized in the scene of Roxy and Jasper joshing each other. Elsewhere, Roxy's internal monologues, briefly interpreted by an omniscient voice, describe her driving fears in caricature. The irony of the narrative begs the question of whether or not Roxy is a victim or an actor in her own defeat. Roxy let us know that she takes tremendous pride in her origins from the Captain Smith-Pocahontases; she believes in the system that enslaves her. The reader must ask whether her victimization is a caricature of a stupid person, a psychological portrait of a true victim, or a burlesque of a person who is degraded in order to relieve the author of discomfort at her race, personal intensity, and sexuality.

The extent to which Twain exploited the fingerprint device as a scientific solution to identity may be a means of sidestepping the problem of race. "Scientific" studies of race were proliferating at the time Twain wrote this book, but Wilson's detective tool is one that determines identity without basing the discovery on race—each "natal signature" is unique. Thus, the key melodramatic moment of the novel uncovers a racial phenomenon without actually playing the race card as its solution. Even more interesting, as scholar Michael Rogan argues, Twain's use of scientific fingerprints as described by Francis Galton's *Finger Prints* (1892) actually makes clear that identity is not fixed (as fingerprints being unique seems to suggest) but rather the opposite; that a person's true identity is socially constructed, a matter of social training that can be, and is, reversed at the end of the novel with substantial consequences. Rogan concludes that in this light the borders of reality are made uncertain, and the readers' and author's own identities are suspect in the face of this discovery, just as Tom is alienated from himself and Chambers is left as an anomaly, comfortable in no world.[10]

Twain provides an intellectualized reality, a reality where humor distances pain through tone and texture. He escapes the more troubling implications of his own buried attitudes and beliefs. The real purpose of the later story may be to put us on our guard that the ideas in the first story are even more true than what Twain has written, which he now claims he was too inept to really do. The "Twins" is an intensifier for the meaning of the earlier work by devaluing the author's role in it—it is the old position of the naïf, translated into a literary burlesque at the level of the structure of the whole volume as a subscription-sales book. Humor is thus a covert but duplicitous way of bringing forth issues without admitting their seriousness—an escape by an author from a difficult and threatening social reality.

NOTES

1. *Mark Twain's Letters to His Publishers, 1867–1894*, Ed. Hamlin Hill (Berkeley: University of California Press, 1967), p. 319.

2. Ibid., p. 355.

3. William Dean Howells, *My Mark Twain* (New York: Harper & Bros., 1910, pp. 29–31). See also Todd S. Purdam, "Black Cadet Gets a Posthumous Commission," *New York Times* (July 25, 1995), p. A10.

4. Brander Matthews, "The Penalty of Humor," *Harper's Monthly* 42 (May 1896): 897–900.

5. Grady is cited in Oliver Jensen, *America's Yesterdays* (New York: American Heritage Publishing Co., 1978), p. 157.

6. Shelley Fisher Fishkin, "Race and Culture at the Century's End: A Social Context for *Pudd'nhead Wilson.*" *Essays in Arts and Sciences* 19 (May 1990): 5, 24n.15.

7. Stephen Greenblatt, "The Politics of Culture," in *Falling into Theory/Conflicting Views on Reading Literature*, Ed. David H. Richter (Boston: Bedford Books, 1994), pp. 289–290. Reprinted from *The Chronicle of Higher Education* (June 12, 1991).

8. Hill, ed., *Mark Twain's Letters to His Publishers*, p. 354.

9. Howells, *My Mark Twain*, pp. 29–31.

10. Michael Ragin, "Francis Galton and Mark Twain/The Natal Autograph in *Pudd'nhead Wilson.*" *Mark Twain's* Pudd'nhead Wilson: *Race, Conflict, and Culture*, Ed. Forrest Robinson and Susan Gillman (Durham, NC: Duke University Press, 1990), p. 80.

Twain's Later Short Writings

As he matured and the end of the century approached, Mark Twain's short stories, sketches, and reportorial writings became more deeply pessimistic about humankind. Thematic issues of greed, self-aggrandizement, moral cowardice, and inhumanity were at the forefront of his thinking. The most important later short works include "The Man That Corrupted Hadleyburg," "King Leopold's Soliloquy," and "To the Person Sitting in Darkness." In addition, "A Dog's Tale" makes the case for man's ingratitude to other forms of life. "The Diaries of Adam and Eve" and "Captain Stormfield's Visit to Heaven," however, define in comic form a poignant spiritual world of possible love and reconciliation in which the right proportions are restored to human relationships. "The Mysterious Stranger" published in 1916 out of fragments left by Twain, is gloomier.

"THE MAN THAT CORRUPTED HADLEYBURG" (1899)

"Hadleyburg" reflects Twain's later canon, that of the more overtly pessimistic Twain. The story features most of the elements that make his works popular: the village setting; characters facing difficult moral decisions; and a comic, folksy figure commenting on the action.

Setting

"Hadleyburg" is a small town full of pride in its ability to shun temptation. Its incorruptibility is envied by outsiders, although the town's virtue is based on ignorance of temptation. Isolated by its vanity, its citizens are more vulnerable than one would think. Twain uses the village concept to represent the small-time hypocrisy that hides humankind's most cowardly, venal, and self-centered delusions. Most of the story takes place in the darkened rooms and streets of the village, climaxing in a large meeting at the town hall festooned with flags.

Plot

An unknown stranger has been mistreated by the townspeople and decides to take revenge on their pettiness by destroying their overblown vanity about their moral incorruptibility. On a dark night, he leaves a bag of gold with Mary Richards, the wife of one of nineteen supposedly incorruptible community leaders in the smugly self-righteous community, as a reward for an unnamed person who supposedly loaned him twenty dollars. The Richardses are immediately corrupted by greed for the gold but let the word out before they can hide the gold for themselves, and soon others are drawn into a greedy competition for the prize. Rev. Mr. Burgess, whose innocence in another matter the Richardses were too cowardly to prove, is called to officiate at the revelation of who should get the money. Jack Halliday, village loafer and skeptic, in the meantime has been sowing seeds of sarcasm that will blossom at the grand meeting where the nineteen "incorruptibles" will attempt to bluff their way into getting the fortune that each thinks another villager, Mr. Goodson, had rightfully earned before his death. Burgess officiates and withholds the Richardses' name after all others are disgraced, but the Richardses are guilt-ridden. Halliday leads the crowd in chanting "You are far from being a bad man," part of the winning formula, which is repeated to chasten the corrupted "incorruptibles," and the stranger purchases and resells the sack of coins to pay the Richardses and humiliate the eighteen others. The outcome is that the Richardses die of grief and humiliation, and Burgess, whom they think has contrived to betray them, is doubly wronged as he is impugned by Richards on his deathbed. The town now wishes to be led into temptation, realizing that its former sham morality was a weakness, not a stength as their vanity had led them to believe.

Characters

Edward and Mary Richards and eighteen other "incorruptible" members of the township's leading families, an unseen Mr. Goodson, Reverend Mr. Burgess, and the town's vagabond iconoclast, irreverent fisherman, and friend of boys, Jack Halliday, the crackerbox philosopher, make up the cast, along with a mysterious stranger. Halliday, like the fools in Shakespeare, teases the follies of others, but he really adds little to the story beyond his skepticism: he is no Hank Morgan or Huck Finn. The reference to him in relation to Sam Lawson of Mrs. Stowe's *Oldtown Folks* (1869) suggests by comparison merely that he is a village loafer with no pretensions to social standing. Burgess is a victim of circumstances and the one truly incorruptible person, and for him, there is no good solution. Other members of the "nineteen" are merely connivers in moral postures befitting their social rank, but without sincerity. Some readers may find the characters are so palpably the demonstration of moral principles that they are hardly believable. At other times, they seem overdrawn. Other readers may find them convincing. Despite varied opinions regarding the success of the story, it demonstrates the intellectual and ethical qualities that caused Twain to write: his preference for wisdom through experience rather than for restrictive morality in an attempt to avoid sin.

Thematic Issues

Twain argues that a prissy, restrictive morality is bad and that many people presumed to be good have a deficient understanding of the responsibilities of humanity. Mr. Richards's failure to state the truth about Burgess is Twain's way of indicting moral cowardice in the face of antagonistic public opinion. The irony develops as characters realize they cannot carry out their own intentions. They become part of a gradually expanding orgy of greed as the plot unfolds around the twin motifs of greed and untested virtue.

The story is based on the greatest statement for freedom of the press penned in the English language, John Milton's "Areopagitica" (1644). Milton argued that good and evil were so intertwined that only those who had been exposed to vice and abstained from it could be true wayfaring Christians. Milton concluded that he could not praise a "fugitive and cloistered virtue, unexercised and unbreathed, that never sallies out and sees her adversary, but slinks out of the race where that immortal garland is to be run for, not without dust and heat." Mary Richards's indictment of the town echoes Milton. Twain thus shows the reader that incorruptibility is not achieved through ignorance of vice but through an open encounter with the world. Common folk, like Halliday, are amused by the travesty of virtue that the leading citizens display; presumably, he is less cowardly than they are because he puts on no false show of rectitude or prosperity.

"A DOG'S TALE" (1903)

One of the most sentimental pieces in Twain's canon, "A Dog's Tale" highlights the inhumanity of humankind in mistaken assumptions about others' actions and in its indifference to the feelings of other living creatures. The story is told by a mother-dog whose father was a St. Bernard and whose mother was a collie that understood human dining-room chat. The narrator mother-dog is a "Presbyterian" who attaches no meaning to the word, but her mother had learned that it seemed important to humans. As the story develops, the application of human concepts to dogs becomes the chilling irony of the story as Twain elaborates the theme of human cruelty toward the weak. The female dog is separated (as slave families were separated in the American South) from her mother, but she is soon comfortable in a new and lovely home. When the loving dog heroically pulls a baby from a burning nursery, however, the father thinks the dog is trying to harm the infant and breaks the animal's leg, causing the animal to hide for days, suffering and terrified. Once the dog is restored to the family and praised and petted, although with a permanent limp that causes the family a minor twinge of guilt, the father takes the dog's puppy and blinds and kills it to settle a scientific argument. He leaves the corpse to be buried by a tender servant who understands the horror of the event and expresses the central theme: that man is the most inhumane of all the animals. The dog herself dies in mourning without understanding what has happened. The theme is intensified as the selflessly innocent voice of the dog conveys a reproach for the inhumanity of its treatment.

"KING LEOPOLD'S SOLILOQUY" (1905)

This satiric soliloquy, or dramatic monologue, was published by the Congo Reform Association, an African liberation society, rather than by a commercial publisher; at this time Twain was writing for a cause, not personal profit. The original publication was accompanied by documentary pictures of mutilated Africans, a "journalistic" exposé as well as a satire. The first-person voice creates irony by recasting the reporter's material as musings by a king. The soliloquy spoken by a single character as if to himself, without plot and characters like a short story, develops tension in the reader's recognition that the king, Leopold, is such a cynical monster that he doesn't regret killing and mutilation at all, only its exposure. Consequently, he does what many politicians do; he blames the sources that bring out the news, dreading reporters and the "kodak" (camera), which doesn't lie. In this work Twain hoped to arouse readers to serious protest, especially by means of his sarcastic and scornful comments on the human race. He used harsh satire, in which the king exposes his own evil as he had since the 1860s in his "Open Letter to Com. Vanderbilt." In "King Leopold's Soliloquy," putting the brutal materialism in the mouth of an important person like a king makes it even more of an affront to the reader's sensibilities. The theme of limitless rapacity, as in Twain's other pieces, is dramatized in the king's ravings.

THE DIARIES OF ADAM AND EVE (1893, 1905)

Twain wrote two diaries, of Adam and Eve, respectively, based on the story of the Garden of Eden and subsequent events. "Extracts from Adam's Diary" was published first; Niagara Falls is mentioned because the story was partly contrived to boost Niagara Falls as a tourist site; "Eve's Diary," a memorial to Livy Clemens, followed. Together they present a picture of a man and a woman that would be termed sexist in the twenty-first century, but their central theme is intended to be a highly sentimentalized recognition of the power of love. The woman is naive and talkative, the man dumb and taciturn, frustrated by the supposedly feminine qualities of the woman. Each recounts the events from the Creation through the Fall (that is, banishment from Eden). Both accounts are strongly sentimental, employing the "innocence" of the diarists to make fun about naming things and animals, about the relations between men and women, and ultimately about what constitutes an ideal state of existence. The conclusion, close to what medieval theology identified as the doctrine of the fortunate fall, holds that it would be better to live together outside of Eden than to live apart inside it. As a comic treatment of the thematic issues of creation and the working out of God's law, the story expresses the frustration of seeking a logical explanation for religious doctrine. Biblical theology is subordinated to Adam's love for Eve, a human sentiment.

"EXTRACTS FROM CAPTAIN STORMFIELD'S VISIT TO HEAVEN" (1907)

Setting

The story is set in celestial space, for Captain Stormfield has died and is first seen traveling to Heaven and, finally, in Heaven itself getting acclimated to the reality of Heaven as opposed to the prevailing Earthly misconceptions of what Heaven must be like. Setting thus becomes the theme, because many of the most self-centered physical assumptions of what Heaven is like are readjusted in the course of Stormfield's experience after being shown up as egocentric vanities.

Plot

The first segment of the plot places Stormfield almost at the end of a thirty-year journey to Heaven. Overtaking a mighty comet that is "the bully of the firmament," Stormfield makes the mistake of annoying the captain of the comet (treated as if it were in a steamboat race with Stormfield), so much that he throws overboard his load of brimstone and leaves Stormfield in his wake, just as if Stormfield had been beaten in a race on the ocean or the Mississippi River. Once Stormfield arrives at the Celestial Gates, a little surprised because he thought he might be headed in another direction, he discovers that the Earth is so small and out of the way that it is hardly known. Nevertheless he is admitted, gets his harp and wings, and is soon introduced to the reality of Heaven. Harps and wings are annoying encumbrances, soon discarded, and Stormfield meets friends including Sam Bartlett and Sandy McWilliams from America who introduce him to the more rational organization of Heaven.

Stormfield soon learns that souls in Heaven come to rest at their natural age, that true integral greatness is recognized even if its possessor never had the opportunity to show it during life, and that heavenly work and activity are an important component of heavenly satisfaction. A Brooklyn preacher named (T. DeWitt) Talmage is an example of someone who thinks he is so important that he can fraternize with the great prophets—a naively egocentric notion, for in this story Heaven is a monarchy, not a republic. Instead, a Tennessee shoemaker named Billings is more appreciated than Shakespeare; a butcher named Duffer who did acts of charity without being seen is considered royalty; and a Boston bricklayer named Absalom Jones, who lost both thumbs and his front teeth and therefore was rejected as a soldier for the Revolutionary War, would have been the greatest general that ever lived. The story concludes when a Hoboken, New Jersey, bartender is welcomed into Heaven with full fanfare and even a glimpse of Moses and Esau. So rare is the appearance of patriarchs, although it occurs here to fulfill the bartender's harmless fantasy, that a monument marking the spot will be erected for tourists to gawk at and scribble their names on for thousands of years thereafter.

Characters

Captain Eli Stormfield, of San Francisco, is the hero of this story. He is an old salt who was religious enough to get into Heaven but remains relaxed enough that he can get a point or so off his compass direction to race with a comet, losing only because he grows too sure of himself. Stormfield is in his seventies and has the practical worldly wisdom to be tolerant and somewhat understanding of his relative place in the universe. Consequently, as first the gatekeepers of Heaven and later an old friend, Sandy McWilliams, introduce him to the organization of Heaven and the logic behind it, he readily accepts the rational hierarchy of Heaven and the rightness of its ordering according to truer values than those expressed by conventional pieties limited by the narrow perspectives of the world he has left. Sandy McWilliams is an already initiated occupant of Heaven who introduces Stormfield to Heaven's arrangements, explaining how people soon tire of wings, have their extraordinary expectations adjusted, and accommodate themselves to the existence of pain in Heaven—for without pain, pleasure would not be felt either.

Minor characters are representative figures more than actors, pictorial and dramatic though the sketch seems. A Pi Ute Injun is the gatekeeper of the Earth section of Heaven, "a mighty good fellow." Others who were modest on Earth but are great in Heaven include the writer Billings, the general Jones, and the butcher Duffer. Each of them was undistinguished in life but recognized as having the stuff of true greatness in Heaven. Somewhat on the negative side are Talmage (a real minister with a large popular following in Twain's period), and the barkeeper, who has reformed but who still seems to represent overblown false expectations. Weird denizens of other planets and universes are represented by a purple one-footed being who precedes Stormfield into Heaven. The universe is represented as a huge place with tremendous variety in it.

Thematic Issues

The main thematic issue of this sketch is the self-deluding self-centeredness of prevailing notions of Heaven as a place where each person will be cast in an angelic model and be the center of attention of God and the prophets, despite the more logical expectation that millions of others have also lived and died in similar hopes. Twain expands the idea to cosmic dimensions but also notices that far more "copper colored" people have lived on Earth than white or black, who are presumed to be color-changed owing to disease. As in his other published works on religion, Twain's theme revolves around a broad, tolerant, and intelligent application of Christian doctrine, based on applying the principles of religion rather than enforcing narrow precepts in cases where they conflict irrationally with other customs. Heaven is seen as ecumenical and universal; narrow doctrines are regarded as inappropriate to a hierarchy far greater than the nationalistic presumptions of American religion.

"THE MYSTERIOUS STRANGER" (1916)

"The Mysterious Stranger" is a concoction published in 1916 by Frederick Duneka of Harper & Brothers and Albert Bigelow Paine, Twain's literary executor, out of a number of Twain manuscripts. The story is set in Eseldorf, Austria, in 1590. Theodor Fischer, the village youth who tells the story, tells the story in his own voice of how a nephew of Satan, Philip Traum, visits himself and two playmates; introduces them to his amoral morality, which prizes neither death nor life; and leads them through a series of tragedies that forestall worse tragedies. The "Moral Sense" is portrayed as one of humankind's most detrimental characteristics in this story, and as village character after village character has his or her life course reversed, death seems to provide a better alternative than life. For example, Frau Brandt is burned at the stake as a blasphemer but is destined to go to Heaven, whereas her accuser, Fischer the weaver, is granted years of prosperity but ultimately is damned to Hell. Thematic issues include the limited vision of humans and the limitless capacity for universal cosmic irony in every event, no matter how innocent and minor it may seem. The story concludes with the ironic rescue of Father Peter from an accusation of theft, which brings grief to his niece, Marget, because Satan makes him a lunatic during the course of the trial. Satan, on parting for the last time from Theodor, declares that Theodor is the only consciousness, "a grotesque and foolish dream," in a space without God, a universe, or any location in empty eternities. Whether Twain would have approved of the story in this manufactured form is an unanswerable question, but the piece is no longer accepted in this form as a legitimate offering by scholars.

So many other important sketches and stories were published both during and after Twain's lifetime that only a review of the collections can reveal their variety, ranging from local color stories to newspaper reporting, to comic sketches, to moral essays. Acrid attacks on patriotic greed and self-interested behavior include "The Battle Hymn of the Republic (Brought down to Date)," "Corn Pone Opinions," "The United States of Lyncherdom," and "The Mysterious Stranger"; they have taken a place in the Twain canon but were not published during his lifetime. A variety of other stories, such as "The Death Disk" and "The £1,000,000 Bank-Note," as well as stylistic commentary such as "Fenimore Cooper's Literary Offences" and "How to Tell a Story," are also worth examining.

Twain was also prolific in platform lectures and after-dinner speeches, a popular medium in his time, and another interesting area related to his short writings. Few Americans were more frequently interviewed for newspapers, gave public lectures that were more fully reported, or provided more trenchant comic statements at major banquets than Twain. "An Encounter with an Interviewer" in 1874 reflects the comic side of his role in the limelight. Some remarkable lines came to the world in such reports, whether by Twain or fabricated: "Reports of my death are greatly exaggerated," for example. "Get your facts first, then you can distort them as much as you want afterward," was recorded by the author Rudyard Kipling after a meeting with Twain. "Plymouth Rock and the Pilgrims," collected in *Mark Twain's Speeches* (1910), is a significant summary of American history from Twain's viewpoint. It is well worth reading and needless to say, its humor is ironic. Twain's "Whittier Dinner Speech" (1877) was supposed to have alienated many members of the literary community; Howells regretted it as "that hideous mistake of poor Clemens," but it may merely show, as one critic argues, that the western and eastern regions of the country had different attitudes toward the "ragging," teasing humor that was characteristic of the frontier. If it represented a major cultural divide, Twain was on both sides of the divide, recognized as a great American writer. Several collections of his speeches have been published, along with many volumes of his letters. All these resources offer characteristic ideas and phrasings that enrich studies of Twain's entire canon.

Bibliography

MAJOR WORKS BY MARK TWAIN

Adventures of Huckleberry Finn. New York: Charles L. Webster & Co., 1885.

The Adventures of Tom Sawyer. Hartford: The American Publishing Co., 1876.

The American Claimant. New York: Charles L. Webster & Co., 1892.

The Celebrated Jumping Frog of Calaveras County. New York: C. H. Webb, 1867.

A Connecticut Yankee in King Arthur's Court. New York: Charles L. Webster & Co., 1889.

Following the Equator. Hartford: The American Publishing Co., 1897.

The Gilded Age: A Tale of To-day. Hartford: The American Publishing Co., 1873; co-authored with Charles Dudley Warner.

The Innocents Abroad. Hartford: The American Publishing Co., 1869.

Life on the Mississippi. Boston: James R. Osgood and Co., 1883.

The Man That Corrupted Hadleyburg, and Other Stories and Essays. New York: Harper & Brothers, 1900.

Personal Recollections of Joan of Arc. New York: Harper & Brothers, 1896.

The Prince and the Pauper. Boston: James R. Osgood and Co., 1881.

Roughing It. Hartford: The American Publishing Co., 1872.

Sketches, New and Old. Hartford: The American Publishing Co., 1875.

To the Person Sitting in Darkness. New York: Anti-Imperialist League of New York, 1901.

The Tragedy of Pudd'nhead Wilson and the Comedy of Those Extraordinary Twins. Hartford: The American Publishing Co., 1894.

A Tramp Abroad. Hartford: The American Publishing Co., 1880.

COLLECTED EDITIONS

Author's National Edition. New York: Harper & Brothers, 1899 and following; various editions including Twain's major works.

The Oxford Mark Twain. Ed. Shelley Fisher Fishkin. 29 vols. New York: Oxford University Press, 1996. 29 vols. Each volume includes an introduction by a modern author or humorist and a concluding analytical essay by a scholar in American literature.

The Iowa-California Edition. Projected to be 72 vols. Berkeley: University of California Press, ongoing with 22 now in print.

OTHER WORKS BY MARK TWAIN

Mark Twain: Collected Tales, Sketches, Speeches, & Essays, 1852–1890 and 1891–1910, vols. 1, 2. Ed. Louis J. Budd, with Chronology and Notes. New York: Library of America, 1992.

Mark Twain's Autobiography. Ed. Albert Bigelow Paine. New York: Harper & Brothers, 1924.

Mark Twain's Fables of Man. Ed. John S. Tuckey. Berkeley: University of California Press, 1972.

Mark Twain's Hannibal, Huck & Tom. Ed. Walter Blair. Berkeley: University of California Press, 1969.

Mark Twain's Letters. Ed. Albert Bigelow Paine. New York: Harper & Brothers, 1917.

Mark Twain's Letters. Vols. 1–5 in print, covering 1853–1873. Berkeley: University of California Press, 1988 and ongoing.

Mark Twain's Letters to His Publishers, 1867–1894. Ed. Hamlin Hill. Berkeley: University of California Press, 1967.

Mark Twain's Mysterious Stranger Manuscripts. Ed. William M. Gibson. Berkeley: University of California Press, 1969.

Mark Twain's Notebook. Ed. Albert Bigelow Paine. New York: Harper & Brothers, 1935.

Mark Twain's Speeches. Ed. Albert Bigelow Paine. New York: Harper & Brothers, 1910.

Mark Twain's Which Was the Dream? Ed. John S. Tuckey. Berkeley: University of California Press, 1967.

What Is Man? and Other Philosophical Writings. Ed. Paul Baender. Berkeley: University of California Press, 1973.

GENERAL STUDIES

Mark Twain at the Buffalo Express. Eds. Joseph B. McCullough and Janice McIntire-Strasburg. Dekalb: Northern Illinois University Press, 1999.

Mark Twain and the Bible. Eds. Howard Baetzhold and Joseph McCullough. Athens: University of Georgia Press, 1995.

Mark Twain's Weapons of Satire: Anti-Imperialist Writings on the Philippine-American War. Ed. by Jim Zwick. Syracuse: Syracuse University Press, 1992.

REFERENCE

Gribben, Alan. *Mark Twain's Library: A Reconstruction*. Boston: G. K. Hall & Co., 1980.

LeMaster, J. R. and James D. Wilson, Eds. *The Mark Twain Encyclopedia*. New York: Garland Publishing, 1993.

Mark Twain: A Bibliography of the Collections of the Mark Twain Memorial and the Stowe-Day Foundation. Comp. by William M. McBride. Hartford: McBride/Publisher, 1984.

Meltzer, Milton. *Mark Twain Himself*. New York: Bonanza Books, 1960.

Rasmussen, R. Kent. *Mark Twain A to Z*. New York: Facts on File, 1995.

Tenney, Thomas. *Mark Twain: A Reference Guide*. Boston: G. K. Hall & Co., 1977.

Wilson, James D. *A Reader's Guide to the Short Stories of Mark Twain*. Boston: G. K. Hall & Co., 1987.

BIOGRAPHIES

Andrews, Kenneth R. *Nook Farm: Mark Twain's Hartford Circle*. Cambridge, MA: Harvard University Press, 1950; rpt. Hamden, CT: Archon Books, 1967.

Brooks, Van Wyck. *The Ordeal of Mark Twain*. New York: E. P. Dutton & Co., 1920.

Budd, Louis J. *Our Mark Twain: The Making of His Public Personality*. Philadelphia: University of Pennsylvania Press, 1983.

DeVoto, Bernard. *Mark Twain's America*. Boston: Little, Brown & Co., 1932.

Dolmetsch, Carl. *"Our Famous Guest": Mark Twain in Vienna*. Athens: University of Georgia Press, 1992.

Emerson, Everett. *The Authentic Mark Twain*. Philadelphia: University of Pennsylvania Press, 1984.

———. *Mark Twain, a Literary Life*. Philadelphia: University of Pennsylvania Press, 2000.

Ferguson, Delancey. *Mark Twain, Man and Legend*. Indianapolis: Bobbs-Merrill Co., 1943.

Geismar, Maxwell. *Mark Twain: An American Prophet*. Boston: Houghton Mifflin Co., 1970.

Hill, Hamlin. *Mark Twain: God's Fool*. New York: Harper & Row, 1973.

Kaplan, Justin. *Mr. Clemens and Mark Twain: A Biography*. New York: Simon & Schuster, 1966.

Kiskis, Michael J. *Mark Twain's Own Autobiography*. Madison: University of Wisconsin Press, 1990.

Leon, Philip W. *Mark Twain & West Point*. Toronto: ECW Press, 1996.

Skandera-Trombley, Laura. *Mark Twain in the Company of Women*. Philadelphia: University of Pennsylvania Press, 1994.

Steinbrink, Jeffrey, *Getting to Be Mark Twain*. Berkeley: University of California Press, 1991.

CONTEMPORARY REVIEWS

Budd, Louis J., ed. *Mark Twain: The Contemporary Reviews*. Cambridge: Cambridge University Press, 1999. Contains hundreds of reviews from newspaper and periodical sources of Mark Twain's major works and his minor works in book form.

Frederick Anderson, ed. *Mark Twain, the Critical Heritage*. New York: Barnes & Noble, 1971. Contains reviews of the following:

The Innocents Abroad or The New Pilgrim's Progress (1869)

Unsigned review, *Nation*, 1869

Unsigned review, *Packard's Monthly*, 1869

Unsigned review, Buffalo *Express*, 1869

William Dean Howells, review, *Atlantic Monthly*, 1869

"Tom Folio," review, Boston *Daily Evening Transcript*, 1869

Bret Harte, review, *Overland Monthly*, 1870

Unsigned review, *Athenaeum*, 1870

Unsigned review, *Saturday Review*, 1870

William Ward, "American Humorists," Macon (Mississippi) *Beacon*, 1870

Roughing It, or The Innocents at Home (1872)

Unsigned review, Manchester *Guardian*, 1872

William Dean Howells, review, *Atlantic Monthly*, 1872

Unsigned review, *Overland Monthly*, 1872

Sketches, New and Old (1875)

William Dean Howells, review, *Atlantic Monthly*, 1875

Matthew Freke Turner, "Artemus Ward and the Humourists of America," *New Quarterly Magazine*, 1876

The Adventures of Tom Sawyer (1876)

William Dean Howells, review, *Atlantic Monthly*, 1876

Moncure D. Conway, review, London *Examiner*, 1876

Unsigned review, *Athenaeum*, 1876

Unsigned review, London *Times*, 1876
Unsigned review, New York *Times*, 1877

A Tramp Abroad (1880)

William Ernest Henley, review, *Athenaeum*, 1880
Unsigned review, *Saturday Review*, 1880
William Dean Howells, review, *Atlantic Monthly*, 1880
H. H. Boyesen, review, *Atlantic Monthly*, 1881
E. Purcell, review, *Academy*, 1881
Unsigned review, *Athenaeum*, 1881
Unsigned review, *Century Magazine*, 1882
John Nichol on Mark Twain, 1882
William Dean Howells, "Mark Twain," *Century Magazine*, 1882
Thomas Sergeant Perry, "An American on American Humour," *St. James's Gazette*,
    1883

Life on the Mississippi (1883)

Lafcadio Hearn, review, New Orleans *Times-Democrat*, 1883
Unsigned review, *Athenaeum*, 1883
Robert Brown, review, *Academy*, 1883
Unsigned review, *Graphic*, 1883

Adventures of Huckleberry Finn (1884–1885)

Unsigned review, *Athenaeum*, 1884
Brander Matthews, review, *Saturday Review*, 1885
Robert Bridges, review, *Life*, 1885
Unsigned article, "Modern Comic Literature," *Saturday Review*, 1885
Thomas Sergeant Perry, review, *Century Magazine*, 1885
Andrew Lang, "The Art of Mark Twain," *Illustrated London News*, 1891
Sir Walter Besant, "My Favourite Novelist and His Best Book," *Munsey's Magazine*,
    1898
Andrew Lang, "Jubilee Ode to Mark Twain," *Longman's Magazine*, 1886

A Connecticut Yankee in King Arthur's Court (1889)

Sylvester Baxter, review, Boston Sunday *Herald*, 1889
William Dean Howells, review, *Harper's Magazine*, 1890
Desmond O'Brien, review, *Truth*, 1890
Unsigned review, *Speaker*, 1890
Unsigned review, London *Daily Telegraph*, 1890

Unsigned review, *Scots Observer*, 1890
William T. Stead, review, *Review of Reviews* (London), 1890
Unsigned review, *Athenaeum*, 1890
Unsigned review, Boston *Literary World*, 1890
Unsigned review, *Plumas National*, 1890
H. C. Vedder, article, New York *Examiner*, 1893

The Tragedy of Pudd'nhead Wilson (1894)

William Livingston Alden, review, *Idler*, 1894
Unsigned review, *Athenaeum*, 1895
Unsigned review, *Critic*, 1895

Personal Recollections of Joan of Arc (1896)

William Peterfield Trent, review, *Bookman* (New York), 1896
Brander Matthews, "Mark Twain—His Work," *Book Buyer*, 1897
Unsigned article, "Mark Twain, Benefactor," *Academy*, 1897
David Masters, "Mark Twain's Place in Literature." *Chautauquan*, 1897
D.C. Murray, "My Contemporaries in Fiction. XII.—The Americans," *Canadian Magazine*, 1897

Following the Equator, or More Tramps Abroad (1897)

Unsigned review, *Academy*, 1897
Unsigned review, *Speaker*, 1897
Unsigned review, *Saturday Review*, 1898
Unsigned review, *Critic*, 1898
Hiram M. Stanley, review, *Dial*, 1898
Theodore De Laguna, "Mark Twain as a Prospective Classic," *Overland Monthly*, 1898
Anne E. Keeling, "American Humour: Mark Twain," *London Quarterly Review*, 1899
Henry Harland, "Mark Twain," London *Daily Chronicle*, 1899
Harry Thurston Peck, "As to Mark Twain," *Bookman* (New York), 1901
R. E. Phillips, "Mark Twain: More Than Humorist," *Book Buyer*, 1901
T. M. Parrott, "Mark Twain: Made in America," *Booklover's Magazine*, 1904
Harry Thurston Peck, "Mark Twain at Ebb Tide," *Bookman* (New York), 1904
Hammond Lamont, "Mark Twain at Seventy," *Nation*, 1905
Unsigned article, "Mark Twain," *Spectator*, 1907
William Lyon Phelps, "Mark Twain," *North American Review*, 1907
Charles Whibley, column, *Blackwood's Magazine*, 1907
H. L. Mencken, review, *Smart Set*, 1909

Unsigned notice, *Saturday Review*, 1910

Frank Jewett Mather, "Two Frontiersmen," *Nation*, 1910

Unsigned notice, *Dial*, 1910

Arnold Bennett, comment, *Bookman* (London), 1910

Sydney Brooks, "England and Mark Twain," *North American Review*, 1910

Harry Thurston Peck, "Mark Twain a Century Hence," *Bookman* (New York), 1910

William Lyon Phelps, "Mark Twain, Artist," *Review of Reviews* (New York), 1910

Simeon Strunsky, "Serious Humorists," *Nation*, 1910

Archibald Henderson, "The International Fame of Mark Twain," *North American Review*, 1910

John Macy on Mark Twain, 1913

H. L. Mencken, "The Burden of Humor," *Smart Set*, 1913

CRITICAL STUDIES

Baldanza, Frank. *Mark Twain: An Introduction and Interpretation*. Totowa, NJ: Barnes & Noble, 1961.

Budd, Louis J. *Critical Essays on Mark Twain, 1910–1980*. Boston: G. K. Hall & Co., 1983.

Camfield, Gregg. *Sentimental Twain: Samuel Clemens in the Maze of Moral Philosophy*. Philadelphia: University of Pennsylvania Press, 1994.

Howells, William Dean. *My Mark Twain: Reminiscences and Criticisms*. New York: Harper & Brothers, 1910.

Messent, Peter. *Mark Twain*. New York: St. Martin's Press, 1997.

Michelson, Bruce. *Mark Twain on the Loose*. Amherst: University of Massachusetts Press, 1995.

Robinson, Forrest. *In Bad Faith: The Dynamics of Deception in Mark Twain's America*. Cambridge: Harvard University Press, 1986. Focuses on *The Adventures of Tom Sawyer* and *Adventures of Huckleberry Finn*.

Sloane, David E. E. *Mark Twain as a Literary Comedian*. Baton Rouge: Louisiana State University Press, 1979.

Smith, Henry Nash. *Mark Twain, the Development of a Writer*. Cambridge: Harvard University Press, 1962.

Wonham, Harry. *Mark Twain and the Art of the Tall Tale*. New York: Oxford University Press, 1993.

SELECTED STUDIES OF INDIVIDUAL WORKS

The Innocents Abroad

Ganzel, Dewey. *Mark Twain Abroad*. Chicago: University of Chicago Press, 1968.

McKeithan, Bryant M. *Travelling with the Innocents Abroad*. Norman: University of Oklahoma Press, 1958.

The Prince and the Pauper

Baetzhold, Howard. *Mark Twain & John Bull*. Bloomington: Indiana University Press, 1970.

Life on the Mississippi

Briden, Earl F. "Through a Glass Eye, Darkly: The Skeptic Design of *Life on the Mississippi*." *Mississippi Quarterly* 48(1995): 225–237.
Kruse, Horst H. *Mark Twain and Life on the Mississippi*. Amherst: University of Massachusetts Press, 1981.

The Adventures of Tom Sawyer

Blair, Walter. "The Structure of Tom Sawyer." *Modern Philology* 37 (August 1930): 75–88.
Robinson, Forrest. *In Bad Faith: The Dynamics of Deception in Mark Twain's America*. Cambridge, MA: Harvard University Press, 1986.
Scharnhorst, Gary, ed. *Critical Essays on "The Adventures of Tom Sawyer."* New York: G. K. Hall, 1993. A comprehensive collection of reviews of the novel.

Adventures of Huckleberry Finn

Barchilon, José, and Joel S. Kovel. "*Huckleberry Finn*: A Psychoanalytic Study." *Journal of the American Psychoanalytic Association* 14 (October 1966): 775–814. A psychoanalysis of Huck Finn as a legitimate patient, excluding Twain's biography.
Chadwick-Joshua, Jocelyn. *The Jim Dilemma*. Jackson: University of Mississippi Press, 1998.
Doyno, Victor A. *Writing Huck Finn*. Philadelphia: University of Pennsylvania Press, 1991.
Fishkin, Shelley Fisher. *Was Huck Black?* New York: Oxford University Press, 1993.
Marks, Barry A., ed. *Mark Twain's "Huckleberry Finn."* Introduction by Barry A. Marks. Boston: D. C. Heath & Co., 1959. "Problems in American Civilization" Series.
Inge, M. Thomas, ed. *Huck Finn among the Critics, a Centennial Selection, 1884–1984*. Washington, DC: United States Information Agency, 1984.
Johnson, Claudia Durst. *Understanding The Adventures of Huckleberry Finn*. Westport, CT: Greenwood Press, 1996.
Leonard, James S., Thomas A. Tenney, and Thadeous M. Davis, eds. *Satire or Evasion? Black Perspectives on Huckleberry Finn*. Durham, NC: Duke University Press, 1992.
Mensh, Elaine, and Harry Mensh. *Black, White, and Huckleberry Finn*. Tuscaloosa: University of Alabama Press, 2000.

Quirk, Tom. *Coming to Grips with Hucklberry Finn.* Columbia: University of Missouri Press, 1993.

Rogers, Franklin R. *Mark Twain's Burlesque Patterns as Seen in the Novels and Narratives 1855–1885.* Dallas: Southern Methodist University Press, 1960.

Sloane, David E. E. *Adventures of Huckleberry Finn: American Comic Vision.* Boston: G. K. Hall-Twayne, 1988.

A Connecticut Yankee in King Arthur's Court

Fulton, Joe B. *Mark Twain in the Margins.* Tuscaloosa: University of Alabama Press, 2000. Closely documents Twain's use of Lecky, Macauley, and Carlyle.

Ketterer, David, ed. *Charles Heber Clark: A Family Memoir.* New York: Peter Lang, 1995. Includes "'Professor Baffin's Adventures' by Max Adeler: The Inspiration for *A Connecticut Yankee in King Arthur's Court*," and "Professor Baffin's Adventures" (1880) by Max Adeler (Charles Heber Clark).

Smith, Henry Nash. *Mark Twain's Fable of Progress.* New Brunswick, NJ: Rutgers University Press, 1964.

The Tragedy of Pudd'nhead Wilson and the Comedy of Those Extraordinary Twins

Anderson, Frederick. "Introduction." *Pudd'nhead Wilson and Those Extraordinary Twins, by Mark Twain.* San Francisco: Chandler Publishing Co., 1968.

Fishkin, Shelley Fisher. "Race and Culture at the Century's End: A Social Context for *Pudd'nhead Wilson.*" *Essays in Arts and Sciences* 19 (May 1990): 1–27.

Hughes, Langston. "Introduction." *Pudd'nhead Wilson.* New York: Bantam Books, 1959.

Matthews, Brander. "The Penalty of Humor." *Harper's Monthly* (May 1896) XCII: 897–900.

McKeithan, Daniel M. *The Morgan Ms. of Pudd'nhead Wilson.* Uppsala: A.-B. Lundequistska Bokhandeln, 1961.

Robinson, Forrest G., and Susan Gillman, eds. *Mark Twain's Pudd'nhead Wilson, Race, Conflict, and Culture.* Durham, NC: Duke University Press, 1990.

Rowlette, Robert. *Mark Twain's Pudd'nhead Wilson: The Development and Design.* Bowling Green, OH: Bowling Green University Popular Press, 1971.

OTHER ANTHOLOGIES OF CRITICISM

Budd, Louis J., ed. *Critical Essays on Mark Twain, 1867–1910.* Boston: G. K. Hall, 1982.

Giddings, Robert, ed. *Mark Twain: A Sumptuous Variety.* London: Vision Press, 1985.

Sloane, David E. E., ed. *Mark Twain's Humor: Critical Essays*. New York: Garland Press, 1993.

Smith, Henry Hash, ed. *Mark Twain: A Collection of Critical Essays*. Englewood Cliffs, NJ: Prentice-Hall, 1963.

SECONDARY SOURCES

Bier, Jesse. *The Rise and Fall of American Humor*. New York: Holt, Rinehart and Winston, 1968.

Blair, Walter. *Native American Humor*. San Francisco: Chandler, 1960 [1937].

Blair, Walter, and Hamlin Hill. *America's Humor from Poor Richard to Doonesbury*. London: Oxford, 1978.

Boorstin, Daniel. *The Americans*. 3 vols. New York: Vintage Books, 1974.

Cohen, Hennig, and William B. Dillingham, eds. *Humor of the Old Southwest*. Athens: Georgia University Press, 1975.

Jensen, Oliver. *America's Yesterdays*. New York: American Heritage Publishing Co., 1978.

Leonard, James S., ed. *Making Mark Twain Work in the Classroom*. Durham, NC: Duke University Press, 1999.

Michaelson, Bruce. *Mark Twain on the Loose: A Comic Writer and the American Self*. Amherst: University of Massachusetts Press, 1995.

Sloane, David E. E. *The Literary Humor of the Urban Northeast, 1830–1890*. Baton Rouge: Louisiana State University Press, 1983.

Wonham, Harry B. *Mark Twain and the Art of the Tall Tale*. New York: Oxford University Press, 1993.

Index

Pages in **boldface** indicate the location of detailed discussion of the work.

New Historicism reading of
Pudd'nhead Wilson, 159–62
"Nigger," as word, 1, 103–4, 106,
110–14, 118, 120–22, 149

Outsiders, 89–90, 95, 128, 147

Pendleton Act of 1883, 140
Picaresque, 22, 125, 130
Politics/law, 26, 38–40, 50, 86, 90,
106–7, 109, 117–18, 139–40, 147
Professional men as theme, 50, 55–57,
76–77, 88, 92, 94–95, 114, 134,
156

Quarles farm, 2, 106, 110

Race/racism, 49, 58, 71–72, 76, 79,
103–4, 111, 133, 145–46, 148–51,
154–55, 157–62. *See also*
Anti-slavery movement and senti-
ments; "A True Story," under Clemens, Samuel L., short stories by
Racial reading of *Huckleberry Finn,*
120–22
Realism/romanticism, 13, 24–27, 51,
57, 76, 79, 105–6, 112, 115–16,
118, 138
Regionalism/regions, 4–5, 45–62, 80,
105–6, 109, 114, 151
Religion, 8, 12, 49–50, 71, 75, 79, 90,
95, 106, 111, 117–18, 126–27,
130, 136, 147, 169–72
Roberts Rules of Order, 39
Romance/melodrama, 75, 78, 99, 112.
See also Realism/romanticism

Scott, Sir Walter, and chivalry, 55, 58,
107, 115
Sentimental and sublime, 48 *ff.,* 57,
61–62, 68–69, 75, 92, 97, 108,
129, 138
Short stories. *See under* Clemens, Samuel L., short stories by

Short stories and sketches deserving
more study, 43
Slavery narratives, 28, 124, 150. *See
also* Anti-slavery movement and sen-
timents; "A True Story," under
Clemens, Samuel L., short stories by
Smith, Henry Nash, on *A Connecticut
Yankee,* 140
Social criticism, 25–27, 54, 43, 80–81,
86, 90, 98–101, 108–11, 115, 124,
132–33
South, 55–57, 59–62, 105, 115
Southwestern humor, 22–23, 108–9
Stowe, Harriet Beecher, *Oldtown Folks,*
167
Swift, Jonathan, "A Modest Proposal,"
40

Tall Tale, 23, 34–40, 43, 52. See also
American humor
Talmage, T. DeWitt, 170
Technology, 48, 125–28, 130–32, 135,
138–39, 142
Travel narratives, 45–62, *passim*
Trowbridge, J. T., 29; *Neighbor
Jackwood,* 153
Trumbull, J. Hammond, 99
Twain, Mark. See Clemens, Samuel L.
Twichell, Joseph, 7–8, 18, 56

Villages and village life, 64, 67–68, 70,
75–80, 86, 105–06, 109, 113, 148,
157, 166

Ward, Artemus, 5, 15, 17, 22, 34, 45,
49
Warner, Charles Dudley, 7–8, 18, 26
West, mid-west, 45–54, 61–62, 114.
See also individual works under
Clemens, Samuel L., major works
by; Clemens, Samuel L., short sto-
ries by

About the Author

DAVID E. E. SLOANE is Professor of English and Education at the University of New Haven. He is past President of the Mark Twain Circle and of the American Humor Studies Association. He has published extensively on Twain and American humor and has lectured nationally and internationally. His publications include *New Directions in American Humor* (1998), *Mark Twain's Humor: Critical Essays* (1993), *Adventures of Huckleberry Finn: American Comic Vision* (1988), *Twain as a Literary Comedian* (1979), and *American Humor Magazines and Comic Periodicals* (Greenwood, 1987).